dog
dog

THE WORLD'S CLASSICS

308

ENGLISH VERSE

VOLUME I

Oxford University Press

ELY HOUSE, LONDON W.I

GLASGOW NEW YORK TORONTO MELBOURNE WELLINGTON
CAPE TOWN SALISBURY IBADAN NAIROBI DAR ES SALAAM
.LUSAKA ADDIS ABABA
BOMBAY CALCUTTA MADRAS KARACHI LAHORE DACCA
KUALA LUMPUR SINGAPORE HONG KONG TOKYO

ENGLISH VERSE

Chosen and edited by

W. PEACOCK

In five volumes
VOLUME I
EARLY LYRICS
TO SHAKESPEARE

London
OXFORD UNIVERSITY PRESS
New York   Toronto

*The first volume of these Selections of English Verse
was published in* The World's Classics *in 1928 and
reprinted in 1932, 1936, 1939, 1944, 1947, 1952, 1956,
1959, 1963, 1966, and 1971*

SBN 19 250308 1

PREFACE

THE origin of the present Selections may be simply stated. Representations were made to the publishers that a Selection of English Verse in five volumes should be issued as a companion work to the Selections of English Prose, also in five volumes, issued in 1921–2. I was invited to undertake the task of editing the book, and the present volumes are the result.

In preparing the work, I have endeavoured to adhere to the object I had in view in editing the companion volumes of English Prose. That object, so far as it applies to the present book, is to provide, for occasional reading, Selections, complete and interesting in themselves, from the works of our great poets, and, incidentally, to illustrate the history of English Poetry, so far indeed as that is possible, within the limits assigned.

As with the Prose Selections, the present book is intended for readers of all classes and of all ages, for ordinary readers as well as students ; and for young as well as old. With the view of making some appeal to the needs and preferences of the young, certain pieces have been included which otherwise might not have found a place here.

The purpose of these volumes being to provide a *corpus* of all great English Poetry, I have endeavoured to choose the best and only the best, undeterred by the fact that many of the pieces presented have been served up again and again in existing anthologies. In this connexion I may be

permitted to quote Sir Arthur Quiller-Couch's re-
marks on the same subject in the preface to his
admirable Selection *The Oxford Book of English
Verse*. He says, 'Having set my heart on choosing
the best, I resolved not to be dissuaded by common
objections against anthologies—that they repeat
one another until the proverb δὶς ἢ τρὶς τὰ καλά loses
all application—or perturbed if my judgement
should often agree with that of good critics.   The
best is the best though a hundred judges have
declared it so ; nor had it been any feat to search
out and insert the second-rate merely because it
happened to be recondite.'

I have arranged the poets in order of birth.   For
convenience, too, I have grouped the majority
of the Ballads, Songs, Carols, and certain other
pieces by unknown writers, in the middle of the
seventeenth century.

Songs from the dramatists have been included,
but, with the exception of Shakespeare's plays,
the drama, properly so called, has been but very
little drawn upon.   This exclusion is due partly to
considerations of space, as several volumes, beyond
the five prescribed by the publishers, would have
been necessary to enable the drama to be ade-
quately represented, partly also to the admitted
difficulty of giving from plays selections intelligible
and interesting in themselves.   But with regard to
Shakespeare, it is assumed that the great majority
of readers are more familiar with his plays than with
those of the other dramatists. Moreover, all readers

must surely possess a copy of his works, to which, if necessary, they can refer.

In dealing with poems of considerable length (e.g. 'The Faerie Queene' and 'Paradise Lost'), I have frequently indulged a preference for the lengthy extract, but not so as to crowd out any indispensable lyrics. Many of the longer poems, indeed, are given in their entirety (e.g. certain of the *Canterbury Tales*, Milton's 'Comus', Pope's 'Rape of the Lock', Shelley's 'Alastor', 'The Sensitive Plant', and 'Adonais', Keats's 'Isabella' and 'The Eve of St. Agnes', Matthew Arnold's 'Sohrab and Rustum', and two of William Morris's tales from *The Earthly Paradise*). This preference for the complete poem, wherever possible, may perhaps, where it is lengthy, tend to give greater prominence to certain poets than to others of greater name; and hence the space allotted to such poets must not always be regarded as an index to their respective rank and importance. However, in dealing with poets of the very highest class, it will, I hope, be found that ample space has been devoted to their works.

As with the Prose Selections, I have begun with the fourteenth century, the age of Chaucer, though a few earlier anonymous lyrics have been included. Living writers are not represented, their exclusion being due to various considerations, among others to difficulties of copyright. These difficulties will also account for the inadequate space given to certain other poets, whose works are still copyright.

With respect to orthography, it was decided that modernization should begin with Shakespeare. The selections from the dialect poets, however, retain throughout their original forms. Notes explanatory of archaic words and phrases have been added.

It remains for me to express my indebtedness to the labours of others in the same field. In particular, I must mention the great help I have received from those two great storehouses of Selections, *Chambers's Cyclopaedia of English Literature*, edited by Dr. David Patrick, and *The English Poets*, edited by Thomas Humphry Ward. In addition, Palgrave's *Golden Treasury* and Sir Arthur Quiller-Couch's *Oxford Book of English Verse* have proved invaluable guides throughout and to both I am greatly indebted. Amongst other works which have been of assistance to me I may mention in particular Archbishop Trench's *Household Book of English Poetry*, Canon Beeching's *Paradise of English Poetry*, Mowbray Morris's *Poet's Walk*, W. E. Henley's *Lyra Heroica*, Mr. R. M. Leonard's *Pageant of English Poetry*, T. W. H. Crosland's *English Song and Ballads*, the Oxford *Treasury of English Literature* by Miss G. E. Hadow and Sir W. H. Hadow, Mr. J. C. Smith's *Book of Verse for Boys and Girls* and his *Book of Verse from Langland to Kipling*, and Mr. Arthur Symons's *Pageant of Elizabethan Poetry*. The various other works which have been of assistance are too numerous for particular mention.

W. P.

10, THE AVENUE, KEW GARDENS.

CONTENTS

CONTENTS

CONTENTS

CONTENTS

CUCKOO SONG

c. 1250

Sumer is icumen in,
  Lhude sing cuccu !
Groweth sed, and bloweth med,
  And springth the wude nu—
      Sing cuccu !

Awe bleteth after lomb,
  Lhouth after calve cu ;
Bulluc sterteth, bucke verteth,
  Murie sing cuccu !

Cuccu, cuccu, well singes thu, cuccu :
  Ne swike thu naver nu ;
Sing cuccu, nu, sing cuccu,
  Sing cuccu, sing cuccu, nu !

SPRING-TIDE

c. 1300

Lenten ys come with loue to toune,
With blosmen and with briddes roune,
  That al this blisse bryngeth.
Dayes-eyes in this dales,
Notes suete of nyhtegales,
  Vch foul song singeth.
The threstelcoc him threteth oo,
Away is huere wynter wo,

lhude] loud.   awe] ewe.   lhouth] loweth.
sterteth] leaps.   swike] cease.   to toune] in its turn.
him threteth oo] is ever chiding them.   huere] their.

When woderoue springeth.
This foules singeth ferly fele,
And wlyteth on huere winter wele,
    That al the wode ryngeth.

The rose rayleth hire rode,
The leves on the lyhte wode
    Waxen al with wille.
The mone mandeth hire bleo,
The lilie is lossom to seo,
    The fenyl and the fille.
Wowes this wilde drakes ;
Miles murgeth huere makes,
    Ase strem that striketh stille.
Mody meneth, so doth mo—
Ichot ycham on of tho,
    For loue that likes ille.

The mone mandeth hire lyht ;
So doth the semly sonne bryht,
    When briddes singeth breme.
Deawes donketh the dounes ;
Deores with huere derne rounes,
    Domes for te deme ;

woderoue] woodruff.   ferly fele] marvellous many. wlyteth] whistle, or look.   rayleth hire rode] clothes herself in red.   mandeth hire bleo] sends forth her light.   lossom to seo] lovesome to see.   fille] thyme. wowes] woo.   miles] males.   murgeth] make merry. makes] mates.   striketh] flows, trickles.   mody meneth] the moody man makes moan.   so doth mo] so do many.   on of tho] one of them.   breme] lustily.   deawes] dews.   donketh] make dank. deores] deares, lovers.   huere derne rounes] their secret tales.   domes for te deme] for to give their decisions.

Wormes woweth vnder cloude;
Wymmen waxeth wounder proude,
   So wel hit wol hem seme.
Yef me shal wonte wille of on,
This wunne weole y wole forgon,
   And wyht in wode be fleme.

ALISON

c. 1300

BYTUENE Mersh and Aueril,
   When spray biginneth to springe,
The lutel foul hath hire wyl
   On hyre lud to synge.
Ich libbe in loue-longinge
For semlokest of alle thynge;
He may me blisse bringe—
   Icham in hire baurdoun.
An hendy hap ichabbe yhent;
Ichot from hevene it is me sent;
From alle wymmen mi loue is lent,
   And lyht on Alysoun.

On heu hire her is fayr ynoh,
   Hire browe broune, hire eye blake;
With lossum chere he on me loh,
   With middel smal and wel ymake.

---

cloude] clod.   wunne weole] wealth of joy.   y wole
forgon] I will forgo.   wyht] wight.   fleme] banished.
on hyre lud] in her language.   ich libbe] I live.
semlokest] seemliest.   he] she.   baurdoun] thraldom.
hendy] gracious.   yhent] seized, enjoyed.   ichot]
I wot.   lyht] alighted.   hire her] her hair.   lossum]
lovesome.   loh] laughed.

Bote he me wolle to hire take,
For to buen hire owen make,
Longe to lyuen ichulle forsake,
   And feye fallen adoun.
An hendy hap, etc.

Nihtes when y wende and wake,
   Forthi myn wonges waxeth won,
Leuedi, al for thine sake
   Longinge is ylent me on.
In world nis non so wyter mon
That al hire bountè telle con;
Hire swyre is whittore then the swon,
   And feyrest may in toune.
An hendy hap, etc.

Icham for wowyng al forwake,
   Wery so water in wore,
Lest eny reue me my make,
   Ychabbe y-yerned yore.
Betere is tholien whyle sore
Then mournen euermore.
Geynest under gore,
   Herkne to my roun.
An hendy hap, etc.

---

bote he] unless she.   buen] be.   make] mate.
feye] like to die.   nihtes] at night.   wende] turn.
forthi] on that account.   wonges waxeth won] cheeks
grow wan.   leuedi] lady.   ylent me on] arrived to
me.   so wyter mon] so wise a man.   swyre] neck.
may] maid.   forwake] worn out with vigils.   so
water in wore] as water in a weir.   reue] rob.   y-yerned
yore] long been distressed.   tholien] to endure.
geynest under gore] comeliest under woman's apparel.
roun] tale, lay.

GEOFFREY CHAUCER

1340–1400

THE CANTERBURY TALES

THE PROLOGUE

WHAN that Aprille with his shoures sote
The droghte of Marche hath perced to the rote,
And bathed every veyne in swich licour,
Of which vertu engendred is the flour;
Whan Zephirus eek with his swete breeth
Inspired hath in every holt and heeth
The tendre croppes, and the yonge sonne
Hath in the Ram his halfe cours y-ronne,
And smale fowles maken melodye,
That slepen al the night with open yē,
(So priketh hem nature in hir corages):
Than longen folk to goon on pilgrimages
(And palmers for to seken straunge strondes)
To ferne halwes, couthe in sondry londes;
And specially, from every shires ende
Of Engelond, to Caunterbury they wende,
The holy blisful martir for to seke,
That hem hath holpen, whan that they were seke.

  Bifel that, in that seson on a day,
In Southwerk at the Tabard as I lay
Redy to wenden on my pilgrimage
To Caunterbury with ful devout corage,
At night was come in-to that hostelrye
Wel nyne and twenty in a companye,

---

swich] such.   hem] them.   hir] their.   corages] dispositions, natures.   ferne] distant, remote.   halwes] shrines of saints.   couthe] well known.   martir] i. e. Becket.

Of sondry folk, by aventure y-falle
In felawshipe, and pilgrims were they alle,
That toward Caunterbury wolden ryde;
The chambres and the stables weren wyde,
And wel we weren esed atte beste.
And shortly, whan the sonne was to reste,
So hadde I spoken with hem everichon,
That I was of hir felawshipe anon,
And made forward erly for to ryse,
To take our wey, ther as I yow devyse.

  But natheles, whyl I have tyme and space,
Er that I ferther in this tale pace,
Me thinketh it acordaunt to resoun,
To telle yow al the condicioun
Of ech of hem, so as it semed me,
And whiche they weren, and of what degree;
And eek in what array that they were inne:
And at a knight than wol I first biginne.   *Knight.*

  A KNIGHT ther was, and that a worthy man,
That fro the tyme that he first bigan
To ryden out, he loved chivalrye,
Trouthe and honour, fredom and curteisye.
Ful worthy was he in his lordes werre,
And therto hadde he riden (no man ferre)
As wel in Cristendom as hethenesse,
And ever honoured for his worthinesse.

  At Alisaundre he was, whan it was wonne;
Ful ofte tyme he hadde the bord bigonne
Aboven alle naciouns in Pruce.
In Lettow hadde he reysed and in Ruce,
No Cristen man so ofte of his degree.
In Gernade at the sege eek hadde he be

  atte] at the.   forward] agreement, covenant.   reysed]
gone on a military expedition.

Of Algezir, and riden in Belmarye.
At Lyeys was he, and at Satalye,
Whan they were wonne; and in the Grete See
At many a noble aryve hadde he be.
At mortal batailles hadde he been fiftene,
And foughten for our feith at Tramissene
In listes thryes, and ay slayn his fo.
This ilke worthy knight had been also
Somtyme with the lord of Palatye,
Ageyn another hethen in Turkye:
And evermore he hadde a sovereyn prys.
And though that he were worthy, he was wys,
And of his port as meke as is a mayde.
He never yet no vileinye ne sayde
In al his lyf, un-to no maner wight.
He was a verray parfit gentil knight.
But for to tellen yow of his array,
His hors were gode, but he was nat gay.
Of fustian he wered a gipoun
Al bismotered with his habergeoun;
For he was late y-come from his viage,
And wente for to doon his pilgrimage. *Squyer.*

With him ther was his sone, a yong SQUYER,
A lovyere, and a lusty bacheler,
With lokkes crulle, as they were leyd in presse.
Of twenty yeer of age he was, I gesse.
Of his stature he was of evene lengthe,
And wonderly deliver, and greet of strengthe.
And he had been somtyme in chivachye,
In Flaundres, in Artoys, and Picardye,

aryve] landing, disembarkation of troops.   prys]
renown, esteem.   gipoun] a short cassock or doublet.
habergeoun] a hauberk, or coat of mail.   crulle] curly.
deliver] quick, active.   chivachye] a military expedition.

And born him wel, as of so litel space,
In hope to stonden in his lady grace.
Embrouded was he, as it were a mede
Al ful of fresshe floures, whyte and rede.
Singinge he was, or floytinge, al the day;
He was as fresh as is the month of May.
Short was his goune, with sleves longe and wyde.
Wel coude he sitte on hors, and faire ryde.
He coude songes make and wel endyte,
Juste and eek daunce, and wel purtreye and wryte.
So hote he lovede, that by nightertale
He sleep namore than dooth a nightingale.
Curteys he was, lowly, and servisable,
And carf biforn his fader at the table.   *Yeman.*

    A YEMAN hadde he, and servaunts namo
At that tyme, for him liste ryde so;
And he was clad in cote and hood of grene;
A sheef of pecok-arwes brighte and kene
Under his belt he bar ful thriftily;
(Wel coude he dresse his takel yemanly:
His arwes drouped noght with fetheres lowe),
And in his hand he bar a mighty bowe.
A not-heed hadde he, with a broun visage.
Of wode-craft wel coude he al the usage.
Upon his arm he bar a gay bracer,
And by his syde a swerd and a bokeler,
And on that other syde a gay daggere,
Harneised wel, and sharp as point of spere;
A Cristofre on his brest of silver shene.
An horn he bar, the bawdrik was of grene;

---

embrouded] embroidered.   floytinge] playing on the
flute.   nightertale] in the night-time.   takel] tackle,
archery-gear.   not-heed] crop-head.   bracer] a guard
for the arm.   bawdrick] baldrick, belt.

A forster was he, soothly, as I gesse.   *Prioresse.*

Ther was also a Nonne, a PRIORESSE,
That of hir smyling was ful simple and coy ;
Hir gretteste ooth was but by sëynt Loy ;
And she was cleped madame Eglentyne.
Ful wel she song the service divyne,
Entuned in hir nose ful semely ;
And Frensh she spak ful faire and fetisly,
After the scole of Stratford atte Bowe,
For Frensh of Paris was to hir unknowe.
At mete wel y-taught was she with-alle ;
She leet no morsel from hir lippes falle,
Ne wette hir fingres in hir sauce depe.
Wel coude she carie a morsel, and wel kepe,
That no drope ne fille up-on hir brest.
In curteisye was set ful muche hir lest.
Hir over lippe wyped she so clene,
That in hir coppe was no ferthing sene
Of grece, whan she dronken hadde hir draughte.
Ful semely after hir mete she raughte,
And sikerly she was of greet disport,
And ful plesaunt, and amiable of port,
And peyned hir to countrefete chere
Of court, and been estatlich of manere,
And to ben holden digne of reverence.
But, for to speken of hir conscience,
She was so charitable and so pitous,
She wolde wepe, if that she sawe a mous
Caught in a trappe, if it were deed or bledde.
Of smale houndes had she, that she fedde

forster] forester.   fetisly] elegantly.   lest] delight.
ferthing] morsel.   raughte] reached.   sikerly] truly.
chere] behaviour.   estatlich] stately.   digne]
worthy.

With rosted flesh, or milk and wastel-breed.
But sore weep she if oon of hem were deed,
Or if men smoot it with a yerde smerte:
And al was conscience and tendre herte.
Ful semely hir wimpel pinched was;
Hir nose tretys; hir eyen greye as glas;
Hir mouth ful smal, and ther-to softe and reed;
But sikerly she hadde a fair forheed;
It was almost a spanne brood, I trowe;
For, hardily, she was nat undergrowe.
Ful fetis was hir cloke, as I was war.
Of smal coral aboute hir arm she bar
A peire of bedes, gauded al with grene;
And ther-on heng a broche of gold ful shene,
On which ther was first write a crowned A,
And after, *Amor vincit omnia.*   *Nonne.*

    Another NONNE with hir hadde she,   *3 Preestes.*
That was hir chapeleyne, and PREESTES THREE.

    A MONK ther was, a fair for the maistrye, *Monk.*
An out-rydere, that lovede venerye;
A manly man, to been an abbot able.
Ful many a deyntee hors hadde he in stable:
And, whan he rood, men mighte his brydel here
Ginglen in a whistling wind as clere,
And eek as loude as dooth the chapel-belle
Ther as this lord was keper of the celle.
The reule of seint Maure or of seint Beneit,
By-cause that it was old and som-del streit,
This ilke monk leet olde thinges pace,
And held after the newe world the space.

yerde] rod, stick.   wimpel] a covering for the head.
tretys] well-proportioned.   fetis] neat, well-made.
shene] beautiful.   a fair] a good one.   maistrye]
mastery.   venerye] hunting.   som-del streit] something narrow.   pace] pass, go.

He yaf nat of that text a pulled hen,
That seith, that hunters been nat holy men;
Ne that a monk, whan he is cloisterlees,
Is lykned til a fish that is waterlees;
This is to seyn, a monk out of his cloistre.
But thilke text held he nat worth an oistre;
And I seyde, his opinioun was good.
What sholde he studie, and make himselven wood,
Upon a book in cloistre alwey to poure,
Or swinken with his handes, and laboure,
As Austin bit? How shal the world be served?
Lat Austin have his swink to him reserved.
Therfore he was a pricasour aright;
Grehoundes he hadde, as swifte as fowel in flight;
Of priking and of hunting for the hare
Was al his lust, for no cost wolde he spare.
I seigh his sleves purfiled at the hond
With grys, and that the fyneste of a lond;
And, for to festne his hood under his chin,
He hadde of gold y-wroght a curious pin:
A love-knotte in the gretter ende ther was.
His heed was balled, that shoon as any glas,
And eek his face, as he had been anoint.
He was a lord ful fat and in good point;
His eyen stepe, and rollinge in his heed,
That stemed as a forneys of a leed;
His botes souple, his hors in greet estat.
Now certeinly he was a fair prelat;
He was nat pale as a for-pyned goost.

pulled] plucked.   wood] mad.   swinken] toil, labour.
Austin] St. Augustine.   bit] bids.   pricasour] hard
rider.   priking] hard riding.   seigh] saw.   purfiled]
trimmed.   grys] gray fur.   in good point] in good case.
stepe] glittering.   forneys] furnace.   leed] leaden vessel.
botes] boots.   souple] pliant.   for-pyned] wasted away.

A fat swan ioved he best of any roost.

His palfrey was as broun as is a berye.   *Frere.*

    A FRERE ther was, a wantown and a merye,

A limitour, a ful solempne man.

In alle the ordres foure is noon that can

So muche of daliaunce and fair langage.

He hadde maad ful many a mariage

Of yonge wommen, at his owne cost.

Un-to his ordre he was a noble post.

Ful wel biloved and famulier was he

With frankeleyns over-al in his contree,

And eek with worthy wommen of the toun :

For he had power of confessioun,

As seyde him-self, more than a curat,

For of his ordre he was licentiat.

Ful swetely herde he confessioun,

And plesaunt was his absolucion ;

He was an esy man to yeve penaunce

Ther as he wiste to han a good pitaunce ;

For unto a povre ordre for to yive

Is signe that a man is wel y-shrive.

For if he yaf, he dorste make avaunt,

He wiste that a man was repentaunt.

For many a man so hard is of his herte,

He may nat wepe al-thogh him sore smerte.

Therfore, in stede of weping and preyeres,

Men moot yeve silver to the povre freres.

His tipet was ay farsed ful of knyves

And pinnes, for to yeven faire wyves.

And certeinly he hadde a mery note ;

limitour] a friar licensed to beg for alms within a certain limit.   famulier] familiar.   ther as] where that.
pitaunce] pittance.   avaunt] vaunt, boast.   tipet]
tippet, cape.   farsed] stuffed.

Wel coude he singe and pleyen on a rote.
Of yeddinges he bar utterly the prys.
His nekke whyt was as the flour-de-lys;
Ther-to he strong was as a champioun.
He knew the tavernes wel in every toun,
And everich hostiler and tappestere
Bet than a lazar or a beggestere;
For un-to swich a worthy man as he
Acorded nat, as by his facultee,
To have with seke lazars aqueyntaunce.
It is nat honest, it may nat avaunce
For to delen with no swich poraille,
But al with riche and sellers of vitaille.
And over-al, ther as profit sholde aryse,
Curteys he was, and lowly of servyse.
Ther was no man no-wher so vertuous.
He was the beste beggere in his hous;
And yaf a certeyn ferme for the graunt;
Noon of his bretheren cam ther in his haunt;
For thogh a widwe hadde noght a sho,
So plesaunt was his ' *In principio*,'
Yet wolde he have a ferthing, er he wente.
His purchas was wel bettre than his rente.
And rage he coude, as it were right a whelpe.
In love-dayes ther coude he muchel helpe.
For there he was nat lyk a cloisterer,
With a thredbar cope, as is a povre scoler,
But he was lyk a maister or a pope.

rote] kind of fiddle.   yeddinges] songs.   hostiler]
innkeeper.   tappestere] barmaid.   bet] better.
lazar] leper.   beggestere] beggar woman.   swich]
poraille] such poor folk.   yaf] gave.   ferme] rent.
purchas] proceeds, gifts acquired.   rage] romp.   love-
dayes] days for settling disputes by arbitration.   clois-
terer] monk.

Of double worsted was his semi-cope,
That rounded as a belle out of the presse.
Somwhat he lipsed, for his wantownesse,
To make his English swete up-on his tonge ;
And in his harping, whan that he had songe,
His eyen twinkled in his heed aright,
As doon the sterres in the frosty night.
This worthy limitour was cleped Huberd. *Marchant.*

    A MARCHANT was ther with a forked berd,
In mottelee, and hye on horse he sat,
Up-on his heed a Flaundrish bever hat ;
His botes clasped faire and fetisly.
His resons he spak ful solempnely,
Souninge alway th'encrees of his winning.
He wolde the see were kept for any thing
Bitwixe Middelburgh and Orewelle.
Wel coude he in eschaunge sheeldes selle.
This worthy man ful wel his wit bisette ;
Ther wiste no wight that he was in dette,
So estatly was he of his governaunce,
With his bargaynes, and with his chevisaunce.
For sothe he was a worthy man with-alle,
But sooth to seyn, I noot how men him calle. *Clerk.*

    A CLERK ther was of Oxenford also,
That un-to logik hadde longe y-go.
As lene was his hors as is a rake,
And he nas nat right fat, I undertake ;
But loked holwe, and ther-to soberly.
Ful thredbar was his overest courtepy ;
For he had geten him yet no benefyce,

semicope] short cope   lipsed] lisped.   mottelee]
motley array.   souninge] tending to.   th'encrees] the
increase.   winning] gain.   sheeldes] French crowns.
chevisaunce] dealing for profit.   overest courtepy] top
cape.

Ne was so worldly for to have offyce.
For him was lever have at his beddes heed
Twenty bokes, clad in blak or reed,
Of Aristotle and his philosophye,
Than robes riche, or fithele, or gay sautrye.
But al be that he was a philosophre,
Yet hadde he but litel gold in cofre;
But al that he mighte of his freendes hente,
On bokes and on lerninge he it spente,
And bisily gan for the soules preye
Of hem that yaf him wher-with to scoleye.
Of studie took he most cure and most hede.
Noght o word spak he more than was nede,
And that was seyd in forme and reverence,
And short and quik, and ful of hy sentence.
Souninge in moral vertu was his speche,
And gladly wolde he lerne, and gladly teche.

Man of Lawe.

A SERGEANT OF THE LAWE, war and wys,
That often hadde been at the parvys,
Ther was also, ful riche of excellence.
Discreet he was, and of greet reverence:
He semed swich, his wordes weren so wyse.
Justyce he was ful often in assyse,
By patente, and by pleyn commissioun;
For his science, and for his heigh renoun
Of fees and robes hadde he many oon.
So greet a purchasour was no-wher noon.
Al was fee simple to him in effect,
His purchasing mighte nat been infect.

lever] rather.   fithele] fiddle.   sautrye] psaltery, kind
of harp.   al be that] although.   hente] get.   scoleye]
to study.   war] prudent.   parvys] church porch.
purchasour] conveyancer.   infect] of no effect.

No-wher so bisy a man as he ther nas,
And yet he semed bisier than he was.
In termes hadde he caas and domes alle,
That from the tyme of king William were falle.
Therto he coude endyte, and make a thing,
Ther coude no wight pinche at his wryting;
And every statut coude he pleyn by rote.
He rood but hoomly in a medlee cote
Girt with a ceint of silk, with barres smale;
Of his array telle I no lenger tale.   *Frankeleyn.*

A FRANKELEYN was in his companye;
Whyt was his berd, as is the dayesye.
Of his complexioun he was sangwyn.
Wel loved he by the morwe a sop in wyn.
To liven in delyt was ever his wone,
For he was Epicurus owne sone,
That heeld opinioun, that pleyn delyt
Was verraily felicitee parfyt.
An housholdere, and that a greet, was he;
Seint Julian he was in his contree.
His breed, his ale, was alwey after oon;
A bettre envyned man was no-wher noon.
With-oute bake mete was never his hous,
Of fish and flesh, and that so plentevous,
It snewed in his hous of mete and drinke,
Of alle deyntees that men coude thinke.
After the sondry sesons of the yeer,
So chaunged he his mete and his soper.

---

termes] pedantic phrases.   caas] cases of law.
domes] decisions.   pinche] find fault.   coude] knew.
medlee] mixed.   ceint] girdle.   by the morwe] early
in the morning.   sop in wyn] wine with bread soaked
in it.   wone] custom.   after oon] equally good.
envyned] stored with wine.   snewed] abounded.

Ful many a fat partrich hadde he in mewe,
And many a breem and many a luce in stewe.
Wo was his cook, but-if his sauce were
Poynaunt and sharp, and redy al his gere.
His table dormant in his halle alway
Stood redy covered al the longe day.
At sessiouns ther was he lord and sire;
Ful ofte tyme he was knight of the shire.
An anlas and a gipser al of silk
Heng at his girdel, whyt as morne milk.
A shirreve hadde he been, and a countour;
Was no-wher such a worthy vavasour.

Haberdassher. Carpenter.

An HABERDASSHER and a CARPENTER,

Webbe. Dyere. Tapicer.

A WEBBE, a DYERE, and a TAPICER,
Were with us eek, clothed in o liveree,
Of a solempne and greet fraternitee.
Ful fresh and newe hir gere apyked was;
Hir knyves were y-chaped noght with bras,
But al with silver, wroght ful clene and weel,
Hir girdles and hir pouches every-deel.
Wel semed ech of hem a fair burgeys,
To sitten in a yeldhalle on a deys.
Everich, for the wisdom that he can,
Was shaply for to been an alderman.
For catel hadde they y-nogh and rente,
And eek hir wyves wolde it wel assente;

but-if] unless. poynaunt] pungent. table dormant] permanent side table. anlas] dagger. gipser] purse. countour] auditor. vavasour] land-holder. webbe] weaver. tapicer] tapestry maker. o] one. gere] clothing. apyked] trimmed. yeldhalle] guildhall. deys] dais. everich] each. catel] goods.

And elles certein were they to blame.
It is ful fair to been y-clept 'ma dame,'
And goon to vigilyës al bifore,
And have a mantel royalliche y-bore. *Cook.*

A COOK they hadde with hem for the nones,
To boille the chiknes with the marybones,
And poudre-marchant tart, and galingale.
Wel coude he knowe a draughte of London ale.
He coude roste, and sethe, and broille, and frye,
Maken mortreux, and wel bake a pye.
But greet harm was it, as it thoughte me,
That on his shine a mormal hadde he;
For blankmanger, that made he with the beste.

Shipman.

A SHIPMAN was ther, woning fer by weste:
For aught I woot, he was of Dertemouthe.
He rood up-on a rouncy, as he couthe,
In a gowne of falding to the knee.
A daggere hanging on a laas hadde he
Aboute his nekke under his arm adoun.
The hote somer had maad his hewe al broun;
And, certeinly, he was a good felawe.
Ful many a draughte of wyn had he y-drawe
From Burdeux-ward, whyl that the chapman sleep.
Of nyce conscience took he no keep.
If that he faught, and hadde the hyer hond,
By water he sente hem hoom to every lond.
But of his craft to rekene wel his tydes,
His stremes and his daungers him bisydes,

vigilyës] festivals, wakes.   for the nones] for this
occasion.   poudre-marchant] kind of spice.   mor-
treux] kind of stew.   mormal] gangrene.   woning]
living.   rouncy] hack.   falding] coarse cloth.   laas]
cord.

His herberwe and his mone, his lodemenage,
Ther nas noon swich from Hulle to Cartage.
Hardy he was, and wys to undertake ;
With many a tempest hadde his berd been shake.
He knew wel alle the havenes, as they were,
From Gootlond to the cape of Finistere,
And every cryke in Britayne and in Spayne ;
His barge y-cleped was the Maudelayne.

Doctour.

With us ther was a DOCTOUR OF PHISYK,
In al this world ne was ther noon him lyk
To speke of phisik and of surgerye ;
For he was grounded in astronomye.
He kepte his pacient a ful greet del
In houres, by his magik naturel.
Wel coude he fortunen the ascendent
Of his images for his pacient.
He knew the cause of everich maladye,
Were it of hoot or cold, or moiste, or drye,
And where engendred, and of what humour ;
He was a verrey parfit practisour.
The cause y-knowe, and of his harm the rote,
Anon he yaf the seke man his bote.
Ful redy hadde he his apothecaries,
To sende him drogges and his letuaries,
For ech of hem made other for to winne ;
Hir frendschipe nas nat newe to biginne.
Wel knew he th'olde Esculapius,
And Deiscorides, and eek Rufus,
Old Ypocras, Haly, and Galien ;
Serapion, Razis, and Avicen ;
Averrois, Damascien, and Constantyn ;

herberwe] harbour.   lodemenage] pilotage.   cryke]
creek.   rote] root.   yaf] gave.   bote] remedy.

Bernard, and Gatesden, and Gilbertyn.
Of his diete mesurable was he,
For it was of no superfluitee,
But of greet norissing and digestible.
His studie was but litel on the bible.
In sangwin and in pers he clad was al,
Lyned with taffata and with sendal ;
And yet he was but esy of dispence ;
He kepte that he wan in pestilence.
For gold in phisik is a cordial,
Therfore he lovede gold in special.   *Wyf of Bathe.*

  A good WYF was ther of bisyde BATHE,
But she was som-del deef, and that was scathe.
Of clooth-making she hadde swiche an haunt,
She passed hem of Ypres and of Gaunt.
In al the parisshe wyf ne was ther noon
That to th' offring bifore hir sholde goon ;
And if ther dide, certeyn, so wrooth was she,
That she was out of alle charitee.
Hir coverchiefs ful fyne were of ground ;
I dorste swere they weyeden ten pound
That on a Sonday were upon hir heed.
Hir hosen weren of fyn scarlet reed,
Ful streite y-teyd, and shoos ful moiste and
  newe.
Bold was hir face, and fair, and reed of hewe.
She was a worthy womman al hir lyve,
Housbondes at chirche-dore she hadde fyve,
Withouten other companye in youthe ;
But therof nedeth nat to speke as nouthe.

<hr>

mesurable] moderate.   sangwin] blood-red.   pers]
sky-blue.   sendal] a thin silk.   dispence] expense.
som-del] somewhat.   haunt] skill.   worthy] respect-
able.   withouten] besides.   nouthe] now.

And thryes hadde she been at Jerusalem;
She hadde passed many a straunge streem;
At Rome she hadde been, and at Boloigne,
In Galice at seint Jame, and at Coloigne.
She coude muche of wandring by the weye:
Gat-tothed was she, soothly for to seye.
Up-on an amblere esily she sat,
Y-wimpled wel, and on hir heed an hat
As brood as is a bokeler or a targe;
A foot-mantel aboute hir hipes large,
And on hir feet a paire of spores sharpe.
In felawschip wel coude she laughe and carpe.
Of remedyes of love she knew perchaunce,
For she coude of that art the olde daunce.

    A good man was ther of religioun,   *Persoun.*
And was a povre PERSOUN of a toun;
But riche he was of holy thought and werk.
He was also a lerned man, a clerk,
That Cristes gospel trewely wolde preche;
His parisshens devoutly wolde he teche.
Benigne he was, and wonder diligent,
And in adversitee ful pacient;
And swich he was y-preved ofte sythes.
Ful looth were him to cursen for his tythes,
But rather wolde he yeven, out of doute,
Un-to his povre parisshens aboute
Of his offring, and eek of his substaunce.
He coude in litel thing han suffisaunce.
Wyd was his parisshe, and houses fer a-sonder,
But he ne lafte nat, for reyn ne thonder,

---

   coude] knew.   gat-tothed] with teeth far apart.
carpe] talk.   persoun of a toun] parish priest.   paris-
shens] parishioners.   y-preved] proved.   sythes] times.
looth] loath, odious.   ne lafte nat] ceased not.

In siknes nor in meschief, to visyte
The ferreste in his parisshe, muche and lyte,
Up-on his feet, and in his hand a staf.
This noble ensample to his sheep he yaf,
That first he wroghte, and afterward he taughte ;
Out of the gospel he tho wordes caughte ;
And this figure he added eek ther-to,
That if gold ruste, what shal iren do ?
For if a preest be foul, on whom we truste,
No wonder is a lewed man to ruste ;
And shame it is, if a preest take keep,
A shiten shepherde and a clene sheep.
Wel oghte a preest ensample for to yive,
By his clennesse, how that his sheep shold live.
He sette nat his benefice to hyre,
And leet his sheep encombred in the myre,
And ran to London, un-to sëynt Poules,
To seken him a chaunterie for soules,
Or with a bretherhed to been withholde ;
But dwelte at hoom, and kepte wel his folde,
So that the wolf ne made it nat miscarie ;
He was a shepherde and no mercenarie.
And though he holy were, and vertuous,
He was to sinful man nat despitous,
Ne of his speche daungerous ne digne,
But in his teching discreet and benigne.
To drawen folk to heven by fairnesse
By good ensample, was his bisinesse :
But it were any persone obstinat,
What-so he were, of heigh or lowe estat,

muche and lyte] great and small.   lewed] ignorant.
shiten] defiled, dirty.   leet] left.   withholde] detained.
despitous] merciless.   daungerous] difficult.   digne]
proud.

Him wolde he snibben sharply for the nones.
A bettre preest, I trowe that nowher noon is.
He wayted after no pompe and reverence,
Ne maked him a spyced conscience,
But Cristes lore, and his apostles twelve,
He taughte, and first he folwed it himselve.

Plowman.

With him ther was a PLOWMAN, was his brother,
That hadde y-lad of dong ful many a fother,
A trewe swinker and a good was he,
Livinge in pees and parfit charitee.
God loved he best with al his hole herte
At alle tymes, thogh him gamed or smerte,
And thanne his neighebour right as himselve.
He wolde thresshe, and ther-to dyke and delve,
For Cristes sake, for every povre wight,
Withouten hyre, if it lay in his might.
His tythes payed he ful faire and wel,
Bothe of his propre swink and his catel.
In a tabard he rood upon a mere.

Ther was also a Reve and a Millere,
A Somnour and a Pardoner also,
A Maunciple, and my-self; ther were namo. *Miller.*

The MILLER was a stout carl, for the nones,
Ful big he was of braun, and eek of bones;
That proved wel, for over-al ther he cam,
At wrastling he wolde have alwey the ram.
He was short-sholdred, brood, a thikke knarre,

---

snibben] chide. nones] occasion. spyced] scru-
pulous. fother] load. swinker] labourer. gamed]
it pleased. swink] labour. catel] goods. tabard]
loose frock. Reve] Reeve, steward, bailiff. Somnour]
summoner. Maunciple] Manciple. ram] wrestler's
prize. knarre] a thickset fellow.

Ther nas no dore that he nolde heve of harre,
Or breke it, at a renning, with his heed.
His berd as any sowe or fox was reed,
And ther-to brood, as though it were a spade.
Up-on the cop right of his nose he hade
A werte, and ther-on stood a tuft of heres,
Reed as the bristles of a sowes eres ;
His nose-thirles blake were and wyde.
A swerd and bokeler bar he by his syde ;
His mouth as greet was as a greet forneys.
He was a janglere and a goliardeys,
And that was most of sinne and harlotryes.
Wel coude he stelen corn, and tollen thryes ;
And yet he hadde a thombe of gold, pardee.
A whyt cote and a blew hood wered he.
A baggepype wel coude he blowe and sowne,
And ther-with-al he broghte us out of towne.

Maunciple.

　A gentil MAUNCIPLE was ther of a temple,
Of which achatours mighte take exemple
For to be wyse in bying of vitaille
For whether that he payde, or took by taille,
Algate he wayted so in his achat,
That he was ay biforn and in good stat.
Now is nat that of God a ful fair grace,
That swich a lewed mannes wit shal pace
The wisdom of an heep of lerned men ?
Of maistres hadde he mo than thryes ten,

heve of harre] lift off its hinges.　　cop] top.　　werte]
wart.　　heres] hairs.　　eres] ears.　　nose-thirles]
nostrils.　　janglere] babbler.　　goliardeys] buffoon.
tollen] take toll.　　thryes] thrice.　　achatours] buyers,
caterers.　　by taille] on trust.　　algate] always.　　achat]
purchase.　　biforn] beforehand.　　lewed] ignorant.
pace] outstrip.

That were of lawe expert and curious ;
Of which ther were a doseyn in that hous
Worthy to been stiwardes of rente and lond
Of any lord that is in Engelond,
To make him live by his propre good,
In honour dettelees, but he were wood,
Or live as scarsly as him list desire ;
And able for to helpen al a shire
In any cas that mighte falle or happe ;
And yit this maunciple sette hir aller cappe. *Reve.*

    The REVE was a sclendre colerik man,
His berd was shave as ny as ever he can.
His heer was by his eres round y-shorn.
His top was dokked lyk a preest biforn.
Ful longe were his legges, and ful lene,
Y-lyk a staf, ther was no calf y-sene.
Wel coude he kepe a gerner and a binne ;
Ther was noon auditour coude on him winne.
Wel wiste he, by the droghte, and by the reyn,
The yelding of his seed, and of his greyn.
His lordes sheep, his neet, his dayerye,
His swyn, his hors, his stoor, and his pultrye,
Was hoolly in this reves governing,
And by his covenaunt yaf the rekening,
Sin that his lord was twenty yeer of age ;
Ther coude no man bringe him in arrerage.
Ther nas baillif, ne herde, ne other hyne,
That he ne knew his sleighte and his covyne ;
They were adrad of him, as of the deeth.
His woning was ful fair up-on an heeth,

dettelees] free from debt.   wood] mad.   scarsly]
parsimoniously.   sette hir aller cappe] befooled.
droghte] drought.   neet] cattle.   dayerye] dairy.
hyne] farm-servant.   covyne] deceitfulness.   adrad]
afraid.   woning] dwelling.

With grene treës shadwed was his place.
He coude bettre than his lord purchace.
Ful riche he was astored prively,
His lord wel coude he plesen subtilly,
To yeve and lene him of his owne good,
And have a thank, and yet a cote and hood.
In youthe he lerned hadde a good mister;
He was a wel good wrighte, a carpenter.
This reve sat up-on a ful good stot,
That was al pomely grey, and highte Scot.
A long surcote of pers up-on he hade,
And by his syde he bar a rusty blade.
Of Northfolk was this reve, of which I telle,
Bisyde a toun men clepen Baldeswelle.
Tukked he was, as is a frere, aboute,
And ever he rood the hindreste of our route.

Somnour.

  A SOMNOUR was ther with us in that place,
That hadde a fyr-reed cherubinnes face,
For sawcefleem he was, with eyen narwe.
As hoot he was, and lecherous, as a sparwe;
With scalled browes blake, and piled berd;
Of his visage children were aferd.
Ther nas quik-silver, litarge, ne brimstoon,
Boras, ceruce, ne oille of tartre noon,
Ne oynement that wolde clense and byte,
That him mighte helpen of his whelkes whyte,

lene] lend.   mister] trade, craft.   stot] horse,
cob.   pers] sky-blue.   clepen] call, name.   tukked]
tukked (i. e. his coat tucked about him).   Somnour]
summoner, apparitor (an officer who summoned delin-
quents before the ecclesiastical courts).   cherubinnes]
cherub's.   sawcefleem] covered with pimples.   scalled]
scabby, scurfy.   piled] very thin.   litarge] ointment
made from protoxide of lead.   ceruce] white lead.
byte] burn.   whelkes] blotches, pimples.

Nor of the knobbes sittinge on his chekes.
Wel loved he garleek, oynons, and eek lekes,
And for to drinken strong wyn, reed as blood.
Than wolde he speke, and crye as he were wood.
And whan that he wel dronken hadde the wyn,
Than wolde he speke no word but Latyn.
A fewe termes hadde he, two or three,
That he had lerned out of som decree ;
No wonder is, he herde it al the day ;
And eek ye knowen wel, how that a jay
Can clepen 'Watte,' as well as can the pope.
But who-so coude in other thing him grope,
Thanne hadde he spent al his philosophye ;
Ay ' *Questio quid iuris* ' wolde he crye.
He was a gentil harlot and a kinde ;
A bettre felawe sholde men noght finde.
He wolde suffre, for a quart of wyn,
A good felawe to have his concubyn
A twelf-month, and excuse him atte fulle :
Ful prively a finch eek coude he pulle.
And if he fond o-wher a good felawe,
He wolde techen him to have non awe,
In swich cas, of the erchedeknes curs,
But-if a mannes soule were in his purs ;
For in his purs he sholde y-punisshed be.
' Purs is the erchedeknes helle,' seyde he.
But wel I woot he lyed right in dede ;
Of cursing oghte ech gilty man him drede—
For curs wol slee, right as assoilling saveth—

knobbes] large pimples.   wood] mad.   clepen]
call, name.   grope] probe.   harlot] rascal, ribald.
atte fulle] entirely.   pulle a finch] pluck a finch, cheat a
novice.   o-wher] anywhere.   erchedeknes] Arch-
deacon's.   but-if] unless.

And **also** war him of a *significavit*.
In daunger hadde he at his owne gyse
The yonge girles of the diocyse,
And knew hir counseil, and was al hir reed.
A gerland hadde he set up-on his heed,
As greet as it were for an ale-stake;
A bokeler hadde he maad him of a cake. *Pardoner.*
  With him ther rood a gentil PARDONER
Of Rouncival, his freend and his compeer,
That streight was comen fro the court of Rome.
Ful loude he song, ' Com hider, love, to me.'
This somnour bar to him a stif burdoun,
Was never trompe of half so greet a soun.
This pardoner hadde heer as yelow as wex,
But smothe it heng, as dooth a strike of flex;
By ounces henge his lokkes that he hadde,
And ther-with he his shuldres over-spradde;
But thinne it lay, by colpons oon and oon;
But hood, for jolitee, ne wered he noon,
For it was trussed up in his walet.
Him thoughte, he rood al of the newe jet;
Dischevele, save his cappe, he rood al bare.
Swiche glaringe eyen hadde he as an hare.
A vernicle hadde he sowed on his cappe.
His walet lay biforn him in his lappe,
Bret-ful of pardoun come from Rome al hoot.

---

  significavit] a writ of excommunication.   in daunger]
within his jurisdiction, under his control.   gyse] way,
manner, fashion.   girles] young people of both sexes.
ale-stake] ale-stake, short pole supporting sign or bush.
stif] strong.   burdoun] burden of a song, bass-accom-
paniment.   heng] hung.   strike] hank.   flex]
flax.   ounces] small portions.   colpons] shreds,
bundles.   jet] fashion, mode.   dischevele] dishevelled.
bret-ful] brim-full.

A voys he hadde as smal as hath a goot.
No berd hadde he, ne never sholde have,
As smothe it was as it were late y-shave;
I trowe he were a gelding or a mare.
But of his craft, fro Berwik into Ware,
Ne was ther swich another pardoner.
For in his male he hadde a pilwe-beer,
Which that, he seyde, was our lady veyl:
He seyde, he hadde a gobet of the seyl
That sëynt Peter hadde, whan that he wente
Up-on the see, til Jesu Crist him hente.
He hadde a croys of latoun, ful of stones,
And in a glas he hadde pigges bones.
But with thise relikes, whan that he fond
A povre person dwelling up-on lond,
Up-on a day he gat him more moneye
Than that the person gat in monthes tweye.
And thus, with feyned flaterye and japes
He made the person and the peple his apes.
But trewely to tellen, atte laste,
He was in chirche a noble ecclesiaste.
Wel coude he rede a lessoun or a storie,
But alderbest he song an offertorie;
For wel he wiste, whan that song was songe,
He moste preche, and wel affyle his tonge,
To winne silver, as he ful wel coude;
Therefore he song so meriely and loude.

Now have I told you shortly, in a clause,
Th'estat, th'array, the nombre, and eek the cause
Why that assembled was this companye

---

male] bag, wallet.   pilwe-beer] pillow-case.   gobet]
shred.   seyl] sail.   hente] caught, seized.   croys]
cross.   latoun] latten, a compound metal.   alder-best]
best of all.   affyle] file, i. e. render smooth.

In Southwerk, at this gentil hostelrye,
That highte the Tabard, faste by the Belle.
But now is tyme to yow for to telle
How that we baren us that ilke night,
Whan we were in that hostelrye alight.
And after wol I telle of our viage,
And al the remenaunt of our pilgrimage.
But first I pray yow, of your curteisye,
That ye n'arette it nat my vileinye,
Thogh that I pleynly speke in this matere,
To telle yow hir wordes and hir chere;
Ne thogh I speke hir wordes properly.
For this ye knowen al-so wel as I,
Who-so shal telle a tale after a man,
He moot reherce, as ny as ever he can,
Everich a word, if it be in his charge,
Al speke he never so rudeliche and large;
Or elles he moot telle his tale untrewe,
Or feyne thing, or finde wordes newe.
He may nat spare, al-thogh he were his brother;
He moot as wel seye o word as another.
Crist spak him-self ful brode in holy writ,
And wel ye woot, no vileinye is it.
Eek Plato seith, who-so that can him rede,
The wordes mote be cosin to the dede.
Also I prey yow to foryeve it me,
Al have I nat set folk in hir degree
Here in this tale, as that they sholde stonde;
My wit is short, ye may wel understonde.
   Greet chere made our hoste us everichon,

---

viage] voyage, journey.   n'arette it nat] impute it
not.   moot] must.   reherce] rehearse, repeat with
exactitude.   al] although.   rudeliche] rudely.   cosin]
cousin, akin, suitable to.

And to the soper sette he us anon;
And served us with vitaille at the beste.
Strong was the wyn, and wel to drinke us leste.
A semely man our hoste was with-alle
For to han been a marshal in an halle;
A large man he was with eyen stepe,
A fairer burgeys is ther noon in Chepe:
Bold of his speche, and wys, and wel y-taught,
And of manhod him lakkede right naught.
Eek therto he was right a mery man,
And after soper pleyen he bigan,
And spak of mirthe amonges othere thinges,
Whan that we hadde maad our rekeninges;
And seyde thus: ' Now, lordinges, trewely,
Ye been to me right welcome hertely:
For by my trouthe, if that I shal nat lye,
I ne saugh this yeer so mery a companye
At ones in this herberwe as is now.
Fayn wolde I doon yow mirthe, wiste I how.
And of a mirthe I am right now bithoght,
To doon yow ese, and it shal coste noght.

Ye goon to Caunterbury; God yow spede,
The blisful martir quyte yow your mede.
And wel I woot, as ye goon by the weye,
Ye shapen yow to talen and to pleye;
For trewely, confort ne mirthe is noon
To ryde by the weye doumb as a stoon;
And therfore wol I maken yow disport,
As I seyde erst, and doon yow som confort.
And if yow lyketh alle, by oon assent,
Now for to stonden at my jugement,

---

leste] was pleasing to.   stepe] bright.   herberwe]
lodging.   quyte] pay.   shapen] planning, devising.
talen] to tell tales.

And for to werken as I shal yow seye,
To-morwe, whan ye ryden by the weye,
Now, by my fader soule, that is deed,
But ye be merye, I wol yeve yow myn heed.
Hold up your hond, withouten more speche.'

　　Our counseil was nat longe for to seche ;
Us thoughte it was noght worth to make it wys,
And graunted him withouten more avys,
And bad him seye his verdit, as him leste.

　　'Lordinges,' quod he, 'now herkneth for the
　　　beste ;
But tak it not, I prey yow, in desdeyn ;
This is the poynt, to speken short and pleyn,
That ech of yow, to shorte with your weye,
In this viage, shal telle tales tweye,
To Caunterbury-ward, I mene it so,
And hom-ward he shal tellen othere two,
Of aventures that whylom han bifalle.
And which of yow that bereth him best of alle,
That is to seyn, that telleth in this cas
Tales of best sentence and most solas,
Shal have a soper at our aller cost
Here in this place, sitting by this post,
Whan that we come agayn fro Caunterbury.
And for to make yow the more mery,
I wol my-selven gladly with yow ryde,
Right at myn owne cost, and be your gyde.
And who-so wol my jugement withseye
Shal paye al that we spenden by the weye.

yeve] give.　　seche] seek.　　us thoughte] it appeared
to us.　　　　to make it wys] to make it a subject for
deliberation, to hesitate.　　　avys] advice, consideration.
verdit] verdict.　　desdeyn] disdain, contempt.　sentence]
meaning, sentiment, instruction.　solas] amusement.
our aller] of us all.

And if ye vouche-sauf that it be so,
Tel me anon, with-outen wordes mo,
And I wol erly shape me therfore.'
  This thing was graunted, and our othes swore
With ful glad herte, and preyden him also
That he wold vouche-sauf for to do so,
And that he wolde been our governour,
And of our tales juge and reportour,
And sette a soper at a certeyn prys;
And we wold reuled been at his devys,
In heigh and lowe; and thus, by oon assent,
We been acorded to his jugement.
And ther-up-on the wyn was fet anon;
We dronken, and to reste wente echon,
With-outen any lenger taryinge.
  A-morwe, whan that day bigan to springe,
Up roos our host, and was our aller cok,
And gadrede us togidre, alle in a flok,
And forth we riden, a litel more than pas,
Un-to the watering of seint Thomas.
And there our host bigan his hors areste,
And seyde; 'Lordinges, herkneth, if yow leste.
Ye woot your forward, and I it yow recorde.
If even-song and morwe-song acorde,
Lat see now who shal telle the firste tale.
As ever mote I drinke wyn or ale,
Who-so be rebel to my jugement
Shal paye for al that by the weye is spent.
Now draweth cut, er that we ferrer twinne;
He which that hath the shortest shal biginne.
Sire knight,' quod he, ' my maister and my lord.

fet] fetohed.   cok] cock or alarum.   pas] foot-pace.
woot] know.   forward] agreement, covenant.   draweth
out] draw lots.   ferrer] farther.   twinne] depart.

Now draweth cut, for that is myn acord.
Cometh neer,' quod he, ' my lady prioresse ;
And ye, sir clerk, lat be your shamfastnesse,
Ne studieth noght ; ley hond to, every man.'
    Anon to drawen every wight bigan,
And shortly for to tellen, as it was,
Were it by aventure, or sort, or cas,
The sothe is this, the cut fil to the knight,
Of which ful blythe and glad was every wight ;
And telle he moste his tale, as was resoun,
By forward and by composicioun,
As ye han herd ; what nedeth wordes mo ?
And whan this gode man saugh it was so,
As he that wys was and obedient
To kepe his forward by his free assent,
He seyde : ' Sin I shal beginne the game,
What, welcome be the cut, a Goddes name !
Now lat us ryde, and herkneth what I seye.'
    And with that word we riden forth our weye ;
And he bigan with right a mery chere
His tale anon, and seyde in this manere.

THE NONNE PREESTES TALE

A POVRE widwe, somdel stape in age,
Was whylom dwelling in a narwe cotage,
Bisyde a grove, stonding in a dale.
This widwe, of which I telle yow my tale,
Sin thilke day that she was last a wyf,
In pacience ladde a ful simple lyf,
For litel was hir catel and hir rente ;
By housbondrye, of such as God hir sente,

aventure] chance.   And he bigan...His tale anon...] *The
Knight's Tale is not included in this Selection.*   somdel]
somewhat.   stape] advanced.   narwe] small.   hir]
her.   catel] possessions.   rente] income.

She fond hir-self, and eek hir doghtren two.
Three large sowes hadde she, and namo,
Three kyn, and eek a sheep that highte Malle,
Ful sooty was hir bour, and eek hir halle,
In which she eet ful many a sclendre meel.
Of poynaunt sauce hir neded never a deel.
No deyntee morsel passed thurgh hir throte ;
Hir dyete was accordant to hir cote.
Repleccioun ne made hir never syk ;
Attempree dyete was al hir phisyk,
And exercyse, and hertes suffisaunce.
The goute lette hir no-thing for to daunce,
N'apoplexye shente nat hir heed ;
No wyn ne drank she, neither whyt ne reed ;
Hir bord was served most with whyt and blak,
Milk and broun breed, in which she fond no lak,
Seynd bacoun, and somtyme an ey or tweye,
For she was as it were a maner deye.

A yerd she hadde, enclosed al aboute
With stikkes, and a drye dich with-oute,
In which she hadde a cok, hight Chauntecleer,
In al the land of crowing nas his peer.
His vois was merier than the mery orgon
On messe-dayes that in the chirche gon ;
Wel sikerer was his crowing in his logge,

---

fond] provided for.   doghtren] daughters.   namo] no more in number.   highte] was called.   sooty] begrimed with soot.   bour] inner room.   poynaunt] pungent.   accordant] according.   cote] coat.   repleccioun] repletion.   attempree dyete] a temperate diet.   lette] hindered.   n'apoplexye] (for ne apoplexye) nor apoplexy.   shente] harmed, injured.   seynd] singed.   ey] egg.   deye] dairy woman.   nas] (for ne was) was not.   messe] mass.   sikerer] surer, more to be trusted.   logge] resting-place.

Than is a clokke, or an abbey orlogge.
By nature knew he ech ascencioun
Of equinoxial in thilke toun ;
For whan degrees fiftene were ascended,
Thanne crew he, that it mighte nat ben amended.
His comb was redder than the fyn coral,
And batailed, as it were a castel-wal.
His bile was blak, and as the jeet it shoon ;
Lyk asur were his legges, and his toon ;
His nayles whytter than the lilie flour,
And lyk the burned gold was his colour.
This gentil cok hadde in his governaunce
Sevene hennes, for to doon al his plesaunce,
Whiche were his sustres and his paramours,
And wonder lyk to him, as of colours.
Of whiche the faireste hewed on hir throte
Was cleped faire damoysele Pertelote.
Curteys she was, discreet, and debonaire,
And compaignable, and bar hir-self so faire,
Sin thilke day that she was seven night old,
That trewely she hath the herte in hold
Of Chauntecleer loken in every lith ;
He loved hir so, that wel was him therwith.
But such a joye was it to here hem singe,
Whan that the brighte sonne gan to springe,
In swete accord, ' my lief is faren in londe.'
For thilke tyme, as I have understonde,
Bestes and briddes coude speke and singe.
    And so bifel, that in a daweninge,
As Chauntecleer among his wyves alle
Sat on his perche, that was in the halle,

---

orlogge] sun-dial, time-piece.   toon] toes.   sustres]
sisters.   cleped] called.   loken] locked.   lith] limb
(viz. of herself).   lief] dear one.

And next him sat this faire Pertelote,
This Chauntecleer gan gronen in his throte,
As man that in his dreem is drecched sore.
And whan that Pertelote thus herde him rore,
She was agast, and seyde, ' O herte dere,
What eyleth yow, to grone in this manere ?
Ye been a verray sleper, fy for shame ! '
And he answerde and seyde thus, ' madame,
I pray yow, that ye take it nat a-grief :
By god, me mette I was in swich meschief
Right now, that yet myn herte is sore afright.
Now god,' quod he, ' my swevene recche aright,
And keep my body out of foul prisoun !
Me mette, how that I romed up and doun
Withinne our yerde, wher-as I saugh a beste,
Was lyk an hound, and wolde han maad areste
Upon my body, and wolde han had me deed.
His colour was bitwixe yelwe and reed ;
And tipped was his tail, and bothe his eres,
With blak, unlyk the remenant of his heres ;
His snowte smal, with glowinge eyen tweye.
Yet of his look for fere almost I deye ;
This caused me my groning, doutelees.'
    ' Avoy ! ' quod she, ' fy on yow, hertelees !
Allas ! ' quod she, ' for, by that god above,
Now han ye lost myn herte and al my love ;
I can nat love a coward, by my feith.
For certes, what so any womman seith,
We alle desyren, if it mighte be,
To han housbondes hardy, wyse, and free,
And secree, and no nigard, ne no fool,

    drecched] vexed, troubled.   eyleth] aileth.   mette]
dreamt.   swevene] dream.   recche] interpret,
expound.   remenant] remainder.   heres] hairs.

Ne him that is agast of every tool,
Ne noon avauntour, by that god above !
How dorste ye seyn for shame unto your love,
That any thing mighte make yow aferd ?
Have ye no mannes herte, and han a berd ?
Allas ! and conne ye been agast of swevenis ?
No-thing, god wot, but vanitee, in sweven is.
Swevenes engendren of replecciouns,
And ofte of fume, and of complecciouns,
Whan humours been to habundant in a wight.
Certes this dreem, which he han met to-night,
Cometh of the grete superfluitee
Of youre rede *colera*, pardee,
Which causeth folk to dreden in here dremes
Of arwes, and of fyr with rede lemes,
Of grete bestes, that they wol hem byte,
Of contek, and of whelpes grete and lyte ;
Right as the humour of malencolye
Causeth ful many a man, in sleep, to crye,
For fere of blake beres, or boles blake,
Or elles, blake develes wole hem take.
Of othere humours coude I telle also,
That werken many a man in sleep ful wo ;
But I wol passe as lightly as I can.

 Lo Catoun, which that was so wys a man,
Seyde he nat thus, ne do no fors of dremes ?
Now, sire,' quod she, ' whan we flee fro the bemes,
For Goddes love, as tak som laxatyf ;

---

avauntour] boaster. engendren] are produced. replecciouns] repletions. fume] vapour. *colera*] (Lat.) choler. arwes] arrows. fyr] fire. rede] red. lemes] flames. contek] strife, contest. lyte] small. boles] bulls. no fors] no matter, no consequence. flee] fly.

Up peril of my soule, and of my lyf,
I counseille yow the beste, I wol nat lye,
That bothe of colere and of malencolye
Ye purge yow; and for ye shul nat tarie,
Though in this toun is noon apotecarie,
I shall my-self to herbes techen yow,
That shul ben for your hele, and for your prow;
And in our yerd tho herbes shal I finde,
The whiche han of hir propretee, by kinde,
To purgen yow binethe, and eek above.
Forget not this, for goddes owene love!
Ye been ful colerik of compleccioun.
Ware the sonne in his ascencioun
Ne fynde yow nat repleet of humours hote;
And if it do, I dar wel leye a grote,
That ye shul have a fevere terciane,
Or an agu, that may be youre bane.
A day or two ye shul have digestyves
Of wormes, er ye take your laxatyves,
Of lauriol, centaure, and fumetere,
Or elles of ellebor, that groweth there,
Of catapuce, or of gaytres beryis,
Of erbe yve, growing in our yerd, that mery is;
Pekke hem up right as they growe, and ete hem in.
Be mery, housbond, for your fader kin!
Dredeth no dreem; I can say yow namore.'
  ' Madame,' quod he, ' *graunt mercy* of your lore.
But nathelees, as touching daun Catoun,
That hath of wisdom such a greet renoun,
Though that he bad no dremes for to drede,

---

colere] choler.   hele] health.   prow] profit.   tho]
those.   kinde] nature.   ware] beware.   leye] lay.
grote] groat, (Dutch) coin.   centaure, fumetere, etc.]
herbs, etc.   fader kin] father's race, ancestry.

By god, men may in olde bokes rede
Of many a man, more of auctoritee
Than ever Catoun was, so mote I thee,
That al the revers seyn of his sentence,
And han wel founden by experience,
That dremes ben significaciouns,
As wel of joye as tribulaciouns
That folk enduren in this lyf present.
Ther nedeth make of this noon argument;
The verray preve sheweth it in dede.
    Oon of the gretteste auctours that men rede
Seith thus, that whylom two felawes wente
On pilgrimage, in a ful good entente;
And happed so, thay come into a toun,
Wher-as ther was swich congregacioun
Of peple, and eek so streit of herbergage
That they ne founde as muche as o cotage
In which they bothe mighte y-logged be.
Wherfor thay mosten, of necessitee,
As for that night, departen compaignye;
And ech of hem goth to his hostelrye,
And took his logging as it wolde falle.
That oon of hem was logged in a stalle,
Fer in a yerd, with oxen of the plough;
That other man was logged wel y-nough,
As was his aventure, or his fortune,
That us governeth alle as in commune.
    And so bifel, that, longe er it were day,
This man mette in his bed, ther-as he lay,
How that his felawe gan up-on him calle,
And seyde, " allas ! for in an oxes stalle

    preve] proof.   wher-as] where that.   herbergage]
lodging, abode.   y-logged] lodged.   fer] far.   yerd]
yard.   mette] dreamt.

This night I shal be mordred there I lye.
Now help me, dere brother, er I dye;
In alle haste com to me," he sayde.
This man out of his sleep for fere abrayde;
But whan that he was wakned of his sleep,
He turned him, and took of this no keep;
Him thoughte his dreem nas but a vanitee.
Thus twyës in his sleping dremed he.
And atte thridde tyme yet his felawe
Cam, as him thoughte, and seide, "I am now
    slawe;
Bihold my blody woundes, depe and wyde!
Arys up early in the morwe-tyde,
And at the west gate of the toun," quod he,
"A carte ful of dong ther shaltow see,
In which my body is hid ful prively;
Do thilke carte aresten boldely.
My gold caused my mordre, sooth to sayn;"
And tolde him every poynt how he was slayn,
With a ful pitous face, pale of hewe.
And truste wel, his dreem he fond ful trewe;
For on the morwe, as sone as it was day,
To his felawes in he took the way;
And whan that he cam to this oxes stalle,
After his felawe he bigan to calle.

    The hostiler answered him anon,
And seyde, "sire, your felawe is agon,
As sone as day he wente out of the toun."
This man gan fallen in suspecioun,

mordred] murdered.   ther] where.   fere] fear.
abrayde] started.   twyës] twice.   thridde] third.
slawe] slain.   in the morwe-tyde] in the morning.
shaltow] shalt thou.   thilke] that same.   do...aresten]
cause to be stopped.   hostiler] innkeeper.

Remembring on his dremes that he mette,
And forth he goth, no lenger wolde he lette,
Unto the west gate of the toun, and fond
A dong-carte, as it were to donge lond,
That was arrayed in the same wyse
As ye han herd the dede man devyse ;
And with an hardy herte he gan to crye
Vengeaunce and justice of this felonye :—
" My felawe mordred is this same night,
And in this carte he lyth gapinge upright.
I crye out on the ministres," quod he,
" That sholden kepe and reulen this citee ;
Harrow ! allas ! her lyth my felawe slayn ! "
What sholde I more un-to this tale sayn ?
The peple out-sterte, and caste the cart to grounde,
And in the middel of the dong they founde
The dede man, that mordred was al newe.

O blisful god, that art so just and trewe !
Lo, how that thou biwreyest mordre alway !
Mordre wol out, that see we day by day.
Mordre is so wlatsom and abhominable
To god, that is so just and resonable,
That he ne wol nat suffre it heled be ;
Though it abyde a yeer, or two, or three,
Mordre wol out, this my conclusioun.
And right anoon, ministres of that toun
Han hent the carter, and so sore him pyned,
And eek the hostiler so sore engyned,
That thay biknewe hir wikkednesse anoon,
And were an-hanged by the nekke-boon.

mette] dreamt.   lette] tarry.   dong-carte] dung cart.
out-sterte] started out.   biwreyest] revealest.   wlat-
som] loathsome.   heled] hidden.   hent] seized.   pyned]
examined by torture.   engyned] tortured, racked.
biknewe] confessed.   nekke-boon] neck-bone.

Here may men seen that dremes been to drede.
And certes, in the same book I rede,
Right in the nexte chapitre after this,
(I gabbe nat, so have I joye or blis,)
Two men that wolde han passed over see,
For certeyn cause, in-to a fer contree,
If that the wind ne hadde been contrarie,
That made hem in a citee for to tarie,
That stood ful mery upon an havensyde.
But on a day, agayn the even-tyde,
The wind gan chaunge, and blew right as hem
    leste.
Jolif and glad they wente un-to hir reste,
And casten hem ful erly for to saille;
But to that oo man fil a greet mervaille.
That oon of hem, in sleping as he lay,
Him mette a wonder dreem, agayn the day;
Him thoughte a man stood by his beddes syde,
And him comaunded, that he sholde abyde,
And seyde him thus, " if thou to-morwe wende,
Thou shalt be dreynt; my tale is at an ende."
He wook, and tolde his felawe what he mette,
And preyde him his viage for to lette;
As for that day, he preyde him to abyde.
His felawe, that lay by his beddes syde,
Gan for to laughe, and scorned him ful faste.
"No dreem," quod he, " may so myn herte agaste,
That I wol lette for to do my thinges,
I sette not a straw by thy dreminges,

to drede] to be dreaded, to be feared,   gabbe] to talk
idly, to prate.   hem leste] them pleased.   hir] their.
oo] one.   mervaille] marvel.   dreynt] drowned.
wook] awoke.   mette] dreamt.   viage] voyage.   lette]
stop.   agaste] terrify.

For swevenes been but vanitees and japes.
Men dreme al-day of owles or of apes,
And eke of many a mase therwithal ;
Men dreme of thing that never was ne shal.
But sith I see that thou wolt heer abyde,
And thus for-sleuthen wilfully thy tyde,
God wot it reweth me ; and have good day."
And thus he took his leve, and wente his way.
But er that he hadde halfe his cours y-seyled,
Noot I nat why, ne what mischaunce it eyled,
But casuelly the shippes botme rente,
And ship and man under the water wente
In sighte of othere shippes it byside,
That with hem seyled at the same tyde.
And therfor, faire Pertelote so dere,
By swiche ensamples olde maistow lere,
That no man sholde been to recchelees
Of dremes, for I sey thee, doutelees,
That many a dreem ful sore is for to drede.

Lo, in the lyf of seint Kenelm, I rede,
That was Kenulphus sone, the noble king
Of Mercenrike, how Kenelm mette a thing ;
A lyte er he was mordred, on a day,
His mordre in his avisioun he say.
His norice him expouned every del
His sweven, and bad him for to kepe him
    wel
For traisoun ; but he nas but seven yeer old,

swevenes] dreams.   jape] trick, jest.   mase] maze,
bewildering position.   for-sleuthen] waste in sloth.
it reweth me] makes me sorry.   y-seyled] sailed.   noot
I nat] know I not.   eyled] ailed.   maistow] mayest
thou.   lere] learn.   recchelees] careless, reckless.
lyte] a little.   avisioun] vision.   say] saw.   norice]
nurse.   del] part.   traisoun] treason.

And therfore litel tale hath he told
Of any dreem, so holy was his herte.
By god, I hadde lever than my sherte
That ye had rad his legende, as have I.
Dame Pertelote, I sey yow trewely,
Macrobeus, that writ th'avisioun
In Affrike of the worthy Cipioun,
Affermeth dremes, and seith that they been
Warning of thinges that men after seen.

 And forther-more, I pray yow loketh wel
In th'olde testament, of Daniel,
If he held dremes any vanitee.
Reed eek of Joseph, and ther shul ye see
Wher dremes ben somtyme (I sey nat alle)
Warning of thinges that shul after falle.
Loke of Egipt the king, daun Pharao,
His bakere and his boteler also,
Wher they ne felte noon effect in dremes.
Who-so wol seken actes of sondry remes,
May rede of dremes many a wonder thing.

 Lo Cresus, which that was of Lyde king,
Mette he nat that he sat upon a tree,
Which signified he sholde anhanged be?
Lo heer Andromacha, Ectores wyf,
That day that Ector sholde lese his lyf,
She dremed on the same night biforn,
How that the lyf of Ector sholde be lorn,
If thilke day he wente in-to bataille;
She warned him, but it mighte nat availle;
He wente for to fighte nathelees,
But he was slayn anoon of Achilles.

tale ... told] made account. lever] rather. sherte]
shirt. remes] realms. biforn] before. lorn]
lost.

But thilke tale is al to long to telle,
And eek it is ny day, I may nat dwelle.
Shortly I seye, as for conclusioun,
That I shal han of this avisioun
Adversitee ; and I seye forther-more,
That I ne telle of laxatyves no store,
For they ben venimous, I woot it wel ;
I hem defye, I love hem never a del.

   Now let us speke of mirthe, and stinte al this ;
Madame Pertelote, so have I blis,
Of o thing god hath sent me large grace ;
For whan I see the beautee of your face,
Ye ben so scarlet-reed about your yen,
It maketh al my drede for to dyen ;
For, also siker as *In principio*,
Mulier est hominis confusio ;
Madame, the sentence of this Latin is—
Womman is mannes joye and al his blis.
For whan I fele a-night your soft syde,
Al-be-it that I may nat on you ryde,
For that our perche is maad so narwe, alas !
I am so ful of joye and of solas
That I defye bothe sweven and dreem.'
And with that word he fley doun fro the beem,
For it was day, and eek his hennes alle ;
And with a chuk he gan hem for to calle,
For he had founde a corn, lay in the yerd.
Royal he was, he was namore aferd ;
He fethered Pertelote twenty tyme,
And trad as ofte, er that it was pryme.

seye] say.   avisioun] vision.   telle of] set by.
venimous] venomous.   woot] know.   hem] them.
never a del] not a bit.   stinte] stop.   yen] eyes.
dyen] die.   siker] sure.   *In principio* etc.] In the beginning,
woman is man's confusion.   pryme] prime (of day).

He loketh as it were a grim leoun ;
And on his toos he rometh up and doun,
Him deyned not to sette his foot to grounde.
He chukketh, whan he hath a corn y-founde,
And to him rennen thanne his wyves alle.
Thus royal, as a prince is in his halle,
Leve I this Chauntecleer in his pasture ;
And after wol I telle his aventure.

   Whan that the month in which the world bigan,
That highte March, whan god first maked man,
Was complet, and [y]-passed were also,
Sin March bigan, thritty dayes and two,
Bifel that Chauntecleer, in al his pryde,
His seven wyves walking by his syde,
Caste up his eyen to the brighte sonne,
That in the signe of Taurus hadde y-ronne
Twenty degrees and oon, and somwhat more ;
And knew by kynde, and by noon other lore,
That it was pryme, and crew with blisful stevene.
' The sonne,' he sayde, ' is clomben up on hevene
Fourty degrees and oon, and more, y-wis.
Madame Pertelote, my worldes blis,
Herkneth thise blisful briddes how they singe,
And see the fresshe floures how they springe ;
Ful is myn herte of revel and solas.'
But sodeinly him fil a sorweful cas ;
For ever the latter ende of joye is wo.
God woot that worldly joye is sone ago ;

---

leoun] lion.   him deyned] he deigned.   rennen
thanne] ran then.   highte] was called.   y-ronne] run.
stevene] voice.   clomben] ascended.   briddes] birds.
solas] solace, pleasure.   sodeinly] suddenly.   him fil]
befell to him.   sorweful cas] sorry chance.   woot]
knows.

And if a rethor coude faire endyte,
He in a cronique saufly mighte it wryte,
As for a sovereyn notabilitee.
Now every wys man, lat him herkne me ;
This storie is al-so trewe, I undertake,
As is the book of Launcelot de Lake,
That wommen holde in ful gret reverence.
Now wol I torne agayn to my sentence.

  A col-fox, ful of sly iniquitee,
That in the grove hadde woned yeres three,
By heigh imaginacioun forn-cast,
The same night thurgh-out the hegges brast
Into the yerd, ther Chauntecleer the faire
Was wont, and eek his wyves, to repaire ;
And in a bed of wortes stille he lay,
Til it was passed undern of the day,
Wayting his tyme on Chauntecleer to falle,
As gladly doon thise homicydes alle,
That in awayt liggen to mordre men.
O false mordrer, lurking in thy den !
O newe Scariot, newe Genilon !
False dissimilour, O Greek Sinon,
That broghtest Troye al outrely to sorwe !
O Chauntecleer, acursed be that morwe,
That thou into that yerd flough fro the bemes !
Thou were ful wel y-warned by thy dremes,

rethor] orator.   endyte] write, relate.   cronique]
chronicle.   saufly] safely.   torne] turn, return.
col-fox] coal fox, fox with black marks.   woned]
lived, dwelt.   heigh] high.   forn-cast] premeditated.
thurgh-out] throughout.   hegges] hedges.   brast]
burst.   wortes] vegetables.   undern] forenoon.
awayte] wait.   liggen] lie.   dissimilour] dissembler.
outrely] utterly.   sorwe] sorrow.   morwe] morrow.
flough] didst fly.

That thilke day was perilous to thee.
But what that god forwoot mot nedes be,
After the opinioun of certeyn clerkis.
Witnesse on him, that any perfit clerk is,
That in scole is gret altercacioun
In this matere, and greet disputisoun,
And hath ben of an hundred thousand men.
But I ne can not bulte it to the bren,
As can the holy doctour Augustyn,
Or Boëce, or the bishop Bradwardyn,
Whether that goddes worthy forwiting
Streyneth me nedely for to doon a thing,
(Nedely clepe I simple necessitee);
Or elles, if free choys be graunted me
To do that same thing, or do it noght,
Though god forwoot it, er that it was wroght;
Or if his witing streyneth nevere a del
But by necessitee condicionel.
I wol not han to do of swich matere;
My tale is of a cok, as ye may here,
That took his counseil of his wyf, with sorwe,
To walken in the yerd upon that morwe
That he had met the dreem, that I yow tolde.
Wommennes counseils been ful ofte colde;
Wommannes counseil broghte us first to wo,
And made Adam fro paradys to go,
Ther-as he was ful mery, and wel at ese.—
But for I noot, to whom it mighte displese,
If I counseil of wommen wolde blame,
Passe over, for I seyde it in my game.
Rede auctours, wher they trete of swich matere,
And what thay seyn of wommen ye may here.

bulte it] sift it.   bren] bran.   forwiting] foreknow-
ledge.   witing] knowledge.

Thise been the cokkes wordes, and nat myne;
I can noon harm of no womman divyne.—
    Faire in the sond, to bathe hir merily,
Lyth Pertelote, and alle hir sustres by,
Agayn the sonne; and Chauntecleer so free
Song merier than the mermayde in the see;
For Phisiologus seith sikerly,
How that they singen wel and merily.
And so bifel that, as he caste his yë,
Among the wortes, on a boterflye,
He was war of this fox that lay ful lowe.
No-thing ne liste him thanne for to crowe,
But cryde anon, 'cok, cok,' and up he sterte,
As man that was affrayed in his herte.
For naturelly a beest desyreth flee
Fro his contrarie, if he may it see,
Though he never erst had seyn it with his yë.
    This Chauntecleer, whan he gan him espye,
He wolde han fled, but that the fox anon
Seyde, 'Gentil sire, allas! wher wol ye gon?
Be ye affrayed of me that am your freend?
Now certes, I were worse than a feend,
If I to yow wolde harm or vileinye.
I am nat come your counseil for t'espye;
But trewely, the cause of my cominge
Was only for to herkne how that ye singe.
For trewely ye have as mery a stevene
As eny aungel hath, that is in hevene;
Therwith ye han in musik more felinge
Than hadde Boëce, or any that can singe.
My lord your fader (god his soule blesse!)

sustres] sisters.   agayn] against.   sonne] sun.
sikerly] truly.   ne liste him] was in no mind.   erst]
before.   seyn] seen.   stevene] voice.

And eek your moder, of hir gentilesse,
Han in myn hous y-been, to my gret ese ;
And certes, sire, ful fayn wolde I yow plese.
But for men speke of singing, I wol saye,
So mote I brouke wel myn eyen tweye,
Save yow, I herde never man so singe,
As dide your fader in the morweninge ;
Certes, it was of herte, al that he song.
And for to make his voys the more strong,
He wolde so peyne him, that with bothe his yĕn
He moste winke, so loude he wolde cryen,
And stonden on his tiptoon ther-with-al,
And strecche forth his nekke long and smal.
And eek he was of swich discrecioun,
That ther nas no man in no regioun
That him in song or wisdom mighte passe.
I have wel rad in daun Burnel the Asse,
Among his vers, how that ther was a cok,
For that a preestes sone yaf him a knok
Upon his leg, whyl he was yong and nyce,
He made him for to lese his benefyce.
But certeyn, ther nis no comparisoun
Bitwix the wisdom and discrecioun
Of youre fader, and of his subtiltee.
Now singeth, sire, for seinte Charitee,
Let see, conne ye your fader countrefete ? '
This Chauntecleer his winges gan to bete,
As man that coude his tresoun nat espye,
So was he ravisshed with his flaterye.

    Allas ! ye lordes, many a fals flatour
Is in your courtes, and many a losengeour,

---

brouke] enjoy, use.   peyne] take pains.   yĕn] eyes.
for that] because.   yaf] gave.   nyce] fastidious.
losengeour] flatterer.

That plesen yow wel more, by my feith,
Than he that soothfastnesse unto yow seith.
Redeth Ecclesiaste of flaterye ;
Beth war, ye lordes, of hir trecherye.

   This Chauntecleer stood hye up-on his toos,
Strecching his nekke, and heeld his eyen cloos,
And gan to crowe loude for the nones ;
And daun Russel the fox sterte up at ones,
And by the gargat hente Chauntecleer,
And on his bak toward the wode him beer,
For yet ne was ther no man that him sewed.
O destinee, that mayst nat been eschewed !
Allas, that Chauntecleer fleigh fro the bemes !
Allas, his wyf ne roghte nat of dremes !
And on a Friday fil al this meschaunce.
O Venus, that art goddesse of plesaunce,
Sin that thy servant was this Chauntecleer,
And in thy service dide al his poweer,
More for delyt, than world to multiplye,
Why woldestow suffre him on thy day to dye ?
O Gaufred, dere mayster soverayn,
That, whan thy worthy king Richard was slayn
With shot, compleynedest his deth so sore,
Why ne hadde I now thy sentence and thy lore,
The Friday for to chyde, as diden ye ?
(For on a Friday soothly slayn was he.)
Than wolde I shewe yow how that I coude pleyne
For Chauntecleres drede, and for his peyne.
   Certes, swich cry ne lamentacioun

beth war] beware.   hir] their.   nones] nonce,
occasion.   gargat] throat.   hente] caught, seized.
sewed] pursued.   roghte] cared.   syn] since.
delyt] delight.   woldestow] wouldst thou.   pleyne]
complain, lament.   peyne] pain.

Was never of ladies maad, whan Ilioun
Was wonne, and Pirrus with his streite swerd,
Whan he hadde hent king Priam by the berd,
And slayn him (as saith us *Eneydos*),
As maden alle the hennes in the clos,
Whan they had seyn of Chauntecleer the sighte.
But sovereynly dame Pertelote shrighte,
Ful louder than dide Hasdrubales wyf,
Whan that hir housbond hadde lost his lyf,
And that the Romayns hadde brend Cartage ;
She was so ful of torment and of rage,
That wilfully into the fyr she sterte,
And brende hir-selven with a stedfast herte.
O woful hennes, right so cryden ye,
As, whan that Nero brende the citee
Of Rome, cryden senatoures wyves,
For that hir housbondes losten alle hir lyves ;
Withouten gilt this Nero hath hem slayn.
Now wol I torne to my tale agayn :—
  This sely widwe, and eek hir doghtres two,
Herden thise hennes crye and maken wo,
And out at dores sterten they anoon,
And syen the fox toward the grove goon,
And bar upon his bak the cok away ;
And cryden, ' Out ! harrow ! and weylaway !
Ha, ha, the fox ! ' and after him they ran,
And eek with staves many another man ;
Ran Colle our dogge, and Talbot, and Ger-
        land,
And Malkin, with a distaf in hir hand ;
Ran cow and calf, and eek the verray hogges
So were they fered for berking of the dogges

clos] close (yard).   shrighte] shrieked.   **brend]**
burnt.   fyr] fire.   malkin] country-wench.

And shouting of the men and wimmen eke,
They ronne so, hem thoughte hir herte breke.
They yelleden as feendes doon in helle;
The dokes cryden as men wolde hem quelle;
The gees for fere flowen over the trees;
Out of the hyve cam the swarm of bees;
So hidous was the noyse, a! *benedicite!*
Certes, he Jakke Straw, and his meynee,
Ne made never shoutes half so shrille,
Whan that they wolden any Fleming kille,
As thilke day was maad upon the fox.
Of bras thay broghten bemes, and of box,
Of horn, of boon, in whiche they blewe and pouped,
And therwithal thay shryked and they houped;
It semed as that heven sholde falle.
Now, gode men, I pray yow herkneth alle!

Lo, how fortune turneth sodeinly
The hope and pryde eek of hir enemy!
This cok, that lay upon the foxes bak,
In al his drede, un-to the fox he spak,
And seyde, 'sire, if that I were as ye,
Yet sholde I seyn (as wis god helpe me),
Turneth agayn, ye proude cherles alle!
A verray pestilence up-on yow falle!
Now am I come un-to this wodes syde,
Maugree your heed, the cok shal heer abyde;
I wol him ete in feith, and that anon.'—
The fox answerde, 'in feith, it shal be don,'—
And as he spak that word, al sodeinly
This cok brak from his mouth deliverly,

dokes] ducks.　　quelle] kill.　　meynee] company.
bemes] trumpets.　　pouped] blew hard.　　houped]
whooped.　　cherles] churls.　　maugree etc.] in spite
of you.　　ete] eat.　　deliverly] adroitly.

And heighe up-on a tree he fleigh anon.
And whan the fox saugh that he was y-gon,
' Allas ! ' quod he, ' O Chauntecleer, allas !
I have to yow,' quod he, ' y-doon trespas,
In-as-muche as I maked yow aferd,
Whan I yow hente, and broghte out of the yerd ;
But, sire, I dide it in no wikke entente ;
Com doun, and I shal telle yow what I mente.
I shal seye sooth to yow, god help me so.'
' Nay than,' quod he, ' I shrewe us bothe two,
And first I shrewe my-self, bothe blood and bones,
If thou bigyle me ofter than ones.
Thou shalt na-more, thurgh thy flaterye,
Do me to singe and winke with myn yë.
For he that winketh, whan he sholde see,
Al wilfully, god lat him never thee ! '
' Nay,' quod the fox, ' but god yeve him meschaunce,
That is so undiscreet of governaunce,
That jangleth whan he sholde holde his pees.'

  Lo, swich it is for to be recchelees,
And necligent, and truste on flaterye.
But ye that holden this tale a folye,
As of a fox, or of a cok and hen,
Taketh the moralitee, good men.
For seint Paul seith, that al that writen is,
To our doctryne it is y-write, y-wis.
Taketh the fruyt, and lat the chaf be stille.

  Now, gode god, if that it be thy wille,
As seith my lord, so make us alle good men ;
And bringe us to his heighe blisse.   Amen.

---

heighe] high.   fleigh] flew.   hente] seized.   wikke]
wicked.   shrewe] beshrew, curse.   bigyle] beguile.
thee] thrive, prosper.   yeve] give.   recchelees]
reckless.   folye] folly.

The Pardoners Tale

In Flaundres whylom was a companye
Of yonge folk, that haunteden folye,
As ryot, hasard, stewes, and tavernes,
Wher-as, with harpes, lutes, and giternes,
They daunce and pleye at dees bothe day and
    night,
And ete also and drinken over hir might,
Thurgh which they doon the devel sacrifyse
With-in that develes temple, in cursed wyse,
By superfluitee abhominable ;
Hir othes been so grete and so dampnable,
That it is grisly for to here hem swere ;
Our blissed lordes body they to-tere ;
Hem thoughte Jewes rente him noght y-nough ;
And ech of hem at otheres sinne lough.
And right anon than comen tombesteres
Fetys and smale, and yonge fruytesteres,
Singers with harpes, baudes, wafereres,
Whiche been the verray develes officeres
To kindle and blowe the fyr of lecherye,
That is annexed un-to glotonye ;
The holy writ take I to my witnesse,
That luxurie is in wyn and dronkenesse.
    Lo, how that dronken Loth, unkindely,
Lay by his doghtres two, unwitingly ;

whylom] once, formerly.   haunteden] practised, gave
themselves up to.   ryot] riotous living.   hasard]
dice-play.   stewes] brothels.   wher-as] where.
dees] dice.   hir] their.   thurgh] through.   grisly]
horrible, terrible, awful.   hem] them.   to-tere] rend,
tear in pieces.   noght y-nough] not enough.   lough]
laughed.   tombesteres] dancing girls, female tumblers.
fetys] neat.   frutesteres] fruit women.   wafereres]
confectioners.   unkindely] unnaturally.

So dronke he was, he niste what he wroghte.
    Herodes, (who-so wel the stories soghte),
Whan he of wyn was replet at his feste,
Right at his owene table he yaf his heste
To sleen the Baptist John ful giltelees.
    Senek seith eek a good word doutelees;
He seith, he can no difference finde
Bitwix a man that is out of his minde
And a man which that is dronkelewe,
But that woodnesse, y-fallen in a shrewe,
Persevereth lenger than doth dronkenesse.
    O glotonye, ful of cursednesse,
O cause first of our confusioun,
O original of our dampnacioun,
Til Crist had boght us with his blood agayn!
Lo, how dere, shortly for to sayn,
Aboght was thilke cursed vileinye;
Corrupt was al this world for glotonye!
    Adam our fader, and his wyf also,
Fro Paradys to labour and to wo
Were driven for that vyce, it is no drede;
For whyl that Adam fasted, as I rede,
He was in Paradys; and whan that he
Eet of the fruyt defended on the tree,
Anon he was out-cast to wo and peyne.
O glotonye, on thee wel oghte us pleyne!
O, wiste a man how many maladyes
Folwen of excesse and of glotonyes,

niste] knew not.   yaf] gave.   heste] command.
to sleen] to slay.   dronkelewe] addicted to drink.
woodnesse] madness, rage.   y-fallen] having befallen.
shrewe] ill-tempered (male) person.   aboght] purchased,
atoned for.   thilke] that.   it is no drede] without
doubt.   defended] forbidden.   pleyne] to complain,
lament.   wiste] (if he) knew.

He wolde been the more mesurable
Of his diete, sittinge at his table.
Allas! the shorte throte, the tendre mouth,
Maketh that, Est and West, and North and South,
In erthe, in eir, in water men to-swinke
To gete a glotoun deyntee mete and drinke!
Of this matere, o Paul, wel canstow trete,
' Mete un-to wombe, and wombe eek un-to mete,
Shal god destroyen bothe,' as Paulus seith.
Allas! a foul thing is it, by my feith,
To seye this word, and fouler is the dede,
Whan man so drinketh of the whyte and rede,
That of his throte he maketh his privee,
Thurgh thilke cursed superfluitee.

The apostel weping seith ful pitously,
' Ther walken many of whiche yow told have I,
I seye it now weping with pitous voys,
That they been enemys of Cristes croys,
Of whiche the ende is deeth, wombe is her god.'
O wombe! O bely! O stinking cod,
Fulfild of donge and of corrupcioun!
At either ende of thee foul is the soun.
How greet labour and cost is thee to finde!
Thise cokes, how they stampe, and streyne, and
          grinde,
And turnen substaunce in-to accident,
To fulfille al thy likerous talent!
Out of the harde bones knokke they
The mary, for they caste noght a-wey

mesurable] moderate.   to-swinke] to labour, toil.
deyntee] dainty.   canstow] canst thou.   trete]
discourse, treat.   wombe] the belly.   croys] cross.
cod] bag; used of the receptacle of the stomach.   soun]
sound.   cokes] cooks.   mary] marrow.

That may go thurgh the golet softe and swote ;
Of spicerye, of leef, and bark, and rote
Shal been his sauce y-maked by delyt,
To make him yet a newer appetyt.
But certes, he that haunteth swich delyces
Is deed, whyl that he liveth in tho vyces.

A lecherous thing is wyn, and dronkenesse
Is ful of stryving and of wrecchednesse.
O dronke man, disfigured is thy face,
Sour is thy breeth, foul artow to embrace,
And thurgh thy dronke nose semeth the soun
As though thou seydest ay 'Sampsoun, Sampsoun';
And yet, god wot, Sampsoun drank never no wyn.
Thou fallest, as it were a stiked swyn ;
Thy tonge is lost, and al thyn honest cure ;
For dronkenesse is verray sepulture
Of mannes wit and his discrecioun.
In whom that drinke hath dominacioun,
He can no conseil kepe, it is no drede.
Now kepe yow fro the whyte and fro the rede,
And namely fro the whyte wyn of Lepe,
That is to selle in Fish-strete or in Chepe.
This wyn of Spayne crepeth subtilly
In othere wynes, growing faste by,
Of which ther ryseth swich fumositee,
That whan a man hath dronken draughtes three,
And weneth that he be at hoom in Chepe,
He is in Spayne, right at the toune of Lepe,
Nat at the Rochel, ne at Burdeux toun ;
And thanne wol he seye, ' Sampsoun, Sampsoun.'

But herkneth, lordings, o word, I yow preye,
That alle the sovereyn actes, dar I seye,

golet] throat, gullet.   swote] sweetly.   a stiked swyn]
a stuck pig.   Lepe] near Cadiz.   fumositee] headiness.

Of victories in th'olde testament,
Thurgh verray god, that is omnipotent,
Were doon in abstinence and in preyere;
Loketh the Bible, and ther ye may it lere.

Loke, Attila, the grete conquerour,
Deyde in his sleep, with shame and dishonour,
Bledinge ay at his nose in dronkenesse;
A capitayn shoulde live in sobrenesse.
And over al this, avyseth yow right wel
What was comaunded un-to Lamuel—
Nat Samuel, but Lamuel, seye I—
Redeth the Bible, and finde it expresly
Of wyn-yeving to hem that han justyse.
Na-more of this, for it may wel suffyse.

And now that I have spoke of glotonye,
Now wol I yow defenden hasardrye.
Hasard is verray moder of lesinges,
And of deceite, and cursed forsweringes,
Blaspheme of Crist, manslaughtre, and wast
    also
Of catel and of tyme; and forthermo,
It is repreve and contrarie of honour
For to ben holde a commune hasardour.
And ever the hyër he is of estaat,
The more is he holden desolaat.
If that a prince useth hasardrye,
In alle governaunce and policye
He is, as by commune opinioun,
Y-holde the lasse in reputacioun.

lere] learn.   wyn-yeving] wine-giving, the giving of
wine.   han] have.   justyse] administration of
justice.   defenden hasardrye] forbid gambling.   moder]
mother.   lesinges] lies, deceits.   catel] goods.
repreve] reproof, shame.   hasardour] gamester.   heyer]
higher.   lasse] less.

Stilbon, that was a wys embassadour,
Was sent to Corinthe, in ful greet honour,
Fro Lacidomie, to make hir alliaunce.
And whan he cam, him happede, par chaunce,
That alle the grettest that were of that lond,
Pleyinge atte hasard he hem fond.
For which, as sone as it mighte be,
He stal him hoom agayn to his contree,
And seyde, ' ther wol I nat lese my name ;
N' I wol nat take on me so greet defame,
Yow for to allye un-to none hasardours.
Sendeth othere wyse embassadours ;
For, by my trouthe, me were lever dye,
Than I yow sholde to hasardours allye.
For ye that been so glorious in honours
Shul nat allyen yow with hasardours
As by my wil, ne as by my tretee.'
This wyse philosophre thus seyde he.

Loke eek that, to the king Demetrius
The king of Parthes, as the book seith us,
Sente him a paire of dees of gold in scorn,
For he hadde used hasard ther-biforn ;
For which he heeld his glorie or his renoun
At no value or reputacioun.
Lordes may finden other maner pley
Honeste y-nough to dryve the day awey.

Now wol I speke of othes false and grete
A word or two, as olde bokes trete.
Gret swering is a thing abhominable,

lond] land.   hem fond] them found.   stal] stole
away, secretly retreated.   nat lese] not lose.   defame]
dishonour.   hasardours] gamesters.   sendeth] send ye.
me were lever dye] I had rather die.   allyen] ally.   tretee]
treaty.   dees] dice.   ther-biforn] beforehand, before
the event.

And false swering is yet more reprevable.
The heighe god forbad swering at al,
Witnesse on Mathew ; but in special
Of swering seith the holy Jeremye,
' Thou shalt seye sooth thyn othes, and nat lye,
And swere in dome, and eek in rightwisnesse ; '
But ydel swering is a cursednesse.
Bihold and see, that in the firste table
Of heighe goddes hestes honurable,
How that the seconde heste of him is this—
' Tak nat my name in ydel or amis.'
Lo, rather he forbedeth swich swering
Than homicyde or many a cursed thing ;
I seye that, as by ordre, thus it stondeth :
This knowen, that his hestes understondeth,
How that the second heste of god is that.
And forther over, I wol thee telle al plat,
That vengeance shal nat parten from his hous,
That of his othes is to outrageous.
' By goddes precious herte, and by his nayles,
And by the blode of Crist, that it is in Hayles,
Seven is my chaunce, and thyn is cink and treye ;
By goddes armes, if thou falsly pleye,
This dagger shal thurgh-out thyn herte go '—
This fruyt cometh of the bicched bones two,
Forswering, ire, falsnesse, homicyde.
Now, for the love of Crist that for us dyde,
Leveth your othes, bothe grete and smale ;
But, sirs, now wol I telle forth my tale.

---

swering] swearing.   othes] oaths.   dome] judgment.   ydel] idle.   hestes] commands.   plat]
plainly.   chaunce] ' chance ', a technical term in the
game of hazard.   cink] cinque, five.   treye] ' tray ',
three.   bicched bones] dice, (lit. evil or accursed bones).

THISE ryotoures three, of whiche I telle,
Longe erst er pryme rong of any belle,
Were set hem in a taverne for to drinke ;
And as they satte, they herde a belle clinke
Biforn a cors, was caried to his grave ;
That oon of hem gan callen to his knave ;
' Go bet,' quod he, ' and axe redily,
What cors is this that passeth heer forby ;
And look that thou reporte his name wel.'

' Sir,' quod this boy, ' it nedeth never-a-del.
It was me told, er ye cam heer, two houres ;
He was, pardee, an old felawe of youres ;
And sodeynly he was y-slayn to-night,
For-dronke, as he sat on his bench upright ;
Ther cam a privee theef, men clepeth Deeth,
That in this contree al the peple sleeth,
And with his spere he smoot his herte a-two,
And wente his wey with-outen wordes mo.
He hath a thousand slayn this pestilence :
And, maister, er ye come in his presence,
Me thinketh that it were necessarie
For to be war of swich an adversarie :
Beth redy for to mete him evermore.
Thus taughte me my dame, I sey na-more.'
' By seinte Marie,' seyde this taverner,
' The child seith sooth, for he hath slayn this yeer,
Henne over a myle, with-in a greet village,
Both man and womman, child and hyne, and page.
I trowe his habitacioun be there ;
To been avysed greet wisdom it were,

---

longe erst er] long first before.   pryme] prime, used
apparently to signify 9 a.m.   cors] corpse.   go bet]
go quickly.   clepeth] call.   Deeth] death.   sleeth]
slays.   swich] such.   henne] hence.   hyne] servant.

Er that he dide a man a dishonour.'
' Ye, goddes armes,' quod this ryotour,
' Is it swich peril with him for to mete ?
I shal him seke by wey and eek by strete,
I make avow to goddes digne bones !
Herkneth, felawes, we three been al ones ;
Lat ech of us holde up his hond til other,
And ech of us bicomen otheres brother,
And we wol sleen this false traytour Deeth ;
He shal be slayn, which that so many sleeth,
By goddes dignitee, er it be night.'

   Togidres han thise three her trouthes plight,
To live and dyen ech of hem for other,
As though he were his owene y-boren brother.
And up they sterte al dronken, in this rage,
And forth they goon towardes that village,
Of which the taverner had spoke biforn,
And many a grisly ooth than han they sworn,
And Cristes blessed body they to-rente—
' Deeth shal be deed, if that they may him hente.'

   Whan they han goon nat fully half a myle,
Right as they wolde han troden over a style,
An old man and a povre with hem mette.
This olde man ful mekely hem grette,
And seyde thus, ' now, lordes, god yow see ! '

   The proudest of thise ryotoures three
Answerde agayn, ' what ? carl, with sory grace,
Why artow al forwrapped save thy face ?
Why livestow so longe in so greet age ? '

   This olde man gan loke in his visage,

digne] worthy, honoured.   togidres] together. han]
have.   her] their.   grisly] horrible.   to-rente]
rent asunder.   hente] seize.   hem] them.   grette]
greeted.   god yow see] God see you.   forwrapped]
wrapped up.   gan] began.   loke] look.

And seyde thus, ' for I ne can nat finde
A man, though that I walked in-to Inde,
Neither in citee nor in no village,
That wolde chaunge his youthe for myn age ;
And therfore moot I han myn age stille,
As longe time as it goddes wille.

Ne deeth, allas ! ne wol nat han my lyf .
Thus walke I, lyk a restelees caityf,
And on the ground, which is my modres gate,
I knokke with my staf, bothe erly and late,
And seye, " leve moder, leet me in !
Lo, how I vanish, flesh, and blood, and skin !
Allas ! whan shul my bones been at reste ?
Moder, with yow wolde I chaunge my cheste,
That in my chambre longe tyme hath be,
Ye ! for an heyre clout to wrappe me ! "
But yet to me she wol nat do that grace,
For which ful pale and welked is my face.

But, sirs, to yow it is no curteisye
To speken to an old man vileinye,
But he trespasse in worde, or elles in dede.
In holy writ ye may your-self wel rede,
" Agayns an old man, hoor upon his heed,
Ye sholde aryse ; " wherfor I yeve yow reed,
Ne dooth un-to an old man noon harm now,
Na-more than ye wolde men dide to yow
In age, if that ye so longe abyde ;
And god be with yow, wher ye go or ryde.
I moot go thider as I have to go.'

' Nay, olde cherl, by god, thou shalt nat so,'

moot] must.   leve moder] dear mother.   leet] let.
heyre clout] hair shroud.   welked] withered.   vileinye]
discourtesy, rudeness.   hoor] hoary, gray.   yeve]
give.   reed] counsel, advice.

Seyde this other hasardour anon ;
' Thou partest nat so lightly, by seint John !
Thou spak right now of thilke traitour Deeth,
That in this contree alle our frendes sleeth.
Have heer my trouthe, as thou art his aspye,
Tel wher he is, or thou shalt it abye,
By god, and by the holy sacrament !
For soothly thou art oon of his assent,
To sleen us yonge folk, thou false theef ! '

  ' Now, sirs,' quod he, ' if that yow be so leef
To finde Deeth, turne up this croked wey,
For in that grove I lafte him, by my fey,
Under a tree, and ther he wol abyde ;
Nat for your boost he wol him no-thing hyde.
See ye that ook ? right ther ye shul him finde.
God save yow, that boghte agayn mankinde,
And yow amende ! '—thus seyde this olde man.
And everich of thise ryotoures ran,
Til he cam to that tree, and ther they founde
Of florins fyne of golde y-coyned rounde
Wel ny an eighte busshels, as hem thoughte.
No lenger thanne after Deeth they soughte,
But ech of hem so glad was of that sighte,
For that the florins been so faire and brighte,
That doun they sette hem by this precious hord.
The worst of hem he spake the firste word.

  ' Brethren,' quod he, ' tak kepe what I seye ;
My wit is greet, though that I bourde and pleye.
This tresor hath fortune un-to us yiven,
In mirthe and jolitee our lyf to liven,

thilke] that very, that same.   aspye] spy.   abye]
suffer for, pay (dearly) for.   yow so leef] so dear to you,
so desired by you.   abyde] remain.   boost] boasting.
ook] oak.   everich] every one.   bourde] jest.   yiven]
given.

And lightly as it comth, so wol we spende.
Ey! goddes precious dignitee! who wende
To-day, that we sholde han so fair a grace?
But mighte this gold be caried fro this place
Hoom to myn hous, or elles un-to youres—
For wel ye woot that al this gold is oures—
Than were we in heigh felicitee.
But trewely, by daye it may nat be;
Men wolde seyn that we were theves stronge,
And for our owene tresor doon us honge.
This tresor moste y-caried be by nighte
As wysly and as slyly as it mighte.
Wherfore I rede that cut among us alle
Be drawe, and lat see wher the cut wol falle;
And he that hath the cut with herte blythe
Shal renne to the toune, and that ful swythe,
And bringe us breed and wyn ful prively.
And two of us shul kepen subtilly
This tresor wel; and, if he wol nat tarie,
Whan it is night, we wol this tresor carie
By oon assent, wher-as us thinketh best.'
That oon of hem the cut broughte in his fest,
And had hem drawe, and loke wher it wol falle;
And it fil on the yongeste of hem alle;
And forth toward the toun he wente anon.
And al-so sone as that he was gon,
That oon of hem spak thus un-to that other,
'Thou knowest wel thou art my sworne brother,
Thy profit wol I telle thee anon.
Thou woost wel that our felawe is agon;

comth] cometh.   wende] weened (supposed).   woot]
know.   doon us honge] have us hanged.   rede] advise.
cut] lot.   herte blythe] blithe heart.   renne] run.
swythe] quickly.   tarie] delay.   wher-as] where.
fest] fist   loke] look.   woost] knowest.

And heer is gold, and that ful greet plentee,
That shal departed been among us three.
But natheles, if I can shape it so
That it departed were among us two,
Hadde I nat doon a freendes torn to thee ? '

   That other answerde, ' I noot how that may be ;
He woot how that the gold is with us tweye,
What shal we doon, what shal we to him seye ? '

   ' Shal it be conseil ? ' seyde the firste shrewe,
' And I shal tellen thee, in wordes fewe,
What we shal doon, and bringe it wel aboute.'

   ' I graunte,' quod that other, ' out of doute,
That, by my trouthe, I wol thee nat biwreye.'

   ' Now,' quod the firste, ' thou woost wel we be
     tweye,
And two of us shul strenger be than oon.
Look whan that he is set, and right anoon
Arys, as though thou woldest with him pleye ;
And I shal ryve him thurgh the sydes tweye
Whyl that thou strogelest with him as in game,
And with thy dagger look thou do the same ;
And than shal al this gold departed be,
My dere freend, bitwixen me and thee ;
Than may we bothe our lustes al fulfille,
And pleye at dees right at our owene wille.'
And thus acorded been thise shrewes tweye
To sleen the thridde, as ye han herd me seye.

   This yongest, which that wente un-to the toun,
Ful ofte in herte he rolleth up and doun
The beautee of thise florins newe and brighte.
' O lord ! ' quod he, ' if so were that I mighte

---

torn] turn.   noot] know not.   tweye] two.   conseil]
a secret.   shrewe] scoundrel.   doon] do.   biwreye]
betray.   ryve] rip.   departed] divided.

Have al this tresor to my-self allone,
Ther is no man that liveth under the trone
Of god, that sholde live so mery as I ! '
And atte last the feend, our enemy,
Putte in his thought that he shold poyson beye,
With which he might sleen his felawes tweye ;
For-why the feend fond him in swich lyvinge,
That he had leve him to sorwe bringe,
For this was outrely his fulle entente
To sleen hem bothe, and never to repente.
And forth he gooth, no lenger wolde he tarie,
Into the toun, un-to a pothecarie,
And preyed him, that he him wolde selle
Som poyson, that he mighte his rattes quelle ;
And eek ther was a polcat in his hawe,
That, as he seyde, his capouns hadde y-slawe,
And fayn he wolde wreke him, if he mighte,
On vermin, that destroyed him by nighte.

The pothecarie answerde, ' and thou shalt have
A thing that, al-so god my soule save,
In al this world ther nis no creature,
That ete or dronke hath of this confiture
Noght but the mountance of a corn of whete,
That he ne shal his lyf anon forlete ;
Ye, sterve he shal, and that in lasse whyle
Than thou wolt goon a paas nat but a myle ;
This poyson is so strong and violent.'

This cursed man hath in his hond y-hent

---

trone] throne.   beye] buy.   sleen] slay.   fond]
found.   sorwe] sorrow.   outrely] utterly.   pothecarie]
apothecary.   rattes quelle] rats kill.   hawe] yard,
enclosure.   wreke] avenge.   nis] is not.   con-
fiture] composition.   mountance] amount.   forlete]
forgo.   sterve] die.   lasse] less.   goon a paas] go
at a footpace.   y-hent] taken.

This poyson in a box, and sith he ran
In-to the nexte strete, un-to a man,
And borwed [of] him large botels three ;
And in the two his poyson poured he ;
The thridde he kepte clene for his drinke.
For all the night he shoop him for to swinke
In caryinge of the gold out of that place.
And whan this ryotour, with sory grace,
Had filled with wyn his grete botels three,
To his felawes agayn repaireth he.

What nedeth it to sermone of it more ?
For right as they had cast his deeth bifore,
Right so they han him slayn, and that anon.
And whan that this was doon, thus spak that oon,
' Now lat us sitte and drinke, and make us merie,
And afterward we wol his body berie.'
And with that word it happed him, par cas,
To take the botel ther the poyson was,
And drank, and yaf his felawe drinke also,
For which anon they storven bothe two.

But, certes, I suppose that Avicen
Wroot never in no canon, ne in no fen,
Mo wonder signes of empoisoning
Than hadde thise wrecches two, er hir ending.
Thus ended been thise homicydes two,
And eek the false empoysoner also.

---

sith] afterwards.   botels] bottles.   thridde] third.
clene] clean. shoop him] purposed, intended. to swinke]
to labour, toil.   sermone] sermonize.   cast] arranged.
han] have.   spak] spake.   oon] one.   wol] will.
par cas] by chance.   ther] wherein.   yaf] gave.
storven] died.   certes] certainly.   wroot] wrote.
canon] Avicenna's book called the Canon.   fen] chapter,
sub-division.   wonder] wondrous.   er] before.

O cursed sinne, ful of cursednesse !
O traytours homicyde, o wikkednesse !
O glotonye, luxurie, and hasardrye !
Thou blasphemour of Crist with vileinye
And othes grete, of usage and of pryde !
Allas ! mankinde, how may it bityde,
That to thy creatour which that thee wroghte,
And with his precious herte-blood thee boghte,
Thou art so fals and so unkinde, allas !

GOOD COUNSEL OF CHAUCER

FLEE fro the prees, and dwelle with sothfastnesse,
Suffyce unto thy good, though hit be smal ;
For hord hath hate, and climbing tikelnesse,
Prees hath envye, and wele blent overal ;
Savour no more than thee bihove shal ;
Werk wel thy-self, that other folk canst rede ;
And trouthe shal delivere, hit is no drede.

Tempest thee noght al croked to redresse,
In trust of hir that turneth as a bal :
Gret reste stant in litel besinesse ;
And eek be war to sporne ageyn an al ;
Stryve noght, as doth the crokke with the wal.

prees] mob, crowd.　　sothfastnesse] truth, honesty.
hit] it.　　hord] avarice.　　tikelnesse] instability.　　wele]
well-being, wealth.　　blent] deceives, beguiles.　　overal]
everywhere.　　savour] taste.　　bihove] suit.　　rede]
counsel, advise.　　hit is no drede] without doubt.
tempest thee noght] do not violently distress thyself.
al croked] all the crooked.　　in trust of hir] trusting to
her.　　that turneth as a bal] Fortune with her wheel.
gret reste] great repose.　　stant] consists.　　besinesse]
meddling.　　sporne ageyn] spurn or kick against.
al] awl.　　crokke] earthenware pot.　　wal] wall.

Daunte thy-self, that dauntest otheres dede ;
And trouthe shal delivere, hit is no drede.
That thee is sent, receyve in buxumnesse,
The wrastling for this worlde axeth a fal.
Her nis non hoom, her nis but wildernesse :
Forth, pilgrim, forth ! Forth, beste, out of thy
    stal !
Know thy contree, look up, thank God of al ;
Hold the hye wey, and lat thy gost thee lede :
And trouthe shal delivere, hit is no drede.

Envoy

Therfore, thou vache, leve thyn old wrecchednesse
Unto the worlde ; leve now to be thral ;
Crye him mercy, that of his hy goodnesse
Made thee of noght, and in especial
Draw unto him, and pray in general
For thee, and eek for other, hevenlich mede ;
And trouthe shal delivere, hit is no drede.

daunte] control.   buxumnesse] submission.   wrastling] wrestling.   axeth a fal] asketh a fall.   her nis non hoom] here is no home.   beste] beast.   stal] stall. hye wey] high way.   gost] spirit.   vache] cow, beast. leve] leave.   thral] enthralled.   mede] mead (drink).

JOHN BARBOUR

d. 1395

FREEDOM

A ! Fredome is a noble thing !
Fredome mays man to haiff liking ;
Fredome all solace to man giffis,
He levys at ese that frely levys !
A noble hart may haiff nane ese,
Na ellys nocht that may him plese,
Gyff fredome fail ; for fre liking
Is yarnyt our all othir thing.
Na he that ay has levyt fre
May nocht knaw weill the propyrtè,
The angyr, na the wretchyt dome
That is couplyt to foule thyrldome.
Bot gyff he had assayit it,
Than all perquer he suld it wyt ;
And suld think fredome mar to prise
Than all the gold in warld that is.

JOHN GOWER

1330(?)–1408

ALEXANDER AND THE PIRATE

Of him whom al this Erthe dradde,
Whan he the world so overladde
Thurgh werre, as it fortuned is,
King Alisandre, I rede this ;
How in a Marche, where he lay,
It fell per chance upon a day

liking] liberty.
yarnyt] yearned for.
Marche] country.

na ellys nocht] nor aught else.
perquer] thoroughly, by heart.

A Rovere of the See was nome,
Which many a man hadde overcome
And slain and take here good aweie :
This Pilour, as the bokes seie,
A famous man in sondri stede
Was of the werkes whiche he dede.
This Prisoner tofor the king
Was broght, and there upon this thing
In audience he was accused :
And he his dede hath noght excused,
Bot preith the king to don him riht,
And seith, ' Sire, if I were of miht,
I have an herte lich to thin :
For if the pouer were myn,
Mi will is most in special
To rifle and geten overal
The large worldes good aboute.
Bot for I lede a povere route
And am, as who seith, at meschief,
The name of Pilour and of thief
I bere ; and thou, which routes grete
Miht lede and take thi beyete,
And dost riht as I wolde do,
Thi name is nothing cleped so,
Bot thou are named Emperour.
Oure dedes ben of o colour
And in effect of o decerte,
Bot thi richesse and my poverte
Tho ben noght taken evene liche.
And natheles he that is riche
This dai, tomorwe he mai be povere ;
And in contraire also recovere

---

nome] taken.   Pilour] pillager.   lich] like.   povere] poor.
route] company.   meschief] ill-luck.   beyete] advantage.

A povere man to gret richesse
Men sen : forthi let rihtwisnesse
Be peised evene in the balance.
 The king his hardi contienance
Behield, and herde hise wordes wise,
And seide unto him in this wise :
' Thin ansuere I have understonde,
Whereof my will is, that thou stonde
In mi service and stille abide.'
And forth withal the same tide
He hath him terme of lif withholde,
The mor and for he schal ben holde,
He made him kniht and yaf him lond,
Which afterward was of his hond
An orped kniht in many a stede,
And gret prouesce of armes dede,
As the Croniques it recorden.

JOHN LYDGATE
1370(?)–1450(?)

THE LONDON LACKPENNY

To London once my stepps I bent,
 Where trouth in no wyse should be faynt,
To Westmynster-ward I forthwith went
 To a man of law to make complaynt ;
 I sayd, ' For Mary's love, that holy saynt,
Pity the poore that wolde proceede ' ;
But for lack of mony I cold not spede.

   .   .   .

peised] weighed. withholde] retained (i. e. for the rest
of his life). orped] bold.
 faynt] feigned.

Then to the Chepe I began me drawne,
  Where mutch people I saw for to stand;
One ofred me velvet, sylke, and lawne,
  An other he taketh me by the hande,
  'Here is Parys thred, the fynest in the land';
I never was use to such thyngs indede,
And wanting mony I might not spede.

    .   .   .

Then into Corn-Hyll anon I yode,
  Where was mutch stolen gere amonge;
I saw where honge myne owne hoode,
  That I had lost amonge the thronge;
  Now by my owne hood I thought it wronge,
I knew it as well as I dyd my crede,
But for lack of mony I could not spede.

    .   .   .

Then hyed I me to Belynsgate;
  And one cryed, 'Hoo! go we hence!'
I prayed a barge-man, for God's sake,
  That he wold spare me my expence.
  'Thou 'scapst not here,' quod he, 'under two
    pence;
I lyst not yet bestow my almes dede.'
Thus lackyng mony, I could not spede.

Then I convayd me into Kent;
  For of the law wold I meddle no more;
Because no man to me tooke entent,
  I dyght me to do as I dyd before,
  Now Jesus, that in Bethlem was bore,
Save London, and send trew lawyers there mede!
For who so wants mony with them shall not spede.

               yode] walked, went.

ROBERT HENRYSON
1435(?)–1506(?)

THE TAILL OF THE UPONLANDIS MOUS
AND THE BURGES MOUS

Esope, my author, makis mentioun
Of twa myis, and thay wer sisteris deir,
Of quhome the eldest duelt in ane borous toun,
The uther wynnit uponland, weill neir,
Soliter, quhile under busk, quhile under breir,
Quhilis in the corne, and uther mennis skaith,
As outlawis dois and levis on their waith.

This rurall mous into the winter tyde
Had hunger, cauld, and tholit gret distres.
The uther mous that in the burgh can byde
Was gild brother and maid ane fre burgess;
Toll fre also, but custum mair or les,
And fredome had to ga quhair ever scho list,
Amang the cheis in ark, and meill in kist.

Ane tyme quhen scho was full and unfutesair,
Scho tuik in mynde hir sister uponland,
And langit for to heir of hir weilfair,
To se quhat lyfe scho led under the wand :
Bairfute, allone, with pykestalf in hir hand,
As pure pilgryme scho passit out of toun,
To seik hir sister baith our daill and doun.

---

borous toun] burgh. wynnit] dwelt. uponland]
in the country. skaith] damage. waith] hunting.
tholit] endured. can] did. but] without. custum]
tax. kist] chest. wand] osier.

Furth mony wilsum wayis can scho walk,
Throw moss and mure, throw bankis, busk, and breir,
Scho ran cryand, quhill scho come to ane balk:
' Cum furth to me, my awin sister deir;
Cry peip anis ! ' With that the mousse culd heir,
And knew hir voce, as kynnisman will do,
Be verray kynd; and furth scho come hir to.

The hartlie joy, Lord God ! gif ye had sene,
Was kythit quhen that thir twa sisteris met;
And gret kyndnes was schawin thame betuene,
For quhillis thay leuch, and quhillis for joy thay
     gret,
Quhile kissit sweit, quhillis in armes plet;
And thus thay fure, quhill soberit was thair mude,
Syne fute for fute unto the chalmer yude.

As I hard say, it was ane sober wane,
Of fog and fairne full febilie was maid,
Ane sillie scheill under ane steidfast stane,
Of quhilk the entres was not hie nor braid;
And in the samyn thay went but mair abaid,
Withoutin fire or candill birnand bricht,
For commonlie sic pykeris luifes nocht licht.

Quhen thay war lugeit thus, thir sillie myis,
The youngest sister in to hir butterie glide,
And brocht furth nuttis and candill in steid of
     spyce ;
Gif this was gude fair, I do it on thame beside.
The burges mous prompit furth in pride,

wilsum] lonesome.   quhill] till.   balk] ridge.
anis] once.   Be] By.   kynd] nature.   kythit]
shown.   gret] wept.   plet] folded.   mude] mood.
yude] went.   wane] abode.   fog] moss.   scheill]
shelter.   abaid] delay.   pykeris] pickers, thieves.
do it on thame beside] leave it to them.

And said, ' Sister, is this your daylie fude ? '
' Quhy not,' quod scho, ' is not this meit richt
   gude ? '

' Na, be my saule, I think it bot ane scorne.'
' Madame,' quod scho, ' ye be the mair to blame.
My mother said, sister, quhen we war borne,
That I and ye lay baith within ane wame :
I keip the rait and custome of my dame,
And of my leving in to povertie,
For landis haif we nane in propertie.'

' My fair sister,' quod scho, ' haif me excusit,
This rude dyat and I can not accord ;
To tender meit my stomok is ay usit,
For quhilis I fair als weill as ony lord ;
Thir widderit peis and nuttis, or thay be bord,
Will brek my teith, and mak my wame full sklender,
Quhilk was befoir usit to meitis tender.'

' Weill, weill, sister,' quod the rurale mous,
' Gif it pleis yow, sic thing as ye se heir,
Baith meit and drink, herberie and hous,
Sall be your awin, will ye remane all yeir ;
Ye sall it haif with blith and mery cheir,
And that sould mak the maissis that ar rude,
Amang friendis, richt tender and wonder gude.

' Quhat plesure is in feistis delicate,
The quhilk ar gevin with ane glowmand brow ?
Ane gentill hart is better recreate
With blith courage, than seith to him ane kow :
Ane modicum is mair for till allow,

  Thir] These.   or] ere.   herberie] lodging.   maissis]
messes.   seith] seethe.

Sua that gude will be carver at the dais,
Than thrawin vult and mony spycit mais.'

For all hir merie exhortatioun,
This burges mous had litill will to sing,
Bot hevilie scho kest hir browis doun,
For all the daynteis that scho culd hir bring.
Yit at the last scho said, half in hething,
' Sister, this victuall and your royell feist
May weill suffice unto ane rurall beist.

' Let be this hole, and cum unto my place,
I sall to yow schaw be experience
My Gude Fryday is better nor your Pace ;
My dische-likkingis is wirth your haill expence.
I haif housis anew of grit defence ;
Of cat nor fall nor trap I haif na dreid.'
' I grant,' quod scho ; and on togidder yeid.

In stubbill array throw rankest gres and corne,
And under bushis, previlie culd thay creip.
The eldest was the gide and went beforne,
The younger to hir wayis tuik gude keip.
On nycht thay ran, and on the day can sleip ;
Quhill in the morning, or the laverok sang,
Thay fand the toun, and in blithlie culd gang.

Not fer fra thine unto ane wirthie wane
This burges brocht thame sone quhair thay suld be ;
Without God speid thair herberie was tane
Into ane spence with victuell grit plentie ;
Baith cheis and butter upoun thair skelfis hie,

---

thrawin vult] cross face.   hething] scorn.   Pace]
Easter.   anew] enough.   fall] trap.   laverok] lark.
culd] did.   thine] thence.   spence] larder.

And flesche and fische aneuch, baith fresche and salt,
And sekkis full of meill and eik of malt.

Efter quhen thay disposit war to dyne,
Withoutin grace thay wesche and went to meit,
With all coursis that cuikis culd defyne,
Muttoun and beif strukkin in tailyeis greit ;
Ane lordis fair thus culd thay counterfeit,
Except ane thing, thay drank the watter cleir
In steid of wyne, bot yit thay maid gude cheir.

With blith upcast and merie countenance,
The eldest sister sperit at hir gest,
Gif that scho be ressone fand differrence
Betuix that chalmer and hir sarie nest.
' Yea dame,' quod scho, ' bot how lang will this
    lest ? '
' For evermair, I wait, and langer to,'
' Gif it be swa, ye ar at eis,' quod scho.

Till eik thair cheir ane subcharge furth scho brocht,
Ane plait of grottis, and ane dische full of meill ;
Thraf caikis als I trow scho spairit nocht,
Aboundantlie about hir for to deill ;
And man fulle fyne scho brocht in steid of geill,
And ane quhite candill out of ane coffer stall,
In steid of spyce to gust thair mouth withall.

Thus maid thay merie quhill thay mycht na mair,
And, ' haill, yuill, haill ! ' thay cryit upone hie.
Yit efter joy oftymes cumis cair,
And troubill efter grit prosperitie.
Thus as thay sat in all thair jolitie,

strukkin] cut.   tailyeis] slices.   upcast] raillery.
sperit] asked.   wait] wot.   eik] eke out.   subcharge]
second course.   grottis] groats.   Thraf] Unleavened.
man] cake.   geill] jelly.

The spensar came with keyis in his hand,
Oppynnit the dur, and thame at denner fand.

Thay taryit nocht to wasche, as I suppois,
Bot on to ga quha that mycht formest win.
The burges had ane hoill, and in scho gois;
Hir sister had na hoill to hide hir in;
To se that selie mous it was grit sin,
So desolate and will of ane gude reid;
For verray dreid scho fell in swoun neir deid.

Bot, as God wald, it fell ane happie cace;
The spensar had na laser for to bide,
Nouther to seik nor serche, to skar nor chace,
Bot on he went, and left the dur up wyde.
The bald burges his passing weill hes spyde;
Out of hir hoill scho come and cryit on hie,
' How fair ye, sister ? cry peip, quhair ever ye be ? '

This rurall mous lay flatling on the ground,
And for the deith scho was full sair dreidand,
For till hir hart straik mony wofull stound,
As in ane fever scho trimblit fute and hand;
And quhen hir sister in sic ply hir fand,
For verray pietie scho began to greit,
Syne confort hir with wordis hunny sweit.

' Quhy ly ye thus ? ryse up, my sister deir,
Cum to your meit, this perrell is over past.'
The uther answerit hir with hevie cheir,
' I may not eit, sa sair I am agast;
I had lever thir fourtie dayis fast,

With watter caill, and to gnaw benis and peis,
Than all your feist in this dreid and diseis.'

With fair tretie yit scho gart hir upryse,
And to the burde thay baith to gidder sat ;
And skantlie had thay drunkin anis or twyse,
Quhen in come Gib-Hunter, our jolie cat,
And bad God speid : the burges up with that,
And till hir hoill scho went as fyre on flint :
Bawdronis the uther be the bak hes hint.

Fra fute to fute he kest hir to and fra,
Quhilis up, quhilis doun, als cant as ony kid ;
Quhilis wald he lat hir rin under the stra,
Quhilis wald he wink, and play with hir bukhid.
Thus to the selie mous grit pane he did,
Quhill at the last, throw fortoun and gude hap,
Betuix the dorsour and the wall scho crap.

And up in haist behind the parraling
Scho clam sa hie, that Gilbert mycht not get hir,
Syne be the cluke thair craftelie can hing,
Till he was gane, hir cheir was all the better.
Syne doun scho lap quhen thair was nane to let hir,
And to the burges mous loud can scho cry :
' Fairweill, sister, thy feist heir I defy !

' Thy mangerie is mingit all with cair,
Thy guse is gude, thy gansell sour as gall ;
The subcharge of thy service is bot sair,
Sa sall thow find heirefterwart may fall.
I thank yone courtyne and yone perpall wall

caill] broth.   Bawdronis] Puss.   hint] caught.
cant] playful.   bukhid] hide-and-seek.   dorsour,
paralling] hanging, curtain.   cluke] claw.   let] prevent.
defy] renounce.   mangerie] eating.   mingit] mingled.
gansell] sauce.   fall] befall.   perpall] partition.

Of my defence now fra yone crewell beist.
Almychtie God, keip me fra sic ane feist!

' Wer I in to the kith that I come fra,
For weill nor wa suld I never cum agane.'
With that scho tuik hir leve and furth can ga,
Quhilis throw the corne, and quhilis throw the plane;
Quhen scho was furth and fre, scho was full fane,
And merilie merkit unto the mure :
I can not tell how efterwart scho fure.

Bot I hard say scho passit to hir den,
Als warme als woll, suppois it was not greit,
Full benelie stuffit, baith but and ben,
Of peiss, and nuttis, beinis, ry, and quheit;
Quhen ever scho list, scho had aneuch to eit,
In quiet and eis, withouttin ony dreid ;
Bot to hir sisteris feist na mair scho yeid.

WILLIAM DUNBAR

1465 (?)–1520 (?)

THE DANCE OF THE SEVIN DEIDLY SYNNIS

> Off Februar the fyiftene nycht,
> Full lang befoir the dayis lycht,
>   I lay in till a trance ;
> And then I saw baith hevin and hell :
> Me thocht, amangis the feyndis fell,
>   Mahoun gart cry ane dance
> Off schrewis that wer nevir schrevin,
> Aganiss the feist of Fasternis evin,

kith] (known) place.   merkit] took her way.   woll]
wool.   suppois] though.   benelie] comfortably.
but and ben] out-room and in-room, kitchen and parlour.
   Mahoun] Mahomet, i. e. the devil.   schrevin] shriven.

To mak thair observance ;
He bad gallandis ga graith a gyiss,
And kast vp gamountis in the skyiss,
That last came out of France.

Heilie harlottes on hawtane wyiss
Come in with mony sindrie gyiss,
Bot yit luche nevir Mahoun ;
Quhill preistis come in with bair schevin nekkis,
Than all the feyndis lewche, and maid gekkis,
Blak Belly and Bawsy Brown.

' Lat se,' quod he, ' Now quha begynnis ; '
With that the fowll Sevin Deidly Synnis
Begowth to leip at anis.
And first of all in dance wes Pryd,
With hair wyld bak and bonet on syd,
Lyk to mak vaistie wanis ;
And round abowt him, as a quheill,
Hang all in rumpillis to the heill
His kethat for the nanis :
Mony prowd trumpour with him trippit
Throw skaldand fyre, ay as they skippit
Thay gyrnd with hiddouss granis.

Than Yre come in with sturt and stryfe ;
His hand wes ay vpoun his knyfe,
He brandeist lyk a beir :
Bostaris, braggaris, and barganeris,
Eftir him passit in to pairis,

graith a gyiss] prepare a masque.   gamountis] gambols.
Heilie] Proud.   hawtane] haughty.   gekkis] mocks.
Begowth] Began.   vaistie] empty.   kethat] cassock.
nanis] nonce.   trumpour] cheat.   sturt] turbulence.
barganeris] wranglers.

All bodin in feir of weir ;
In iakkis and stryppis and bonnettis of steill,
Thair leggis wer chenyeit to the heill,
Ffrawart wes their affeir :
Sum vpoun vdir with brandis beft,
Sum jaggit vthiris to the heft,
With knyvis that scherp cowd scheir.

Nixt in the dance foll_owit Invy,
Fild full of feid and fellony,
Hid malyce and dispyte ;
Ffor pryvie hatrent that tratour trymlit.
Him follow_it mony freik dissymlit,
With fenyeit wirdis quhyte ;
And flattereris in to menis facis ;
And bakbyttaris of sindry racis,
To ley that had delyte ;
And rownaris of fals lesingis ;
Allace ! that courtis of noble kingis
Of thame can nevir be quyte.

Nixt him in dans come Cuvatyce,
Rute of all evill and grund of vyse,
That nevir cowd be content ;
Catyvis, wrechis and okkeraris,
Hud-pykis, hurdaris and gadderaris.
All with that warlo went :
Out of thair throttis thay schot on vdder
Hett moltin gold, me thocht a fudder,

bodin in feir of weir] arrayed in guise of war.   chen-
yeit] clad in chain-mail.   Ffrawart] Froward.   affeir]
bearing.   beft] beat.   jaggit] pricked.   feid] fued.
freik] wag.   rownaris] whisperers.   lesingis] lies.
okkeraris] usurers.   Hud-pykis] Misers.   hurdaris]
hoarders.   gadderaris] gatherers.   warlo] wizard.
fudder] hundredweight.

As fyreflawcht maist fervent ;
Ay as thay tomit thame of schot,
Ffeyndis fild thame new vp to the thrott
With gold of allkin prent.

Syne Sweirnes, at the secound bidding,
Come lyk a sow out of a midding,
Full slepy wes his grunyie :
Mony sweir bumbard belly huddroun,
Mony slute daw and slepy duddroun,
Him serwit ay with sounyie ;
He drew thame furth in till a chenyie,
And Belliall, with a brydill renyie,
Evir lascht thame on the lunyie :
In dance thay war so slaw of feit,
Thay gaif thame in the fyre a heit,
And maid thame quicker of counyie.

Than Lichery, that lathly corss,
Berand lyk a bawkit horss,
And Ydilness did him leid ;
Thair wes with him ane ugly sort,
And mony stynkand fowll tramort,
That had in syn bene deid.
Quhen thay wer entrit in the dance,
Thay wer full strenge of countenance,
Lyk turkass birnand reid.

Than the fowll monstir Glutteny,
Off wame vnsasiable and gredy,

fyreflawcht] wildfire.   tomit] emptied.   allkin prent]
all kind(s) of stamp.   Sweirnes] Sloth.   grunyie]
snout.   bumbard belly huddroun] tun-bellied glutton.
slute] sluttish.   daw] sluggard.   duddroun] sloven.
sounyie] care.   lunyie] loins.   counyie] apprehension.
Berand] Neighing.   tramort] corpse.   turkass] pincers.
wame] belly.

To dance he did him dress :
Him followit mony fowll drunckart,
With can and collep, cop and quart,
In surffet and excess ;
Full mony a waistless wallydrag,
With wamiss vnweildable, did furth wag,
In creische that did incress ;
Drynk ! ay thay cryit, with mony a gaip ;
The feyndis gaif thame hait leid to laip,
Their lovery wes na less.

Na menstrallis playit to thame but dowt,
Ffor glemen thair wer haldin owt,
Be day, and eik by nycht ;
Except a menstrall that slew a man,
Swa till his heretage he wan,
And entirt be breif of richt.

Than cryd Mahoun for a Heleiand padyane ;
Syne ran a feynd to feche Makfadyane,
Ffar northwart in a nuke ;
Be he the correnoch had done schout,
Erschemen so gadderit him abowt,
In Hell grit rowme thay tuke.
Thae tarmegantis, with tag and tatter,
Ffull lowd in Ersche begowth to clatter,
And rowp lyk revin and ruke :
The Devill sa devit wes with thair yell,
That in the depest pot of hell
He smorit thame with smuke.

wallydrag] weakling.   creische] grease.   lovery]
desire.   but] without.   padyane] pageant.   Be] By
the time that.   Erschemen] Gaels.   rowp] croak.
devit] deafened.   smorit] smothered.

IN HONOUR OF THE CITY OF LONDON

LONDON, thou art of townes *A per se*.
  Soveraign of cities, seemliest in sight,
Of high renoun, riches and royaltie ;
  Of lordis, barons, and many a goodly knyght ;
  Of most delectable lusty ladies bright ;
Of famous prelatis, in habitis clericall ;
  Of merchauntis full of substaunce and of myght :
London, thou art the flour of Cities all.

Gladdith anon, thou lusty Troynovaunt,
  Citie that some tyme cleped was New Troy ;
In all the erth, imperiall as thou stant,
  Pryncesse of townes, of pleasure and of joy,
  A richer restith under no Christen roy ;
For manly power, with craftis naturall,
  Fourmeth none fairer sith the flode of Noy :
London, thou art the flour of Cities all.

Gemme of all joy, jasper of jocunditie,
  Most myghty carbuncle of vertue and valour ;
Strong Troy in vigour and in strenuytie ;
  Of royall cities rose and geraflour ;
  Empress of townes, exalt in honour ;
In beawtie beryng the crone imperiall ;
  Swete paradise precelling in pleasure ;
London, thou art the flour of Cities all.

Above all ryvers thy Ryver hath renowne,
  Whose beryall stremys, pleasaunt and preclare,
Under thy lusty wallys renneth down,

  gladdith] rejoice.   Troynovaunt] Troja nova or
Trinovantum.   fourmeth] appeareth.   geraflour]
gillyflower.

Where many a swan doth swymme with wyngis
    fair ;
Where many a barge doth saile and row with are ;
Where many a ship doth rest with top-royall.
  O, towne of townes ! patrone and not compare,
London, thou art the flour of Cities all.

Upon thy lusty Brigge of pylers white
    Been merchauntis full royall to behold ;
Upon thy stretis goeth many a semely knyght
    In velvet gownes and in cheynes of gold.
    By Julyus Cesar thy Tour founded of old
May be the hous of Mars victoryall,
    Whose artillary with tonge may not be told :
London, thou art the flour of Cities all.

Strong be thy wallis that about thee standis ;
    Wise be the people that within thee dwellis ;
Fresh is thy ryver with his lusty strandis ;
    Blith by thy chirches, wele sownyng be thy bellis ;
    Rich be thy merchauntis in substaunce that
      excellis ;
Fair be their wives, right lovesom, white and small ;
    Clere be thy virgyns, lusty under kellis :
London, thou art the flour of Cities all.

Thy famous Maire, by pryncely governaunce,
    With sword of justice thee ruleth prudently.
No Lord of Parys, Venyce, or Floraunce
    In dignitye or honour goeth to hym nigh.
    He is exampler, loode-ster, and guye ;
Principall patrone and rose orygynalle,
    Above all Maires as maister most worthy :
London, thou art the flour of Cities all.

are] oar.   small] slender.   kellis] hoods, head-
dresses.   guye] guide.

THE NUT-BROWN MAID
15th century

He.   Be it right or wrong, these men among
       On women do complaine ;
       Affermyng this, how that it is
       A labour spent in vaine
       To love them wele ; for never a dele
       They love a man agayne,
       For lete a man do what he can
       Ther favour to attayne,
       Yet yf a newe to them pursue,
       Ther furst trew lover than
       Laboureth for nought, and from her thought
       He is a bannisshed man.

She.   I say not nay, but that all day
       It is bothe writ and sayde
       That woman's fayth is, as who saythe,
       All utterly decayed :
       But nevertheles, right good witnes
       In this case might be layde,
       That they love trewe, and contynew,—
       Recorde THE NUT-BROWNE MAIDE ;
       Whiche from her love, whan her to prove,
       He cam to make his mone,
       Wolde not departe, for in her herte
       She lovyd but hym allone.

He.   Than betwene us lete us discusse
       What was all the maner
       Betwene them too : we wyl also
       Telle all the peyne in-fere
       That she was in ; now I begynne,
       Soo that ye me answere :

never a dele] never a bit.   **than**] then.   **in-fere**] in company together.

Wherfore all ye that present be,
I pray you geve an eare.
I am the knyght, I cum be nyght,
As secret as I can,
Saying, Alas! thus stondyth the case,
I am a bannisshed man!

She. *And I your wylle for to fulfylle*
In this wyl not refuse,
Trusting to shewe, in wordis fewe,
That men have an ille use,
To ther owne shame, wymen to blame,
And causeles them accuse:
Therefore to you I answere now,
Alle wymen to excuse,
Myn owne hert dere, with you what chiere
I prey you telle anoon:
For in my mynde, of all mankynde
I love but you allon.

He. *It stondith so: a dede is do*
Wherof moche harme shal growe.
My desteny is for to dey
A shamful dethe, I trowe,
Or ellis to flee,—the ton must be:
None other wey I knowe,
But to withdrawe as an outlaw,
And take me to my bowe.
Wherfore, adew, my owne hert trewe,
None other red I can;
For I muste to the grene-wode goo,
Alone, a bannysshed man.

She. *O Lorde, what is this worldis blisse,*
That chaungeth as the mone!

red I can] counsel I know.

My somers day in lusty May
  Is derked before the none.
I here you saye, Farwel : nay, nay,
  We departe not soo sone.
Why say ye so ? Wheder wyl ye goo ?
  Alas, what have ye done ?
Alle my welfare to sorow and care
  Shulde chaunge, yf ye were gon :
For in my mynde, of all mankynde
  I love but you alone.

He. I can beleve it shal you greve,
    And somwhat you distrayne ;
But aftyrwarde your paynes harde
  Within a day or tweyne
Shal sone aslake, and ye shal take
  Confort to you agayne.
Why shuld ye nought ? for, to make thought,
  Your labur were in vayne,
And thus I do, and pray you, too,
  As hertely as I can :
For I muste too the grene-wode goo,
  Alone, a banysshed man.

She. Now syth that ye have shewed to me
    The secret of your mynde,
I shal be playne to you agayne,
  Lyke as ye shal me fynde :
Syth it is so that ye wyll goo,
  I wol not leve behynde ;
Shal never be sayd the Nutbrowne Mayd
  Was to her love unkind.

derked] darkened. departe] part. wheder] whither.
distrayne] disquiet. aslake] lessen. syth[since.
leve] remain.

Make you redy, for soo am I,
   All though it were anoon :
For in my mynde, of all mankynde
   I love but you alone.

He. Yet I you rede to take good hede
     What men wyl thinke and sey ;
Of yonge and olde it shal be tolde,
     That ye be gone away
Your wanton wylle for to fulfylle,
     In grene-wood you to play ;
And that ye myght from your delyte
     Noo lenger make delay.
Rather than ye shuld thus for me
     Be called an ylle woman
Yet wolde I to the grene-woode goo
     Alone, a banyshed man.

She. Though it be songe of olde and yonge
     That I shuld be to blame,
Theirs be the charge that speke so large
     In hurting of my name.
For I wyl prove that feythful love
     It is devoyd of shame,
In your distresse and hevynesse
     To parte wyth you the same ;
And sure all thoo that doo not so,
     Trewe lovers ar they noon ;
But in my mynde, of all mankynde
     I love but you alone.

He. I councel yow remembre how
     It is noo maydens lawe,
Nothing to dought, but to renne out
     To wod with an outlawe.

parte wyth] share with.   thoo] those.

For ye must there in your hande bere
   A bowe redy to drawe,
And as a theef thus must ye lyve,
   Ever in drede and awe ;
By whiche to yow gret harme myght grow ;—
   Yet had I lever than
That I had too the grene-wod goo,
   Alone, a banysshyd man.

She. I thinke not nay, but as ye saye,
   It is noo maydens lore ;
But love may make me for your sake,
   As ye have said before,
To com on fote, to hunte and shote,
   To gete us mete and store ;
For soo that I your company
   May have, I aske noo more ;
From whiche to parte it makith myn herte
   As colde as ony ston ;
For in my mynde, of all mankynde
   I love but you alone.

He. For an outlawe this is the lawe,
   That men hym take and binde,
Wythout pytee, hangèd to bee,
   And waver with the wynde.
Yf I had neede, as God forbede,
   What rescous coude ye finde ?
For sothe, I trowe, you and your bowe
   Shuld drawe for fere behynde :
And noo marveyle ; for lytel avayle
   Were in your councel than ;
Wherfore I too the woode wyl goo,
   Alone, a banysshd man.

lever than] rather then.   rescous] rescue, aid.

She. Ful wel knowe ye that wymen bee
    Ful febyl for to fyght ;
No womanhed is it, indeede,
    To bee bolde as a knight.
Yet in suche fere yf that ye were
    Amonge enemys day and nyght,
I wolde wythstonde, with bowe in hande,
    To greve them as I myght,
And you to save, as wymen have
    From deth many one :
For in my mynde, of all mankynde
    I love but you alone.

He. Yet take good hede ; for ever I drede
    That ye coude not sustein
The thorney wayes, the depe valeis,
    The snowe, the frost, the reyn,
The colde, the hete ; for, drye or wete,
    We must lodge on the playn ;
And us aboove noon other rove
    But a brake bussh or twayne ;
Whiche sone shulde greve you, I beleve,
    And ye wolde gladly than
That I had too the grene-wode goo,
    Alone, a banysshyd man.

She. Syth I have here ben partynere
    With you of joy and blysse,
I muste also parte of your woo
    Endure, as reason is ;
Yet am I sure of oo plesure,
    And shortly, it is this;
That where ye bee, mesemeth, perdé,
    I coude not fare amysse.

        rove] roof.   **oo]** one.

Wythout more speche, I you beseche
   That we were soon agone ;
For in my mynde, of all mankynde
   I love but you alone.

He. Yf ye goo thedyr, ye must consider,
   Whan ye have lust to dyne,
Ther shal no mete be for to gete,
   Nor drinke, bere, ale, ne wine ;
Ne shetis clene, to lye betwene,
   Made of thred and twyne ;
Noon other house but levys and bowes,
   To kever your hed and myn.
Loo, myn herte swete, this ylle dyet
   Shuld make you pale and wan :
Wherfore I to the wood wyl goo,
   Alone, a banysshid man.

She. Amonge the wylde dere suche an archier
   As men say that ye bee,
Ne may not fayle of good vitayle
   Where is so grete plente :
And watir cleere of the ryvere
   Shal be ful swete to me ;
Wyth whiche in hele I shal right wele
   Endure, as ye shal see ;
And, er we go, a bed or twoo
   I can provide anoon ;
For in my mynde, of all mankynde
   I love but you alone.

He. Loo, yet before, ye must doo more,
   Yf ye wyl goo with me,
As cutte your here up by your ere,
   Your kirtel by the knee ;

      ne] nor.   hele] health.

Wyth bowe in hande for to withstonde
Your enmys, yf nede bee ;
And this same nyght, before daylyght,
To woodward wyl I flee ;
And yf ye wyl all this fulfylle
Doo it shortely as ye can :
Ellis wil I to the grene-wode goo,
Alone, a banysshyd man.

She. I shal as now do more for you
Than longeth to womanhed,
To short my here, a bowe to bere,
To shote in tyme of nede :
O my swete moder, before all other,
For you have I most drede !
But now, adiew ! I must ensue
Wher fortune duth me leede.
All this make ye : now lete us flee ;
The day cumeth fast upon ;
For in my mynde, of all mankynde
I love but you alone.

He. Nay, nay, not soo ; ye shal not goo,
And I shal telle you why ;
Your appetyte is to be lyght
Of love, I wele aspie :
For right as ye have sayd to me,
In lyke wyse, hardely,
Ye wolde answere, whosoever it were,
In way of company.
It is sayd of olde, sone hote, sone colde,
And so is a woman ;
Wherfore I too the woode wyl goo,
Alone, a banysshid man.

shortely] quickly.   longeth] belongeth.   hardely] boldly.

She.   Yef ye take hede, yt is noo nede
  Suche wordis to say bee me ;
For ofte ye preyd, and longe assayed,
  Or I you lovid, perde :
And though that I of auncestry
  A barons doughter bee,
Yet have you proved how I you loved,
  A squyer of lowe degree ;
And ever shal, what so befalle,
  To dey therfore anoon ;
For in my mynde, of al mankynde
  I love but you alone.

He.   A baron's childe to be begyled,
  It were a curssèd dede !
To be felow with an outlawe—
  Almyghty God forbede !
Yet bettyr were the power squyer
  Alone to forest yede
Than ye shal saye another day,
  That be my wyked dede
Ye were betrayed ; wherfore, good maide,
  The best red that I can,
Is that I too the grene-wode goo,
  Alone, a banysshed man.

She.   Whatsoever befalle, I never shal
  Of this thing you upbraid :
But yf ye goo, and leve me soo,
  Than have ye me betraied.
Remember you wele, how that ye dele,
  For yf ye, as ye sayde,
Be so unkynde to leve behynde
  Your love, the Nutbrowne Maide,

bee me] regarding me. to dey] were I to die. yede] went.

Trust me truly, that I shal dey,
   Sone after ye be gone ;
For in my mynde, of all mankynde
   I love but you alone.

He. Yef that ye went, ye shulde repent,
   For in the forest now
I have purveid me of a maide,
   Whom I love more than you :
Another fayrer than ever ye were
   I dare it wel avowe ;
And of you bothe eche shulde be wrothe
   With other, as I trowe.
It were myn ease to lyve in pease ;
   So wyl I, yf I can :
Wherfore I to the wode wyl goo,
   Alone, a banysshid man.

She. Though in the wood I undirstode
   Ye had a paramour,
All this may nought remeve my thought,
   But that I will be your ;
And she shal fynde me softe and kynde
   And curteis every our,
Glad to fulfylle all that she wylle
   Commaunde me, to my power :
For had ye, loo, an hondred moo,
   Yet wolde I be that one.
For in my mynde, of all mankynde
   I love but you alone.

He. Myn owne dere love, I see the prove
   That ye be kynde and trewe ;
Of mayde, and wyf, in all my lyf,
   The best that ever I knewe.

moo] more.   that one] one of them.   prove] proof.

Be mery and glad, be no more sad,
 The case is chaungèd newe ;
For it were ruthe that for your trouth
 Yow shuld have cause to rewe.
Be not dismayed : whatsoever I sayd
 To you whan I began,
I wyl not too the grene-wod goo ;
 I am noo banysshyed man.

She. Theis tidingis be more glad to me
 Than to be made a quene,
Yf I were sure they shuld endure ;
 But it is often seen,
When men wyl breke promyse, they speke
 The wordis on the splene.
Ye shape some wyle me to begyle,
 And stele fro me, I wene :
Then were the case wurs than it was,
 And I more woo-begone :
For in my mynde, of al mankynde
 I love but you alone.

He. Ye shal not nede further to drede :
 I wyl not disparage
You, God defende, sith you descende
 Of so grete a lynage.
Now understonde : to Westmerlande,
 Whiche is my herytage,
I wyl you bringe, and wyth a rynge,
 Be wey of maryage
I wyl you take, and lady make,
 As shortly as I can :
Thus have ye wone an erles son,
 And not a banysshyd man.

on the splene] that is, in haste.   defende] forbid.

Here may ye see that wymen be
*   In love meke, kinde, and stable :*
Late never man repreve them than,
*   Or calle them variable ;*
But rather prey God that we may
*   To them be confortable ;*
Whiche somtyme provyth suche as loveth,
*   Yf they be charitable.*
For sith men wolde that wymen sholde
*   Be meke to them echeon,*
Moche more ought they to God obey,
*   And serve but hym alone.*

BELL MY WIFE

16th cent. (?)

THIS winters weather itt waxeth cold
    & ffrost it ffreeseth on euery hill
& Boreas blowes his blaste soe bold
    yt all our cattell are like to spill
Bell my wiffe she loues noe strife
    she sayd vnto me quietlye
rise vp & saue Cow crumbockes liff
    man put thine old cloake about thee

He. O Bell my wiffe why dost thou flyte
        thou kens my cloake is verry thin
    Itt is soe sore ouer worne
        a crickè theron cannott runn
    Ile goe ffind the court wth in
    Ile noe longer lend nor borrow
    Ile goe ffind the court wth in
    for Ile haue a new cloake about me

            flyte] scold.

She.   Cow Crumbocke is a very good cowe
      Shee has alwayes beene good to the pale
  Shee has helpt vs to butter & cheese I trow
      & other things shee will not fayle
  for I wold be loth to see her pine
  therfore good husband ffollow my counsel
      now
  forsake the cowe & follow the ploughe
  man take thine old coate about thee

He.   my Cloake itt was a verry good cloake
      It hath beene alwayes good to the weare
  Itt hath cost mee many a groat
      I have had itt this 44 yere
  sometime itt was of the cloth in graine
      Itt is now but a sigh clout as yo^u may see
  It will neither hold out winde nor raine
      & Ile haue a new Cloake about mee

She.   It is 44 yeeres agoe
      since the one of vs the other did ken
  & wee haue had betwixt vs both
      children either nine or ten
  wee haue brought them vp to women & men
      In the feare of god I trow they bee
  & why wilt thou thyselfe misken
      Man take thine old cloake about thee

He.   O Bell my wiffe, why doest thou flyte
      now is nowe & then was then
  seeke all the world now throughout
      thou kens not Clownes from gentlemen

cloth in graine] scarlet cloth.   sigh clout] a rag for
straining.

they are cladd in blacke greene yellow & blew
 soe farr aboue their owne degree
once in my liffe Ile take a vew
 ffor Ile haue a new cloake about mee

She. King Harry was a verry good k——
  I trow his hose cost but a Crowne
he thought them 12d ouer to deere
  Therfore he called the taylor Clowne
he was king & wore the Crowne
  & thouse but of a low degree
Itts pride yᵗ putts this cuntrye downe
  man put thy old Cloake about thee

He. O Bell my wiffe why dost thou fflyte
  now is now & then was then
wee will liue now obedyent liffe
  thou the woman & I the man
Itts not for a man wᵗʰ a woman to threape
  vnlesse he ffirst giue ouer the play
wee will liue nowe as wee began
and Ile haue mine old Cloake about me

BALOW

16th cent. (?)

BALOW, my babe, Lye still & sleepe
Itt greeues me sore to see thee weepe
wouldst thou be quiet I'se be glad
thy mourning makes my sorrow sad
Balowe my boy thy mothers ioy
thy ffather breeds me great anoy
   Balow la-low

threape] argue.

when he began to court my loue
& wth his sugred words me moue
his ffaynings false & fflattering Chere
to me y^t time did not appeare
but now I see most cruellye
he cares neither for my babe nor mee
   Balow la-low

Lye still my darling sleepe awhile
& when thou wakest thoule sweetly smile
but smile not as thy father did
to cozen maids nay god forbid
but yett I ffeare thou will goe neere
thy fathers hart & fface to beare
   Balow la-low

I Cannott chuse but euer will
be louing to thy father still ;
where ere he goes where ere he ryde
my loue wth him doth still abyde
In weale or woe where ere he goe
my hart shall neere depart him ffroe
   Balow la-low

But doe not doe not pretty mine
to ffaynings false thy hart incline
be loyall to thy lover true
& neuer Change her ffor a new
If good or faire of her haue Care
ffor womens baninge is wonderous sare
   Balow la-low

Bearne by thy face I will beware
like Sirens words Ile not come neere
my babe & I together will liue
heele Comfort mee when Cares doe greeue

 neere] ne'er. bearne] bairn. heele] he'll.

> my babe & I right soft will lye
> & neere respect mans crueltye
> > Balow la-low
>
> ffarwell ffarwell the falsest youth
> y^t euer kist a womans mouth
> I wish all maids be warned by mee
> neere to trust mans curtesye
> for if wee doe but chance to bowe
> theyle use vs then they care not how
> > Balow la-low

JOHN SKELTON

1460–1529(?)

TO MISTRESS MARGARET HUSSEY

> Mirry Margarete,
> As mydsomer flowre,
> Jentill as fawcoun,
> Or hawke of the towre ;
> With solace and gladnes,
> Moche mirthe and no madnes,
> All good and no badnes ;
> So ioyously,
> So maidenly,
> So womanly
> Her demenyng
> In every thynge,
> Far, far passynge
> That I can endyght,
> Or suffyce to wryght

Jentill as fawcoun] gentle as falcon.   endyght] indite.   wryght] write.

Of Mirry Margarete
As mydsomer flowre,
Jentyll as fawcoun,
Or hawke of the towre,
As pacient and as styll
And as full of good wyll
As fayre Isaphill,
Colyaunder,
Swete pomaunder,
Good Cassaunder ;
Stedfast of thought,
Wele made, wele wrought,
Far may be sought,
Erst that ye can fynde
So corteise, so kynde,
As mirry Margarete,
This midsomer flowre,
Jentyll as fawcoun,
Or hawke of the towre.

THE TRAGEDY OF THE SPARROW AND THE CURSING OF THE CAT

O cat of carlyshe kynde
The fynde was in thy mynde
Whan thou my byrde untwynde
I wold thou haddest ben blynde
The leopardes sauage
The lyons in theyr rage
Myght catche ye in theyr pawes
And gnawe the in theyr iawes
These serpens of Lybany

carlyshe kynde] churlish nature. fynde] fiend.
untwynde] tore to pieces.

Myght stynge the venymously
The dragones with their tonges
Might poyson thy lyver and longes
The mantycors of ye montaynes
Myght fede them on thy braynes
      Melanchates that hounde
That plucked Acteon to the grounde
Gaue hym his mortall wounde
Chaunged to a dere
The story doth appere
Was chaunged to an harte
So thou foule cat that thou arte
The selfe same hounde
Myght the confounde
That his owne Lorde bote
Myght byte asondre thy throte
      Of Inde the gredy grypes
Myght tere out all thy trypes
Of Arcady the beares
Might plucke awaye thyne eares
The wylde wolfe Lycaon
Byte asondre thy backe bone
Of Ethna the brennynge hyll
That day and night brenneth styl
Set in thy tayle a blase
That all the world may gase
And wonder upon the
From Occyan the great se
Unto the Iles of Orchady
From Tyllbery fery
To the playne of Salysbery
So trayterously my byrde to kyll
That never ought the euyll wyll.

bote] bit.   grypes] griffins.   ought] owned.

TO MISTRESS MARGERY WENTWORTH

WITH margerain ientyll,
　The flowre of goodly hede,
Enbrowdred the mantill
　Is of your maydenhede.
Plainly I can not glose ;
　Ye be, as I diuyne,
The praty primrose,
　The goodly columbyne.
With margerain iantill,
　The flowre of goodly hede,
Enbrawderyd the mantyll
Is of yowre maydenhede.

Benygne, corteise, and meke,
　With wordes well deuysid ;
In you, who list to seke,
　Be virtus well comprysid.
With margerain iantill
　The flowre of goodly hede,
Enbrawderid the mantill
　Is of yowr maydenhede.

margerain] marjoram.

SIR THOMAS WYATT

1503–1542

FORGET NOT YET

*The Lover Beseecheth his Mistress not to Forget
his Steadfast Faith and True Intent*

Fforget not yet the tryde entent,
Of suche a truthe as I have ment,
My great travayle so gladly spent,
Fforget not yet!

Fforget not yet when fyrst began,
The wery lyffe ye know syns when
The sute, the servys, none tell can,
Fforget not yet!

Fforget not yet the gret assays,
The cruell wrong, the skornfull ways,
The paynfull pacyence in denays.
Fforget not yet!

Fforget not yet, forget not thys,
How long ago hathe beyn, and ys
The mynd, that never ment amys,
Fforget not yet.

Fforget not then thyne owne aprovyd,
The whyche so long hathe thee so lovyd,
Whose stedfast faythe yet never movyd,
Fforget not thys.

THE APPEAL

An Earnest Suit to his Unkind Mistress, not to
Forsake him.

AND wylt thow leve me thus ?
Say nay, say nay, ffor shame,
To save thee from the blame
Of all my greffe and grame ;
And wylt thou leave me thus ?
    Say nay ! Say nay !

And wylt thow leve me thus
That hathe lovyd the so long
In welthe and woo among :
And ys thy hart so strong
As for to leve me thus ?
    Say nay ! Say nay !

And wylt thow leve me thus,
That hathe gevyn the my hart
Never for to depart
Neyther for payn nor smart :
And wylt thow leve me thus ?
    Say nay ! Say nay !

And wylt thow leve me thus,
And have nomore pyttye
Of hym that lovythe the ?
Helas thy crueltye !
And wylt thow leve me thus ?
    Say nay ! Say nay !

grame] sorrow.

THOMAS, LORD VAUX

1510–1557(?)

YOUTH

WHEN I looke backe, and in my selfe behold
The wandering wayes that youth could not
descry ;
And markt the fearful course that youth did hold,
And mette in mind, eache steppe youth strayd
aewry ;
My knees I bowe, and from my hart I call,
O Lord, forget these faultes and folies all !

For now I see, how voyde youth is of skill,
I see also his prime time and his end :
I doo confess my faultes and all my ill,
And sorow sore, for that I did offend,
And with a mind repentant of all crimes,
Pardon I aske for youth, ten thousand times.

The humble hart, hath daunted the proud mind ;
Eke wysedome hath giuen ignorance a fall :
And wit hath taught, that folly could not find,
And age hath youth, her subiect and her thrall.
Therfore I pray, O Lord of life and truth,
Pardon the faultes committed in my youth.

Thou that diddest graunt the wise-king his requeste
Thou that in the Whale Thy prophet didst preserve :
Thou that forgavst the wounding of Thy brest :
Thou that didst save the thefe in state to sterve :
Thou onely God, the giuer of all grace :
Wipe out of mind the path of youthes vaine race.

sterve] die.

Thou that, by power, to life didst raise the dead :
Thou that [of grace] restorest the blind to sight :
Thou that for loue, Thy life and loue outbled :
Thou that of fauour madest the lame goe right :
Thou that canst heal, and helpe in all assayes,
Forgive the gilth, that grewe in youthes vaine
     wayes.

And now since I, with faith and doubtlesse mind,
Doo flye to Thee by prayer, to appease Thy yre :
And since that Thee I onely seeke to finde,
And hope, by faith, to attaynè my iust desire ;
Lord, mind no more youthes error and unskill,
And able age to doo Thy holy will.

OF A CONTENTED MIND

When all is doen and saied, in the ende this shall
     you finde,
The moste of all doeth bath in blisse that hath a
     quiet minde :
And, cleare from worldlie cares, to deame can bee
     content
The sweetest tyme in all this life in thinkyng to
     bee spent.

The body subiecte is to fickle Fortunes power,
And to a million of mishapps is casuall every
     hower :
And death in tyme doeth chaunge it to a clodde of
     claie ;
When as the mynde, whiche is devine, runnes
     neuer to decaie.

gilth] guilt.

Companion none is like unto the mynde alone ;
For many have been harmde by speach, through
    thinking few or none.
Feare often tymes restraineth words, but maks
    not thoughts to cease ;
And he speaks beste, that hath the skill when for
    to holde his peace.

Our wealth leaues vs at death, our kinsmen at the
    graue ;
But vertues of the mynde vnto the heauens with
    vs we have.
Wherefore for vertue's sake, I can be well content,
The sweetest tyme of all my life, to deeme in
    thinkyng spent.

HENRY HOWARD, EARL OF SURREY

1517(?)–1547

THE LOVER COMFORTETH HIMSELF, WITH
THE WORTHINESS OF HIS LOVE

WHEN raging loue with extreeme paine,
Most cruelly disdaines my hart,
When that my teares as flouds of raine,
Beare witnes of my wofull smarte,
When sighes haue wasted so my breath,
That I lye at the point of death.
I call to mind the nauie great,
That the Greekes brought to Troyē towne,
And how the boystrous windes did beate,
Their ships and rent their sailes a downe

boystrous] boisterous.

Till Agamemnons daughters bloud,
Appeased the Gods that them withstood.

And how in these ten yeres warre
Full many a bloudy deede was done,
And many a Lord that came from farre,
There caught his bane alas to sone,
And many a good knight ouercome,
Before the Greekes had Helene wonne.

Then think I thus sith such repaire,
So long time warre of valiant men,
Was all to winne a ladie faire,
Shall I not learn to suffer then,
And thinke my time well spent to be,
Seruing a worthier wight then shee.

Therefore I neuer will repent,
But paines contented still indure,
For like as when rough winter spent,
The pleasant spring straight draweth in ure,
So after raging stormes of *care*,
Joyfull at length may be my *fare*.

THE MEANS TO ATTAIN HAPPY LIFE

Martial, the things that do attain
    The happy life, be these I find,
The richesse left, not got with pain ;
    The fruitfull grounde, the quiet minde,

The egall frend, no grudge no strife,
    No charge of rule, nor gouernance ;
Without disease the helthfull life ;
    The houshold of continuance ;

sith] since.   egall] equal.

The meane diet, no delicate fare;
  True wisdome ioyndè with simplenesse;
The night dischargèd of all care,
  Where wine the wit may not oppresse,

The faithfull wife, without debate;
  Such slepes as may begile the night:
Contented wyth thine owne estate
  Ne wish for death, ne feare his might.

A PRAISE OF HIS LOVE

WHEREIN HE REPROVETH THEM THAT COMPARE THEIR LADIES WITH HIS

Geve place ye louers here before
  That spent your boastes and bragges in vaine
My Ladyes beautie passeth more
The best of yours I dare well sayne
Then doth the sunne the candle light,
Or brightest day the darkest night
  And there to hath a troth as iust,
as had Penelope the faire,
For what she saith ye may it trust
as it by writing sealed were,
and vertues hath she many moe
Than I with pen haue skill to showe
  I could rehearse, if that I woulde
The wholl effect of natures plaint
when she had lost the perfite mould,
The like to whom she could not paint
with wringing hands how she did cry,
And what she said, I know it I

ioynde] join'd.   then] than.   moe] more.

I know she swore with raging mind,
Her kingdome onely set a part,
There was no losse by law of kind,
That could haue gone so neere her hart.
And this was cheefly all hir paine,
She could not make the like againe.
    Sith nature this gaue her the praise
To be the cheefest worke she wrought,
In faith me thinke some better waies
On your behalfe might well be sought.
Then to compare (as ye haue done)
To match the candle with the sunne.

RICHARD EDWARDES

1523–1566

AMANTIUM IRAE

In going to my naked bed as one that would have
    slept,
I herd a wife sing to her child, that long before had
    wept ;
She sighèd sore and sang ful sweete, to bring the
    babe to rest,
That would not cease but cryèd still, in sucking at
    her brest.
She was full wearie of her watch, and greevèd with
    her child,
She rockèd it and rated it, till that on her it smilde :
Then did she say, Now have I found this proverbe
    true to proue,
The falling out of faithfull frends renuing is of loue.

sith] since.

Then tooke I paper, penne, and ynke, this proverbe
    for to write,
In regester for to remaine of such a worthy wight :
As she proceeded thus in song unto her little
    bratt,
Much matter vttered she of waight, in place whereas
    shee satt :
And prouèd plaine there was no beast, nor creature
    bearing life,
Could well be knowne to liue in loue without
    discord and strife :
Then kissèd she her little babe, and sware by God
    above,
The falling out of faithfull frendes renuing is of loue.

She said that neither king ne prince, ne lord could
    live aright,
Until their puissaunce the did prove, their manhode
    and their might.
When manhode shal be matched so that feare can
    take no place,
Then weary workes make warriours each other to
    embrace,
And leaued their forse that faylèd them, which did
    consume the rout,
That might before have lived their time, their
    strength and nature out :
Then did she sing as one that thought no man could
    her reprove,
The falling out of faithful frendes renuing is of loue.

She sayd she saw no fish ne fowl, nor beast within
    her haunt,
That mett a stranger in their kind, but could give
    it a taunt :

Since fleshe might not endure, but rest must wrath
    succede,
And forse the fight to fall to play in pasture where
    they feede,
So noble nature can well ende the worke she hath
    begone,
And bridle well that will not cease her tragedy in
    some :
Thus in song she oft reherst, as dyd her wel behoue,
The falling out of faithful frendes is the renuing of
    loue.

I meruaile much pardy (quoth she) for to behold
    the route,
To see man, woman, boy and beast, to toss the
    world about :
Some knele, some crouch, some beck, some chek,
    and some can smoothly smile,
And some embrace others in arme, and there thinke
    many a wile,
Some stand aloufe at cap and knee, some humble
    and some stoute,
Yet are they never frendes in deede untill they
    once fall out :
Thus ended she her song and sayd, before she did
    remove,
The falling out of faithful freends is the renuing
    of loue.

meruaile] marvel.

GEORGE GASCOIGNE
1525(?)–1577

THE LULLABY OF A LOVER

Sing lullaby, as women doe,
   Wherewith they bring their babes to rest;
And lullaby can I sing to,
   As womanly as can the best.
With lullaby they still the childe,
And if I be not much beguild,
Full many wanton babes have I,
Which must be stild with lullabie.

First lullaby my youthfull yeares,
   It is nowe time to go to bed:
For croockèd age and hoary heares,
   Have wone the hauen with in my head.
With Lullaby then youth be still;
With lullaby content thy will;
Since courage quayles, and commes behind,
Go sleepe, and so beguile thy minde!

Next Lullaby my gazing eyes,
   Which wonted were to glaunce apace;
For every Glasse may nowe suffice
   To shewe the furrowes in thy face.
With Lullabye then winke awhile;
With Lullabye your lookes beguile;
Lette no fayre face, nor beautie brighte,
Entice you efte with vayne delighte.

heares] hairs.

And Lullaby my wanton will;
  Lette reason's rule nowe reigne thy thought;
Since all too late I finde by skyll
Howe deare I have thy fancies bought;
With Lullaby nowe tak thyne ease,
With Lullaby thy doubtes appease;
For trust to this, if thou be styll,
My body shall obey thy will.

Eke Lullabye my louing boye,
  My little Robyn take thy rest,
Since age is colde, and nothing coye,
  Keepe close thy coyne, for so is best:
With Lullaby be thou content,
With Lullaby thy lustes relente,
Lette others pay which hath mo pence,
Thou art to pore for such expence.

Thus Lullabye my youth, myne eyes,
  My will, my ware, and all that was:
I can no moer delayes devise;
  But welcome payne, let pleasure passe:
With Lullaby now take your leave;
With Lullaby your dreames deceive;
And when you rise with waking eye,
Remember then this Lullabye.

THE ARRAIGNMENT OF A LOVER

At Beautyes barre as I dyd stande,
When false suspect accused mee,
George (quod the Judge) holde vp thy hande,
Thou art arraignde of Flatterye:
Tell therefore howe thou wylt bee tryde,
Whose judgement here wylt thou abyde?

My Lord (quod I) this Lady here,
Whome I esteeme aboue the rest,
Doth knowe my guilte if any were :
Wherefore hir doome shall please me best,
Let hir bee Judge and Juror boathe,
To trye mee guiltlesse by myne oathe.

Quod Beautie, no, it fitteth not,
A Prince hir selfe to iudge the cause :
Wyll is our Justice well you wot,
Appointed to discusse our Lawes :
If you wyll guiltlesse seeme to goe,
God and your countrey quitte you so.

Wyll is
dame bew-
ties chiefe
Iustice of
Oyre and
terminer.

Then crafte the cryer cal'd a quest,
Of whome was falshoode formost feere,
A packe of pickethankes were the rest,
Which came false witnesse for to beare,
The Jurye suche, the Judge uniust,
Sentence was sayde I should be trust.

Jelous the Jayler bound mee fast,
To heare the verdite of the byll,
George (quod the Judge) nowe thou art cast,
Thou must goe hence to heauie hill,
And there be hangde all but the head,
God rest thy soule when thou art dead.

Downe fell I then vpon my knee,
All flatte before Dame Beauties face,
And cryed, good Ladye pardon mee,
Which here appeale vnto your grace,
You knowe if I haue beene vntrue,
It was in too much praysing you.

doome] verdict.   trust] trussed.

And though this Judge doe make suche
    haste,
To shead with shame my guiltlesse blood :
Yet let your pittie first bee plaste,
To saue the man that meant you good,
So shall you shewe your selfe a Queene,
And I maye bee your seruaunt seene.

    (Quod Beautie) well : bicause I guesse,
What thou dost meane hencefoorth to bee,
Although thy faultes deserue no lesse,
Than Justice here hath iudged thee,
Wylt thou be bounde to stynt all strife, .
And be true prisoner all thy lyfe ?

    Yea Madame (quod I) that I shall,
Loe fayth and trueth my suerties :
Why then (quod shee) come when I call, Common
I aske no better warrantise.   Bayll.
Thus am I Beauties bounden thrall,
At hir commaunde when shee doth call.

EDWARD DE VERE, EARL OF OXFORD

1534–1604

FAIR FOOLS

If woemen could be fayre and yet not fonde,
  Or that theire loue were firme, not fickell still,
I woulde not meruayle that they make men bonde,
  By seruise longe to purchase theyre good will ;
But when I se how frayll those creatures are,
I muse that men forget themselues so farr.

    plaste] placed.
    fonde] foolish.   or that] if that, if.   meruayle]
marvel.   bonde] bound.

To marcke the choyse they make, and how they
    change,
    How ofte from Phoebus they do flee to Pann,
Vnsettled still, like haggardes willd, theye range,
    These gentlle byrdes that flye from man to man ;
Who woulde not scorne and shake them from the
    fyste,
And let them flye, fayre fooles, which waye they
    lyste.

Yet, for disporte we fawne and flatter bothe,
    To passe the tyme when nothinge else can please ;
And trayne them to our lure with subtylle othe,
    Till, wearye of thyre wiles, ourselues we ease ;
And then we saye, when we theire fancye trye,
To playe with fooles, oh, what a foole was I.

THOMAS SACKVILLE, EARL OF DORSET

1536(?)–1608

THE PORCH OF HELL

AND, first, within the porch and iawes of hell,
Sate deepe Remorse of conscience, all be sprent
With teares : and to herselfe oft would she tell
Her wretchednes, and cursing neuer stent
To sob and sighe ; but ever thus lament,
With thoughtful care, as she that all in vaine
Would weare and wast continually in paine.

Her eyes unstedfast, rolling here and there,
Whurld on ech place, as place that vengeaunce
    brought,
So was her minde continually in feare,

       haggardes] wild hawks.   stent] cease.

Tossed and tormented with tedious thought
Of those detested crimes which she had wrought;
With dreadful cheare and lookes throwen to the
  skye,
Wishing for death, and yet she could not dye.

Next saw we Dread, all trembling how he shooke,
With foote uncertaine, profered here and there:
Benummbd of speach, and, with a ghastly looke,
Searcht every place all pale and dead for feare,
His cap borne up with staring of his heare,
Stoynd and amazde at his owne shade for drede,
And fearing greater daungers than was nede.

And next within the entry of this lake
Sate fell Revenge gnashing her teeth for ire,
Deuising meanes how she may vengeaunce take,
Neuer in rest till she haue her desire:
But frets within so farforth with the fier
Of wreaking flames, that now determines she
To dye by death, or vengde by death to be.

When fell Revenge with bloudy foule pretence
Had showd her selfe as next in order set,
With trembling lims we softly parted thence,
Till in our eyes another sight we met:
When fro my hart a sigh forthwith I fet,
Rewing, alas! upon the wofull plight
Of Misery, that next appeard in sigt.

His face was leane, and somedeale pyned away,
And eke his hands consumed to the bone,
But what his body was I cannot say,
For on his carkas rayment had he none,

cheare] countenance, expression. heare] hair. stoynd]
astonished. fet] fetched. somedeale] somewhat.

Save clouts and patches peeced one by one ;
With staffe in hand, and script on shoulder cast,
His chiefe defence against the winters blast.

His foode for most, was wild fruites of the tree,
Unlesse sometime some crums fel to his share,
Which in his wallet long, God wot, kept hee,
As on the which full daintely would fare :
His drincke, the running streame, his cup, the bare
Of his palme closde, his bed, the hard cold ground :
To this poore life was Misery ybound.

Whose wretched state when we had well beheld
With tender ruth on him, and on his feres.
In thoughtfull cares, forth then our pace we helde.
And, by and by, another shape apperes,
Of greedye Care, still brushing up the breres,
His knuckles knobde, his flesh deepe dented in,
With tawed hands, and hard ytanned skin.

The morrow gray no soner hath begon
To spreade his light, even peeping in our eyes,
When he is up, and to his worke yrun :
But let the nights blacke misty mantles rise,
And with foule darke neuer so much disguise
The fayre bright day, yet ceasseth he no while,
But hath his candels to prolong his toile.

By him lay heavy Slepe, the cosin of Death,
Flat on the ground, and still as any stone,
A very corps, saue yeldinge forth a breath :
Small kepe toke he whom Fortune frowned on,
Or whom she lifted vp into the trone
Of high renowne, but as a lyving death,
So, ded alive, of life hee drew the breath.

feres] comrades.   breres] briars.

The bodies rest, the quiet of the hart,
The trauailes ease, the still nights feare was hee,
And of our life in earth the better part;
Reuer of sight, and yet in whom we see
Things oft that tyde, and oft that neuer bee,
Without respect, esteeming equally
King *Cresus* pompe, and *Irus* pouerty.

And next in order sad Olde Age we founde:
His beard all hoare, his eyes hollow and blind,
With drouping chere still poring on the ground,
As on the place where nature him assinde,
To rest, when that the sisters had untwind
His vitall thred, and ended with their knife
The fleeting course of fast declyning life.

There heard we him with broke and hollow plaints
Rewe with himselfe his ende approching fast,
And all for nought his wretched minde torment
With sweete remembraunce of his pleasures past,
And fresh delites of lusty youth forewaste;
Recounting which, how would he sob and shrike,
And to be yong againe of *Ioue* beseke.

But, and the cruell fates so fixed be,
That time forepast cannot retourne againe,
This one request of *Ioue* yet prayed hee:
That in such withred plight, and wretched paine,
As elde (accompanied with his lothsome traine),
Had brought on him, all were it woe and griefe,
He might a while yet linger forth his lief,

And not so soone descend into the pit,
Where death, when he the mortall corps hath slaine,
With retchlesse hand in graue doth couer it,

feare] brother.   forewaste] wasted.   retchlesse] reckless.

Thereafter neuer to enioye againe
The gladsome light, but in the ground ylaine,
In depth of darknesse wast and weare to nought,
As he neuer into the world bin brought.

But who has seene him sobbing, how he stoode
Unto himselfe, and how he would bemone
His youth forepast, as though it wrought him good
To talke of youth, all were his youth foregone,
He would have mused, and meruayled much
    whereon
This wretched Age should life desire so faine,
And knowes full well life doth but length his paine.

Crookebackt he was, toothshaken, and blere iyed,
Went on three feete, and sometime crept on foure,
With olde lame boones that ratled by his syde,
His scalpe all pild, and he with eld forlore :
His withred fist still knocking at deathes dore,
Fumbling and driueling as he drawes his breath ;
For briefe, the shape and messenger of death.

ANONYMOUS

17th century

JOLLY GOOD ALE AND OLD

I CAN not eate, but lytle meate
    my stomacke is not good ;
But sure I thinke, that I can drynke
    with him that weares a hood.
Thoughe I go bare, take ye no care,
    I am nothinge a colde :
I stuffe my skyn, so full within,
    of ioly good Ale and olde.

meruayled] marvelled.   pild] bare, bald.   eld]
old age.   driueling] drivelling.

Backe and syde go bare, go bare,
   booth foote and hand go colde ;
But Bellye god send the good ale inoughe,
   whether it be new or olde.

I love no rost, but a nut browne toste,
   and a crab layde in the fyre ;
A lytle bread, shall do me stead
   much breade I not desyre :
No froste nor snow, no winde, I trowe,
   can hurte mee if I wolde ;
I am so wrapt, and throwly lapt
   of ioly good ale and olde.
      Backe and syde go bare, &c.

And Tyb my wyfe, that as her lyfe
   loueth well good ale to seeke,
Full ofte drynkes shee, tyll ye may see
   the teares run downe her cheekes :
Then dooth she trowle, to mee the bowle
   euen as a mault worme shuld,
And, sayth sweethart, I tooke my parte
   of this ioly good ale and olde.
      Backe and syde go bare, &c.

Now let them drynke, tyll they nod and winke,
   euen as good felowes shoulde doe ;
They shall not mysse, to haue the blisse
   good ale doth bringe men to ;
And all poore soules that haue scowred boules
   or haue them lustely trolde,
God saue the lyues, of them and theyr wyues
   whether they be yonge or olde.
      Backe and syde go bare, go bare,
        booth foote and hande go colde :
      But Bellye god sende thee good ale ynoughe,
        whether it be newe or olde.

ANONYMOUS PIECES FROM ELIZABETHAN MISCELLANIES

A CRADLE SONG

The Arbor of Amorous Devices, 1597

Come little babe, come silly soule,
Thy fathers shame, thy mothers griefe,
Borne as I doubt to all our dole,
And to thy selfe vnhappie chiefe :
    Sing Lullabie and lap it warme,
    Poore soule that thinkes no creature harme.

Thou little thinkst and lesse doost knowe,
The cause of this thy mothers moane,
Thou wantst the wit to waile her woe,
And I my selfe am all alone :
    Why doost thou weepe ? why doost thou
      waile ?
    And knowest not yet what thou doost ayle.

Come, little wretch, ah silly heart,
Mine onely joy what can I more :
If there be any wrong thy smart,
That may the destinies implore :
    Twas I, I say, against my will,
    I wayle the time, but be thou still.

And doest thou smile oh thy sweete face,
Would God himselfe he might thee see,
No doubt thou wouldst soone purchace grace,
I know right well for thee and mee :
    But come to mother babe and play,
    For father false is fled away.

      dole] grief, sorrow.   lap] to fold, wrap up.

Sweet boy if it by fortune chance,
Thy father home againe to send,
If death do strike me with his launce,
Yet mayst thou me to him commend :
 If any aske thy mothers name,
 Tell how by loue she purchast blame.

Then will his gentle heart soone yeeld,
I know him of a noble minde,
Although a Lyon in the field,
A Lamb in towne thou shalt him finde :
 Aske blessing babe, be not afrayde,
 His sugred words hath me betrayde.

Then mayst thou ioy and be right glad,
Although in woe I seeme to moane,
Thy father is no Rascall lad,
A noble youth of blood and boane :
 His glancing lookes if he once smile,
 Right honest women may beguile.

Come little boy and rocke a sleepe,
Sing lullabie and be thou still,
I that can doe nought else but weepe,
Wil sit by thee and waile my fill :
 God blesse my babe and lullabie,
 From this thy fathers qualitie.

MADRIGAL

Davison's *Poeticall Rapsodie*, 1602

In praise of two.

FAUSTINA hath the fairer face,
And Phillida the better grace,
    Both haue mine eye enriched.
This sings full sweetly with her voyce,
Her fingers make as sweet a noyse,
    Both haue mine eare bewitched:
Ay me! sith Fates haue so prouided,
My heart (alas) must be divided.

PHILLIDA'S LOVE-CALL

England's Helicon, 1600

Phillida. CORIDON, arise, my *Coridon*,
        Titan shineth cleare:
Coridon. Who is it that calleth *Coridon*,
        who is it that I heare?
Phil. Phillida thy true-Loue calleth thee,
        arise then, arise then;
        arise and keepe thy Flock with me:
Cor. *Phillida* my true-Loue, is it she?
        I come then, I come then,
        I come and keepe my flocke with thee.

Phil. Here are cherries ripe my *Coridon*,
        eate them for my sake:
Cor. Here's my Oaten pipe my louely one,
        sport for thee to make.

sith] since.

Phil. Here are threds my true-Loue, fine as silke,
  to knit thee, to knit thee
   a paire of stockings white as milke.
Cor. Here are Reedes my true-Loue, fine and neate,
  to make thee, to make thee,
   a bonnet to with stand the heate.

Phil. I will gather flowers my *Coridon*,
  to set in thy Cap :
Cor. I will gather Peares my louely one,
  To put in thy lap.
Phil. I will buy my true-Loue Garters gay,
  for Sundayes, for Sundayes,
   to weare about his legges so tall :
Cor. I will buy my true-Loue yellow Say,
  for Sundayes, for Sundayes,
   to weare about her middle small.

Phil. When my *Coridon* sits on a hill,
  making melody :
Cor. When my louely one goes to her wheele,
  Singing cherily.
Phil. Sure me thinks my true-Loue doth excell
  for sweetnesse, for sweetnesse,
   our Pan, that old Arcadian Knight :
Cor. And me thinks my true-Loue beares the bell
  for clearenesse, for clearenesse,
   beyond the Nimphs that be so bright.

Phil. Had my *Coridon*, my *Coridon*,
  been (alack) her swaine :
Cor. Had my louely one, my louely one,
  beene in *Ida* plaine.

Say] *soie*, silk.

Phil. *Cinthia Endimion* had refus'd,
   preferring, preferring,
    My *Coridon* to play with-all :
Cor. The Queene of Loue had beene excus'd
   bequeathing, bequeathing,
    my *Phillida* the golden ball.

Phil. Yonder comes my Mother, *Coridon*,
   whether shall I flie ?
Cor. Vnder yonder Beech my louely one,
   while she passeth by.
Phil. Say to her thy true-Loue was not here,
   remember, remember,
    to morrow is another day :
Cor. Doubt me not, my true-Loue, do not feare,
   farewell then, farewell then,
    heauen keepe our loues alway.

FAIN WOULD I CHANGE THAT NOTE

Capt. Tobias Hume's *First Part of Ayres*, 1605.

FAIN would I change that note
To which fond loue hath charmd me,
Long, long to sing by roate,
Fancying that that harmde me.
  Yet when this thought doth come,
  Love is the perfect summe
    Of all delight
   I have no other choice
   Either for pen or voyce,
    To sing or write.

O Loue they wrong thee much,
That say thy sweete is bitter.
When thy ripe fruit is such,
As nothing can be sweeter,

Faire house of ioy and blisse,
Where truest pleasure is,
   I doe adore thee ;
I know thee what thou art,
I serue thee with my hart,
   And fall before thee.

HEY NONNY NO!

Christ Church MS.

Hay nonny no !
Men are fooles that wish to dye !
Is 't not fyne to dance and singe
When the bells of death doe ringe ?
Is 't not fyne to swym in wyne,
And turne uppon the toe,
And singe hay noninо !
When the winds doe blowe and the seas flow ?
Hay noninо !

PREPARATIONS

Christ Church MS.

Yet if his Maiestie, our Soueraigne Lord,
Should of his owne accord
Friendly himselfe inuite,
And saye ' I'le be your guest to morrowe night,'
How should we stir our selues, call and command
All hands to worke ! ' Let no man idle stand !

' Set me fine Spanish tables in the hall,
See they be fitted all ;
Let there be rome to eate,
And order taken that there want no meate.
See euery sconce and candlestick made bright,
That without tapers they may giue a light.

' Looke to the presence : are the carpets spred,
The dazie o're the head,
The cushions in the chayres
And all the candles lighted on the stayres ?
Perfume the chambers, and in any case
Let each man giue attendance in his place ! '

Thus, if the king were coming, would we doe ;
And 'twere good reason too ;
For 'tis a duteous thing
To show all honor to an earthly king,
And after all our trauayle and our cost,
So he be pleased, to think no labour lost.

But at the coming of the King of Heauen
All 's set at six and seuen ;
We wallow in our sinn,
Christ cannot finde a chamber in the Inn.
We entertaine Him always like a stranger,
And, as at first, still lodge Him in the manger.

THE MARRIAGE OF THE FROG AND THE MOUSE

Thomas Ravenscroft's *Melismata*

'Twas the Frogge in the well,
    Humble-dum, humble-dum.
And the merrie Mouse in the Mill,
    tweedle tweedle, twino.

The Frogge would a woing ride,
Sword and buckler by his side.

When he was vpon his high horse set,
His boots they shone as blacke as iet.

When she came to the merry mill pin,
Lady Mouse been you within ?

Then came out the dusty Mouse,
I am Lady of this house.

Hast thou any minde of me ?
I haue e'ne great minde of thee.

Who shall this marriage make ?
Our Lord which is the rat.

What shall we haue to our supper ?
Three beanes in a pound of butter.

When supper they were at,
The Frog, the Mouse, and euen the Rat,

Then came in gib our cat
And catcht the mouse euen by the backe.

Then did they separate,
And the frog leapt on the floore so flat.

Then came in Dicke our Drake,
And drew the frogge euen to the lake.

The Rat run vp the wall
   humble-dum, humble-dum.
A goodly company, the diuell goe with all
   tweedle, tweedle, twino.

the diuell] the Devil.

WE MUST NOT PART

Egerton MS.

Wᴇᴇ must not parte as others doe
with sighs & teares as wee weare two,
though with these outward formes wee parte
wee keepe each other in our hart,
what search hath found a beinge where
I am not if that thou be there,
true Loue hath winges and can as [soone]
survey the world as Sun and Moone,
and euery where our Triumphes keepe,
ouer absence which makes others weepe,
by which alone a power is giuen,
to liue one Earth as they in heauen.

THE FAITHLESS SHEPHERDESS

*William Byrd's Songs of
Sundry Natures,* 158

Wʜʏʟᴇ that the *Sunne* with his beames hot,
    Scorched the fruits in vale and mountaine,
Philon the shepherd late forgot,
    Sitting besides a Christall fountaine,
        In shadow of a greene Oke tree,
        Vppon his pipe this song playd he.
Adew loue, adew loue, vntrue loue, vntrue loue
Vntrue loue, adew loue, adew loue,
Your minde is light, soone lost for new loue.

So long as I was in your sight,
    I was as your hart, your soule, your treasure,
And euermore you sob'd, you sigh'd,
    Burning in flames beyond all measure,

        Christall] crystal.   adew] adieu.

Three dayes endur'd your loue to me,
   And it was lost in other three.
Adew loue, adew loue, vntrue loue, vntrue loue
Vntrue loue, adew loue, adew loue,
Your minde is light, soone lost for new loue.

Another shepherd you dyd see,
   To whome your hart was soone enchayned,
Full soone your loue was leapt from me,
   Full soone my place he had obtayned.
      Soone came a third your loue to winne,
      And we were out and he was in.
Adew loue, adew loue, vntrue loue, vntrue loue
Vntrue loue, adew loue, adew loue,
Your minde is light, soone lost for new loue.

Sure you haue made me passing glad,
   That you your mynd so soone remoued,
Before that I the leysure had,
   To chuse you for my best beloued.
      For all my loue was past and doonne,
      Two dayes before it was begoonne.
Adew loue, adew loue, vntrue loue, vntrue loue
Vntrue loue, adew loue, adew loue,
Your minde is light, soone lost for new loue.

LOVE NOT ME FOR COMELY GRACE

John Wilbye's *Second Set of Madrigals,* 1609

LOUE not me for comely grace,
For my pleasing eye or face,
Nor for any outward part,
No, nor for my constant heart :
    For those may faile or turne to ill,
    So thou and I shall sever:
Keepe therfore a true womans eye,
And love me still, but know not why,
    So hast thou the same reason still,
    To dote vpon me euer !

MADRIGAL

Davison's *Poeticall Rapsodie,* 1602

My loue in her attire doth shew her wit,
It doth so well become her :
For every season she hath dressings fit :
    For Winter, Spring, and Summer.
    No beautie she doth misse,
        When all her Robes are on,
    But beauties selfe she is
        When all her Robes are gone.

THE NEW JERUSALEM

First printed 1601

HIERUSALEM my happie home
    When shall I come to thee
When shall my sorrows have an end
    Thy ioyes when shall I see

O happie harbour of the saints
  O sweete and pleasant soyle
In thee noe sorrow may be founde
  Noe greefe, noe care, noe toyle

In thee noe sickenesse may be seene
  Noe hurt, noe ache, noe sore
There is noe death, nor uglie devill
  There is life for euermore

Noe dampishe mist is seene in thee
  Noe could, nor darksome night
There everie soule shines as the sunne
  There god himself giues light

There lust and lukar cannot dwell
  There envie beares noe sway
There is noe hunger heate nor could
  But pleasure everie way

Hierusalem : Hierusalem
  God grant I once may see
Thy endless ioyes and of the same
  Partaker aye to bee

Thy wales are made of precious stones
  Thy bulwarkes Diamondes square
Thy gates are of right orient pearle
  Exceedinge riche and rare

Thy terrettes and thy pinacles
  With carbuncles doe shine
Thy verie streetes are paued with gould
  Surpassinge cleare and fine

Thy houses are of Ivorie
  Thy windoes cristale cleare
Thy tyles are mad of beaten gould
  O god that I were there

Within thy gates nothinge doeth come
    That is not passinge cleane
Noe spiders web, noe durt noe dust
    Noe filthe may there be seene

Ah my sweete home Hierusaleme
    Would god I were in thee
Would god my woes were at an end
    Thy ioyes that I might see

Thy saints are crownd with glorie great
    They see god face to face
They triumph still, they still reioyce
    Most happie is their case

Wee that are heere in banishment
    Continuallie doe mourne
We sighe and sobbe, we weepe and weale
    Perpetually we groane

Our sweete is mixt with bitter gaule
    Our pleasure is but paine
Our ioyes scarce last the lookeing on
    Our sorrowes still remaine

But there they liue in such delight
    Such pleasure and such play
As that to them a thousand yeares
    Doth seeme as yeaster day

Thy viniardes and thy orchardes are
    Most beautiful and faire
Full furnished with trees and fruits
    Most wonderfull and rare

Thy gardens and thy gallant walkes
    Continually are greene
There groes such sweete and pleasant flowers
    As noe where eles are seene

There is nector and ambrosia made
   There is muske and civette sweete
There manie a faire and daintie drugge
   Are trodden under feete

There cinomon there sugar groes
   There narde and balme abound
What tounge can tell or hart conceieue
   The ioyes that there are found

Quyt though the streets with siluer sound
   The flood of life doe flowe
Upon whose bankes on everie syde
   The wood of life doth growe

There trees for euermore beare fruite
   And evermore doe springe
There euermore the Angels sit
   And evermore doe singe

There David standes with harpe in hand
   As maister of the Queere
Tenne thousand times that man were blest
   That might this musicke hear

Our Ladie singes magnificat
   With tune surpassinge sweete
And all the virginns beare their parts
   Sitting about her feete

Te Deum doth Sant Ambrose singe
   Saint Augustine dothe the like
Ould Simeon and Zacharie
   Have not their songes to seeke

There Magdalene hath left her mone
   And cheerfullie doth singe
With blessed Saints whose harmonie
   In everie streete doth ringe

Hierusalem my happie home
    Would god I were in thee
Would god my woes were at an end
    Thy ioyes that I might see

MY LADY'S TEARS

John Dowland's *Second Book
of Songs or Airs*, 1600

I SAW my Lady weepe,
    And sorrow proud to bee aduancèd so :
In those faire eies, where all perfections keepe,
    Hir face was full of woe.
But such a woe (beleeue me) as wins more hearts,
Then mirth can doe, with hir intysing parts.

Sorow was there made faire,
And passion wise, teares a delightfull thing,
Silence beyond all speech a wisdome rare,
    Shee made hir sighes to sing,
And all things with so sweet a sadnesse moue
As made my heart at once both grieue and loue.

O fayrer then ought ells,
The world can shew, leaue of in time to grieue,
Inough, inough, your ioyfull lookes excells,
    Teares kills the heart belieue,
O striue not to bee excellent in woe,
Which onely breeds your beauties ouerthrow.

ells] else.

TEARS

John Dowland's *Third and last
Book of Songs or Airs*, 1603

WEEPE you no more sad fountaines,
   What need you flowe so fast,
Looke how the snowie mountaines,
   Heau'ns sunne doth gently waste.
But my sunnes heau'nly eyes
   View not your weeping,
   That nowe lie sleeping
Softly, now softly lies
   Sleeping.

Sleepe is a reconciling,
   A rest that peace begets ;
Doth not the sunne rise smiling,
   When faire at euen he sets,
Rest you then, rest sad eyes,
   Melt not in weeping,
   While she lies sleeping
Softly, now softly lies
   Sleeping.

SINCE FIRST I SAW YOUR FACE

Thomas Ford's *Music of
Sundry Kinds*, 1607

SINCE first I saw your face I resolued to honour and
   renowne yee ;
If now I be disdayned I wishe my hart had neuer
   knowne yee,
What I that lou'de and you that likte shal wee
   beginne to wrangle ?
No, no, no, my hart is fast and cannot disentangle.
If I admire or prayse you too much, that fault you
   may forgiue mee,

Or if my hands had stray'd but a touch, then iustly
    might you leaue me,
I askt you leaue, you bad me loue, ist now a time
    to chide me ?
No, no, no, ile loue you still, what fortune ere
    betide me.
The Sunne, whose beames most glorious are, re-
    iecteth no beholder,
And your sweet beautie past compare, made my
    poore eyes the boulder,
Where beautie moues, and wit delights, and signes
    of kindnes bind me
There, O there where ere I go, ile leaue my hart
    behinde mee.

THE SHEPHERDS' SONG: A CAROL OR HYMN
FOR CHRISTMAS

England's Helicon, 1600

    SWEET Musicke, sweeter farre
    Then any Song is sweet :
    Sweet Musicke heauenly rare,
    Mine eares (O peeres) doth greete.
You gentle Flocks, whose fleeces pearl'd with dewe,
Resemble heauen, whom golden drops make bright:
Listen, O listen, now, O not to you
Our pipes make sport to shorten wearie night.
    But voyces most diuine,
    Make blisfull Harmonie :
    Voyces that seeme to shine,
    For what else cleares the skie ?
Tunes can we heare, but not the Singers see :
The tunes diuine, and so the Singers be.

        peeres] mates.

Loe how the firmament,
Within an azure fold :
The flock of starres hath pent,
That we might them behold :
Yet from their beames proceedeth not this light,
Nor can their Christals such reflection giue :
What then doth make the Element so bright ?
The heauens are come downe vpon earth to liue.

But harken to the Song,
Glory to glories King :
And peace all men among,
These Queristers doe sing.
Angels they are, as also (Shepheards) hee,
Whom in our feare we doe admire to see.

Let not amazement blinde
Your soules (said he) annoy :
To you and all mankinde,
My message bringeth ioy.
For loe the worlds great Shepheard now is borne
A blessed Babe, an infant full of power :
After long night, vp-risen is the morne,
Renowning *Bethlem* in the Sauiour.

Sprung is the perfect day,
By Prophets seene a farre :
Sprung is the mirthfull May,
Which Winter cannot marre.
In *Dauids* Citie doth this Sunne appeare :
Clouded in flesh, yet Shepheards sit we here.

Element] sky.   renowning] making famous.

NICHOLAS BRETON

1542–1626.

PHILLIDA AND CORYDON

In the merry moneth of May,
In a morne by breake of day,
Foorth I walked by the Woodside,
Whenas May was in his pride:
There I spied all alone,
Phillida and *Coridon*.
Much a-doo there was God wot,
He would loue, and she would not.
She sayd neuer man was true,
He sayd, none was false to you.
He sayd, he had lou'd her long,
She sayd, Loue should haue no wrong.
Coridon would kisse her then,
She said, Maides must kisse no men
Till they did for good and all.
Then she made the Sheepheard call
All the heauens to witnesse truth:
Neuer lou'd a truer youth.
Thus with many a pretty oath,
Yea and nay, and faith and troth,
Such as silly Sheepheards vse,
When they will not Loue abuse;
Loue, which had beene long deluded,
Was with kisses sweete concluded.
And *Phillida* with garlands gay:
Was made the Lady of the May.

silly] simple.

A PASTORAL OF PHILLIS AND CORYDON

On a hill there growes a flower,
    faire befall the dainty sweete :
By that flower there is a Bower,
    where the heauenly Muses meete.

In that Bower there is a chaire,
    fringdèd all about with gold ;
Where dooth sit the fairest faire,
    that euer eye did yet behold.

It is *Phillis* faire and bright,
    shee that is the Sheepheards ioy :
Shee that *Venus* did despight,
    and did blind her little boy.

This is she, the wise, the rich,
    that the world desires to see :
This is *ipsa quæ* the which,
    there is none but onely shee.

Who would not this face admire ?
    who would not this Saint adore ?
Who would not this sight desire,
    though he thought to see no more ?

Oh faire eyes, yet let me see,
    one good looke, and I am gone :
Looke on me, for I am hee,
    thy poore silly *Coridon*.

Thou that art the Sheepheards Queene,
    Looke vpon thy silly Swaine :
By thy comfort haue beene seene
    dead men brought to life againe.

despight] anger.

THE THIRD PASTOR'S SONG

Who can liue in heart so glad,
As the merrie countrie lad?
Who vpon a faire greene balke,
May at pleasures sit and walke?
And amidde the Azure skies,
See the morning Sunne arise?
While hee heares in euery spring,
How the Birdes doe chirpe and sing:
Or, before the houndes in crie,
See the Hare goe stealing by:
Or along the shallow brooke,
Angling with a baited hooke:
See the fishes leape and play,
In a blessed Sunny day:
Or to heare the Partridge call,
Till shee haue her Couye all:
Or to see the subtill foxe,
How the villaine plies the box:
After feeding on his pray,
How he closely sneakes away,
Through the hedge and downe the furrow,
Till he geets into his burrowe.
Then the Bee to gather honey,
And the little blacke-haird Cony,
On a banke for Sunny place,
With her fore-feete wash her face:
Are not these with thousandes moe,
Then the Courts of Kinges doe knowe?
The true pleasing spirits sights,
That may breede true loue's delightes,

balke] ridge or piece of land left unploughed by accident.
couye] covey.　　　then] than.

But with all this happinesse,
To beholde that Shepheardesse,
To whose eyes all Shepheards yeelde,
All the fairest of the fielde.
Faire *Aglaia* in whose face,
Liues the Shepheards highest Grace :
In whose worthy wonder praise,
See what her true Shepheard saies.
Shee is neither proude nor fine,
But in spirit more diuine :
Shee can neither lower nor leere,
But a sweeter smiling cheere :
She had neuer painted face,
But a sweeter smiling grace :
Shee can neuer loue dissemble,
Truth doth so her thoughts assemble,
That where wisdome guides her will,
Shee is kind and constant still,
All in summe she is that creature,
Of that truest comfortes Nature,
That doth shewe (but in exceedinges)
How their praises had their breedings :
Let then poetts faine their pleasure,
In their fictions of loue's treasure :
Proud high spirits seeke their graces,
In their Idoll painted faces :
My loues spirits lowlinesse,
In affections humblenesse,
Vnder heau'n no happines
Seekes but in this Shepheardesse.
For whose sake I say and sweare,
By the passions that I beare,

cheere] countenance, aspect.   all in summe] entirely,
altogether.   faine] feign.

Had I got a Kinglie grace,
I would leaue my Kinglie place.
And in heart be trulie glad :
To become a Country Lad.
Hard to lie, and goe full bare,
And to feede on hungry fare :
So I might but liue to bee,
Where I might but sit to see,
Once a day, or all day long,
The sweet subiect of my song :
In *Aglaiae's* onely eyes,
All my worldly paradise.

SIR EDWARD DYER

1545(?)–1607

MY MIND TO ME A KINGDOM IS

My mynde to me a kindome is
    Suche preasente ioyes therin I fynde
That it excells all other blisse
    That earth affords or growes by kynde
Thoughe muche I wante wch moste would haue
    Yet still my mynde forbides to craue

No princlye pompe, no wealthy store,
    No force to winn the victorye
No wilye witt to salue a sore
    No shape to feade a lounge eye
To none of these I yealde as thrall
For why my minde dothe serue for all.

wch moste] which [what] most.   princlye] princely.
for why] because.

I see how plenty suffers ofte
   And hasty clymers sone do fall
I see that those whiche are alofte
   Myshapp dothe threaten moste of all
They get withe toylle theye keepe withe feare
Suche cares my mynde coulde neuer beare.

Contente I liue, this is my staye
   I seeke no more than maye suffyse
I press to beare no haughtye swaye
   Look what I lack my minde suppleise
Lo thus I tryumphe lyke a kynge
Content withe that my mynde doth bringe.

Some haue to muche yet still do craue
   I litle haue and seeke no more.
They are but poore thoughe much they haue
   And I am ryche wth lyttle store.
They poore, I ryche ; theye begg, I geue
They lacke, I leaue, they pyne I lyue.

I laughe not at an others loss
   I grudge not at an others payne
No worldly waues my mynde cann toss
   My state at one dothe still remayne
I feare no foe, I fawne no freende,
I lothe not lyfe nor dreade my ende

Some waye theyre pleasure by theyre luste
   Their wisdom by theyre rage of will.
Theire treasure is theyre onlye truste
   A cloked crafte theyre store of skyll.
But all the pleasure that I fynde
Is to mayntayne a quiet mynde.

---

suppleise] supplies.   withe that] with what.   pyne]
pine. lyue] live. payne] ? gayne. freende] friend.
lothe] loathe. waye] weigh. cloked] cloakèd.

My wealthe is healthe and perfecte ease,
　　My conscience cleere my choyse defense,
I neither seeke by brybes to please.
　　Nor by deceyte to breede offence
Thus do I lyue thus will I dye
Would all did so as well as I.

SIR WALTER RALEIGH

1552-1618

AS YOU CAME FROM THE HOLY LAND

As you came from the holy land
　　of Walsinghame
Mett you not wth my true loue
　　by the way as you came
How shall I know your trew loue
That haue mett many one
As I went to the holy lande
That haue come that haue gone
She is neyther whyte nor browne
Butt as the heauens fayre
There is none hathe a powre so diuine
In the earth or the ayre
Such an one did I meet good S^r
Suche an Angelyke face
Who lyke a queene lyke a nymph did appere
by her gate by her grace :
She hath lefte me here all alone
All allone as vnknowne
Who somtymes did me lead wth her selfe
And me loude as her owne :—

choyse] choice.　　　powre] form.
gate] gait.　　　loude] loved.

Whats the cause that she leaues you alone
And a new waye doth take :
Who loued you once as her owne
And her ioye did you make :
I haue loude her all my youth
Butt no ould as you see
Loue lykes not the fallyng frute
From the wythered tree :
Know that loue is a careless chylld
And forgett promysse paste :
He is blynd, he is deaff when he lyste
And in faythe neuer faste :
His desyre is a dureless contente
And a trustless ioye
He is won wth a world of despayre
And is Lost with a Ioye :
Of women kynde suche indeed is the loue
Or the word Loue abused
Vnder wch many chyldysh desyres
And conceytes are excusde :
But Loue is a durable fyre
In the mynde euer burnynge :
Neuer sycke neuer ould neuer dead
From itt selfe neuer turnynge :

loued] loved.   no ould] now old.   chylld] child.
forgett promysse paste] forgets promise past.   lyste] list.
abused] abusèd.   excusde] excusèd.   but Loue] but
[true] love.

VERSES MADE BY SIR WALTER RALEIGH THE NIGHT BEFORE HE WAS BEHEADED

Giue mee my Escallope shell of Quiett
My staffe of faith to walke vppon
My scripp of Joy Immortall dyett
My Bottle of Saluation
My Gowne of Glorye, hopes true gage
And thus I take my pilgrimage

Blood must bee my Bodyes Balmer
No other Balme will there be giuen
Whilst my Soule like Quitte Palmer
Trauills towardes the land of heauen
Ouer the Siluer Mountaines
Whear Springes the Nectar fountaines
    And here Ile kiss
    the boule of bliss
    Drinck my eternall fill
    on euery Milky Hill
    My Soule will bee adry before
    But after ytt shall thirst no more

And In that bliss-full day
More peacefull Pillgrimms I shall see
That haue shooke of their gownes of Clay
And goe apparreld fresh-like mee
    Ile take them first
    to slacke thire thirst
    And then to tast of Nectars Suckettes
    Att these Clere Wells
    Whear Sweetnes dwells
    Drawne vpp by Sainctes in heauenly buckettes

escallope] scallop.   Quiett] quiet.   ytt] it.   shooke of] cast off.

And when our Bottles & All wee
Are fild wth Immortallite
Then those holye pathes well trauill
Strewd wth Rubies thicke as grauill
From thence to Heauens Bliss-full hall
Wheare noe Corrupted Lawyers brawle
  Noe Conscience Moulten Into gould
  Noe forge accuser bought or sould
  Noe cause defer'd, noe vayne spent Journye
  For there Christ is the Kinge's Attournye
  Who pleades for All, w^thout degrees
  And hee hath Angells but noe fees

When the Grande twelue million Jurye
of our sines wth dreadfull furye
Gainst our soules blacke verdictes giue
Christ pleades his death, and then wee liue
  bee thou my speaker, taintles pleader
  Vnblotted Lawyer true proceder
  Thou wone'st Saluation euen by Almes
  Not wth a bribed Lawyers palmes
  And this is my eternall plea
  To hym that made heauen Earth & Sea

Seeing my selfe must dye soe soone
And wante a head to dyne next noon
Just att the stroake when my vaynes start &
  spread
Sett on my Soule an Euerlasting head
  Then am I readye like a Palmer fitt
  To tredd those blest pathes wch before I
  writt

---

trauill] travel. grauill] gravel. forge accuser]
forged accuser.

THE SHEPHERD'S DESCRIPTION OF LOVE

Melibœus.   SHEEPHEARD, what's Loue, I pray thee
                    tell ?
Faustus.   It is that Fountaine, and that Well,
                 Where pleasure and repentance dwell.
                 It is perhaps that sauncing bell
                     That tolls all into heauen or hell,
                     And this is Loue as I heard tell.

Meli.   Yet what is Loue, I pre-thee say ?
Fau.   It is a worke on holy-day,
           It is December match'd with May,
           When lustie-bloods in fresh aray,
               Heare ten moneths after of the play,
               And this is Loue, as I heare say.

Meli.   Yet what is Loue, good Sheepheard saine ?
Fau.   It is a Sun-shine mixt with raine,
           It is a tooth-ach, or like paine,
           It is a game where none dooth gaine,
               The Lasse saith no, and would full
                   faine :
               And this is Loue, as I heare saine.

Meli.   Yet Sheepheard, what is Loue, I pray ?
Fau.   It is a yea, It is a nay,
           A pretty kind of sporting fray,
           It is a thing will soone away,
               Then Nimphs take vantage while ye
                   may :
               And this is loue as I heare say.

saine] say.

Meli. Yet what is Loue, good Sheepheard show ?
Fau. A thing that creepes, it cannot goe,
A prize that passeth too and fro,
A thing for one, a thing for moe,
    And he that prooues shall finde it so ;
    And Sheepheard this is loue I troe.

THE AUTHOR'S EPITAPH, MADE *BY HIMSELF*
THE NIGHT BEFORE HIS DEATH

EVEN such is Time, which takes in trust
    Our youth, and Ioy's, and all we haue,
And payes vs but with age and dust,
    Which in the darke and silent graue,
When we have wandred all our wayes,
Shuts vp the story of our dayes :
But from which Earth, Graue, and Dust,
The Lord shall raise me vp I trust.

THE NYMPH'S REPLY TO MARLOWE'S
PASSIONATE SHEPHERD

IF all the world and loue were young,
And truth in euery Sheepheards tongue,
These pretty pleasures might me moue,
To liue with thee, and be thy loue.

Time driues the flocks from field to fold,
When Riuers rage, and Rocks grow cold,
And Philomell becommeth dombe,
The rest complaines of cares to come.

    moe] more.   troe] believe, think.

The flowers doe fade, & wanton fieldes,
To wayward winter reckoning yeelds,
A honny tongue, a hart of gall,
Is fancies spring, but sorrowes fall.

Thy gownes, thy shooes, thy beds of Roses,
Thy cap, thy kirtle, and thy poesies,
Soone breake, soone wither, soone forgotten :
In follie ripe, in reason rotten.

Thy belt of straw and Iuie buddes,
Thy Corall claspes and Amber studdes,
All these in mee no meanes can moue,
To come to thee, and be thy loue.

But could youth last, and loue still breede,
Had ioyes no date, nor age no neede,
Then these delights my minde might moue
To liue with thee, and be thy loue.

    Iuie buddes] ivy buds.   ioyes] joys.

EDMUND SPENSER

1552(?)–1599

THE FAERIE QUEENE

The Story of the Red Cross Knight or of Holiness

(1) *The Knight and Una (Truth)*

A GENTLE Knight was pricking on the plaine,
  Y cladd in mightie armes and siluer shielde,
Wherein old dints of deepe wounds did remaine,
  The cruell markes of many a bloudy fielde ;
Yet armes till that time did he neuer wield :
  His angry steede did chide his foming bitt,
As much disdayning to the curbe to yield :
  Full iolly knight he seemd, and faire did sitt,
As one for knightly giusts and fierce encounters fitt.

But on his brest a bloudie Crosse he bore,
  The deare remembrance of his dying Lord,
For whose sweete sake that glorious badge he
      wore,
  And dead as liuing euer him ador'd :
Vpon his shield the like was also scor'd,
  For soueraine hope, which in his helpe he had :
Right faithfull true he was in deede and word,
  But of his cheere did seeme too solemne sad ;
Yet nothing did he dread, but euer was ydrad.

pricking] spurring, riding fast.   y cladd] clothed.
giusts] jousts, tournaments.   cheere] countenance.
ydrad] dreaded.

Vpon a great aduenture he was bond,
   That greatest *Gloriana* to him gaue,
   That greatest Glorious Queene of *Faerie* lond,
   To winne him worship, and her grace to haue,
   Which of all earthly things he most did craue ;
   And euer as he rode, his hart did earne
   To proue his puissance in battell braue
   Vpon his foe, and his new force to learne ;
Vpon his foe, a Dragon horrible and stearne.

A louely Ladie rode him faire beside,
   Vpon a lowly Asse more white then snow,
   Yet she much whiter, but the same did hide
   Vnder a vele, that wimpled was full low,
   And ouer all a blacke stole she did throw,
   As one that inly mournd : so was she sad,
   And heauie sat vpon her palfrey slow :
   Seemed in heart some hidden care she had,
And by her in a line a milke white lambe she
   lad.

So pure an innocent, as that same lambe,
   She was in life and euery vertuous lore,
   And by descent from Royall lynage came
   Of ancient Kings and Queenes, that had of
      yore
   Their scepters stretcht from East to Westerne
      shore,
   And all the world in their subiection held ;
   Till that infernall feend with foule vprore
   Forwasted all their land, and them expeld :
Whom to auenge, she had this Knight from far
   compeld.

          wimpled] laid, lay in plaits or folds.

Behind her farre away a Dwarfe did lag,
  That lasie seemd in being euer last,
  Or wearied with bearing of her bag
  Of needments at his backe. Thus as they past,
  The day with cloudes was suddeine ouercast,
  And angry *Ioue* an hideous storme of raine
  Did poure into his Lemans lap so fast,
  That euery wight to shrowd it did constrain,
And this faire couple eke to shroud themselues were
    fain.

Enforst to seeke some couert nigh at hand,
  A shadie groue not far away they spide,
  That promist ayde the tempest to withstand :
  Whose loftie trees yclad with sommers pride,
  Did spred so broad, that heauens light did hide,
  Not perceable with power of any starre :
  And all within were pathes and alleies wide,
  With footing worne, and leading inward farre :
Faire harbour that them seemes ; so in they entred
    arre.

And foorth they passe, with pleasure forward led,
  Ioying to heare the birdes sweete harmony,
  Which therein shrouded from the tempest dred,
  Seemd in their song to scorne the cruell sky.
  Much can they prayse the trees so straight and
    hy,
  The sayling Pine, the Cedar proud and tall,
  The vine-prop Elme, the Poplar neuer dry,
  The builder Oake, sole king of forrests all,
The Aspine good for staues, the Cypresse funerall.

Ioue] Jove.   Lemans] lover's.   perceable] pene-
trable.   Aspine] Aspen.

The Laurell, meed of mightie Conquerours
  And Poets sage, the Firre that weepeth still,
  The Willow worne of forlorne Paramours,
  The Eugh obedient to the benders will,
  The Birch for shaftes, the Sallow for the mill,
  The Mirrhe sweete bleeding in the bitter wound,
  The warlike Beech, the Ash for nothing ill,
  The fruitfull Oliue, and the Platane round,
The caruer Holme, the Maple seeldom inward
    sound.

(2) *The House of Pride*

A STATELY Pallace built of squared bricke,
  Which cunningly was without morter laid,
  Whose wals were high, but nothing strong, nor
    thick,
  And golden foile all ouer them displaid,
  That purest skye with brightnesse they dismaid:
  High lifted vp were many loftie towres,
  And goodly galleries farre ouer laid,
  Full of faire windowes, and delightfull bowres;
And on the top a Diall told the timely howres.

It was a goodly heape for to behould,
  And spake the praises of the workmans wit;
  But full great pittie, that so faire a mould
  Did on so weake foundation euer sit:
  For on a sandie hill, that still did flit,
  And fall away, it mounted was full hie,
  That euery breath of heauen shaked it:
  And all the hinder parts, that few could spie,
Were ruinous and old, but painted cunningly.

Eugh] Yew.   foile] a thin sheet of metal.

Arriued there they passed in forth right ;
   For still to all the gates stood open wide,
   Yet charge of them was to a Porter hight
   Cald *Maluenù*, who entrance none denide :
   Thence to the hall, which was on euery side
   With rich array and costly arras dight :
   Infinite sorts of people did abide
   There waiting long, to win the wished sight
Of her, that was the Lady of that Pallace
   bright.

By them they passe, all gazing on them round,
   And to the Presence mount ; whose glorious
     vew
   Their frayle amazed senses did confound :
   In liuing Princes court none euer knew
   Such endlesse richesse, and so sumptuous
     shew ;
   Ne *Persia* selfe, the nourse of pompous pride
   Like euer saw. And there a noble crew
   Of Lordes and Ladies stood on euery side,
Which with their presence faire, the place muche
   beautifide.

High aboue all a cloth of State was spred,
   And a rich throne, as bright as sunny day,
   On which there sate most braue embellished
   With royall robes and gorgeous array,
   A mayden Queene, that shone as *Titans* ray,
   In glistring gold, and peerelesse pretious stone :
   Yet her bright blazing beautie did assay
   To dim the brightnesse of her glorious throne,
As enuying her selfe, that too exceeding shone.

   hight]committed, entrusted.   dight]deoked, equipped,
adorned.   ne]not, nor.

Exceeding shone, like *Phœbus* fairest childe,
  That did presume his fathers firie wayne,
  And flaming mouthes of steedes vnwonted wilde
  Through highest heauen with weaker hand to
    rayne ;
  Proud of such glory and aduancement vaine,
  While flashing beames do daze his feeble eyen,
  He leaues the welkin way most beaten plaine,
  And rapt with whirling wheeles, inflames the
    skyen,
With fire not made to burne, but fairely for to
  shyne.

So proud she shyned in her Princely state,
  Looking to heauen ; for earth she did disdayne,
  And sitting high ; for lowly she did hate :
  Lo vnderneath her scornefull feete, was layne
  A dreadfull Dragon with an hideous trayne,
  And in her hand she held a mirrhour bright,
  Wherein her face she often vewed fayne,
  And in her selfe-lou'd semblance tooke delight ;
For she was wondrous faire, as any liuing wight.

Of griesly *Pluto* she the daughter was,
  And sad *Proserpina* the Queene of hell ;
  Yet did she thinke her pearelesse worth to pas
  That parentage, with pride so did she swell,
  And thundring *Ioue*, that high in heauen doth
    dwell,
  And wield the world, she claymed for her syre,
  Or if that any else did *Ioue* excell :
  For to the highest she did still aspyre,
Or if ought higher were then that, did it desyre.

firie wayne] fiery wain.   fayne] gladly, with pleasure.

And proud *Lucifera* men did her call,
   That made her selfe a Queene, and crownd to be,
   Yet rightfull kingdome she had none at all,
   Ne heritage of natiue soueraintie,
   But did vsurpe with wrong and tyrannie
   Vpon the scepter, which she now did hold :
   Ne ruld her Realmes with lawes, but pollicie,
   And strong aduizement of six wisards old,
That with their counsels bad her kingdome did vp-
   hold.

Soone as the Elfin knight in presence came,
   And false *Duessa* seeming Lady faire,
   A gentle Husher, *Vanitie* by name
   Made rowme, and passage for them did prepaire :
   So goodly brought them to the lowest staire
   Of her high throne, where they on humble knee
   Making obeyssance, did the cause declare,
   Why they were come, her royall state to see,
To proue the wide report of her great Maiestee.

With loftie eyes, halfe loth to looke so low,
   She thanked them in her disdainefull wise,
   Ne other grace vouchsafed them to show
   Of Princesse worthy, scarse them bad arise.
   Her Lordes and Ladies all this while deuise
   Themselues to setten forth to straungers sight :
   Some frounce their curled haire in courtly guise,
   Some prancke their ruffes, and others trimly
   dight
Their gay attire : each others greater pride does
   spight.

rowme] place, space, room.   frounce] to gather in
folds.   prancke] to fold, plait.   spight] to grudge,
envy.

Goodly they all that knight do entertaine,
   Right glad with him to haue increast their crew :
   But to *Duess'* each one himself did paine
   All kindnesse and faire courtesie to shew ;
   For in that court whylome her well they knew :
   Yet the stout Faerie mongst the middest crowd
   Thought all their glorie vaine in knightly vew,
   And that great Princesse too exceeding prowd,
That to strange knight no better countenance allowd.

Suddein vpriseth from her stately place
   The royall Dame, and for her coche doth call :
   All hurtlen forth, and she with Princely pace,
   As faire *Aurora* in her purple pall,
   Out of the East the dawning day doth call :
   So forth she comes : her brightnesse brode doth
     blaze ;
   The heapes of people thronging in the hall,
   Do ride each other, vpon her to gaze :
Her glorious glitterand light doth all mens eyes
     amaze.

So forth she comes, and to her coche does clyme,
   Adorned all with gold, and girlonds gay,
   That seemd as fresh as *Flora* in her prime,
   And stroue to match, in royall rich array,
   Great *Iunoes* golden chaire, the which they say
   The Gods stand gazing on, when she does ride
   To *Ioues* high house through heauens braspaued
     way
   Drawne of faire Pecocks, that excell in pride,
And full of *Argus* eyes their tailes dispredden wide.

coche] coach.   hurtlen] rushing, dashing.   glitterand] glittering, shining.   dispredden] spread out.

(3) *The Knight and Una meet an armed Knight flying from Despair. The Cave of Despair*

So as they traueild, lo they gan espy
　An armed knight towards them gallop fast,
　That seemed from some feared foe to fly,
　Or other griesly thing, that him agast.
　Still as he fled, his eye was backward cast,
　As if his feare still followed him behind ;
　Als flew his steed, as he his bands had brast,
　And with his winged heeles did tread the wind,
As he had beene a fole of *Pegasus* his kind.

Nigh as he drew, they might perceiue his head
　To be vnarmd, and curld vncombed heares
　Vpstaring stiffe, dismayd with vncouth dread ;
　Nor drop of bloud in all his face appeares
　Nor life in limbe : and to increase his feares,
　In fowle reproch of knighthoods faire degree,
　About his neck an hempen rope he weares,
　That with his glistring armes does ill agree ;
But he of rope or armes has now no memoree.

The *Redcrosse* knight toward him crossed fast,
　To weet, what mister wight was so dismayd :
　There him he finds all sencelesse and aghast,
　That of him selfe he seemd to be afrayd ;
　Whom hardly he from flying forward stayd,
　Till he these wordes to him deliuer might ;
　Sir knight, aread who hath ye thus arayd,
　And eke from whom make ye this hasty flight :
For neuer knight I saw in such misseeming plight.

traueild] travelled.　agast] frightened, terrified.　Als]
also.　brast] burst.　fole] foal.　heares] hairs.
to weet] to know.　what mister wight] what kind of
person.　aread] tell, shew.　eke] also.

He answerd nought at all, but adding new
   Feare to his first amazment, staring wide
   With stony eyes, and hartlesse hollow hew,
   Astonisht stood, as one that had aspide
   Infernall furies, with their chaines vntide.
   Him yet againe, and yet againe bespake
   The gentle knight ; who nought to him-replide,
   But trembling euery ioynt did inly quake,
And foltring tongue at last these words seemd forth
   to shake.

For Gods deare loue, Sir knight, do me not stay ;
   For loe he comes, he comes fast after mee.
   Eft looking backe would faine haue runne away ;
   But he him forst to stay, and tellen free
   The secret cause of his perplexitie :
   Yet nathemore by his bold hartie speach,
   Could his bloud-frosen hart emboldned bee,
   But through his boldnesse rather feare did
   reach,
Yet forst, at last he made through silence suddein
   breach.

And am I now in safetie sure (quoth he)
   From him, that would haue forced me to dye ?
   And is the point of death now turnd fro mee,
   That I may tell this haplesse history ?
   Feare nought : (quoth he) no daunger now is
   nye.
   Then shall I you recount a ruefull cace,
   (Said he) the which with this vnlucky eye
   I late beheld, and had not greater grace
Me reft from it, had bene partaker of the place.

aspide] espied.   Eft] afterwards.   nathemore] never
the more.

I lately chaunst (Would I had neuer chaunst)
   With a faire knight to keepen companee,
   Sir *Terwin* hight, that well himselfe aduaunst
   In all affaires, and was both bold and free,
   But not so happie as mote happie bee :
   He lou'd, as was his lot, a Ladie gent,
   That him againe lou'd in the least degree :
   For she was proud, and of too high intent,
And ioyd to see her louer languish and lament.

From whom returning sad and comfortlesse,
   As on the way together we did fare,
   We met that villen (God from him me blesse)
   That cursed wight, from whom I scapt whyleare,
   A man of hell, that cals himselfe *Despaire* :
   Who first vs greets, and after faire areedes
   Of tydings strange, and of aduentures rare :
   So creeping close, as Snake in hidden weedes,
Inquireth of our states, and of our knightly deedes.

Which when he knew, and felt our feeble harts
   Embost with bale, and bitter byting griefe,
   Which loue had launched with his deadly darts,
   With wounding words and termes of foule re-
      priefe
   He pluckt from vs all hope of due reliefe,
   That earst vs held in loue of lingring life ;
   Then hopelesse hartlesse, gan the cunning thiefe
   Perswade vs die, to stint all further strife :
To me he lent this rope, to him a rustie knife.

chaunst] chanced.   hight] named, called.   aduaunst]
advanced.   mote] might.   gent] gentle.   scapt]
escaped.   whyleare] erewhile, lately.   areedes] tells,
describes, shows.   embost with bale] exhausted.
earst] formerly, lately.   stint] to stop, cease.

With which sad instrument of hastie death,
    That wofull louer, loathing lenger light,
    A wide way made to let forth liuing breath.
    But I more fearefull, or more luckie wight,
    Dismayd with that deformed dismall sight,
    Fled fast away, halfe dead with dying feare :
    Ne yet assur'd of life by you, Sir knight,
    Whose like infirmitie like chaunce may beare :
But God you neuer let his charmed speeches
      heare.

How may a man (said he) with idle speach
    Be wonne, to spoyle the Castle of his health ?
    I wote (quoth he) whom triall late did teach,
    That like would not for all this worldes wealth :
    His subtill tongue, like dropping honny, mealt'th
    Into the hart, and searcheth euery vaine,
    That ere one be aware, by secret stealth
    His powre is reft, and weakenesse doth remaine.
O neuer Sir desire to try his guilefull traine.

Certes (said he) hence shall I neuer rest,
    Till I that treachours art haue heard and tride ;
    And you Sir knight, whose name mote I re-
      quest,
    Of grace do me vnto his cabin guide.
    I that hight *Treuisan* (quoth he) will ride
    Against my liking backe, to doe you grace :
    But nor for gold nor glee will I abide
    By you, when ye arriue in that same place ;
For leuer had I die, then see his deadly face.

---

    lenger] longer.   wote] to know.   mealt'th] melteth.
reft] seized, taken away.   treachours] traitor's.   leuer]
rather.

Ere long they come, where that same wicked wight
  His dwelling has, low in an hollow caue,
  Farre vnderneath a craggie clift ypight,
  Darke, dolefull, drearie, like a greedie graue,
  That still for carrion carcases doth craue :
  On top whereof aye dwelt the ghastly Owle,
  Shrieking his balefull note, which euer draue
  Farre from that haunt all other chearefull
    fowle ;
And all about it wandring ghostes did waile and
    howle.

And all about old stockes and stubs of trees,
  Whereon nor fruit, nor leafe was euer seene,
  Did hang vpon the ragged rocky knees ;
  On which had many wretches hanged beene,
  Whose carcases were scattered on the greene,
  And throwne about the cliffs. Arriued there,
  That bare-head knight for dread and dolefull
    teene,
  Would faine haue fled, ne durst approchen neare,
But th'other forst him stay, and comforted in
    feare.

That darkesome caue they enter, where they find
  That cursed man, low sitting on the ground,
  Musing full sadly in his sullein mind ;
  His griesie lockes, long growen, and vnbound,
  Disordred hong about his shoulders round,
  And hid his face ; through which his hollow eyne
  Lookt deadly dull, and stared as astound ;
  His raw-bone cheekes through penurie and pine,
Were shronke into his iawes, as he did neuer dine.

ypight] placed, set.   teene] grief, sorrow.

His garment nought but many ragged clouts,
  With thornes together pind and patched was,
  The which his naked sides he wrapt abouts;
  And him beside there lay vpon the gras
  A drearie corse, whose life away did pas,
  All wallowd in his owne yet luke-warme blood,
  That from his wound yet welled fresh alas;
  In which a rustie knife fast fixed stood,
And made an open passage for the gushing flood.

Which piteous spectacle, approuing trew
  The wofull tale that *Treuisan* had told,
  When as the gentle *Redcrosse* knight did vew,
  With firie zeale he burnt in courage bold,
  Him to auenge, before his bloud were cold,
  And to the villein said, Thou damned wight
  The author of this fact, we here behold,
  What iustice can but iudge against thee right,
With thine owne bloud to price his bloud, here shed in sight?

What franticke fit (quoth he) hath thus distraught
  Thee, foolish man, so rash a doome to giue?
  What iustice euer other iudgement taught,
  But he should die, who merites not to liue?
  None else to death this man despayring driue,
  But his owne guiltie mind deseruing death.
  Is then vniust to each his due to giue?
  Or let him die, that loatheth liuing breath?
Or let him die at ease, that liueth here vneath?

vneath] with difficulty, uneasily.

Who trauels by the wearie wandring way,
  To come vnto his wished home in haste,
  And meetes a flood, that doth his passage stay,
  Is not great grace to helpe him ouer past,
  Or free his feet, that in the myre sticke fast ?
  Most enuious man, that grieues at neighbours
    good,
  And fond, that ioyest in the woe thou hast,
  Why wilt not let him passe, that long hath stood
Vpon the banke, yet wilt thy selfe not passe the
  flood ?

He there does now enioy eternall rest
  And happie ease, which thou doest want and
    craue,
  And further from it daily wanderest :
  What if some litle paine the passage haue,
  That makes fraile flesh to feare the bitter waue ?
  Is not short paine well borne, that brings longease,
  And layes the soule to sleepe in quiet graue ?
  Sleepe after toyle, port after stormie seas,
Ease after warre, death after life does greatly please.

The knight much wondred at his suddeine wit,
  And said, The terme of life is limited,
  Ne may a man prolong, nor shorten it ;
  The souldier may not moue from watchfull sted,
  Nor leaue his stand, vntill his Captaine bed.
  Who life did limit by almightie doome,
  (Quoth he) knowes best the termes established ;
  And he, that points the Centonell his roome,
Doth license him depart at sound of morning droome.

  fond] foolish.   sted] place, situation.   bed] to order,
command.   Centonell] sentinel.   roome] place, position.
droome] drum.

Is not his deed, what euer thing is donne,
  In heauen and earth ? did not he all create
  To die againe ? all ends that was begonne.
  Their times in his eternall booke of fate
  Are written sure, and haue their certaine date.
  Who then can striue with strong necessitie,
  That holds the world in his still chaunging state,
  Or shunne the death ordayned by destinie ?
When houre of death is come, let none aske whence,
    nor why.

The lenger life, I wote the greater sin,
  The greater sin, the greater punishment :
  All those great battels, which thou boasts to win,
  Through strife, and bloud-shed, and auenge-
    ment,
  Now praysd, hereafter deare thou shalt repent :
  For life must life, and bloud must bloud repay.
  Is not enough thy euill life forespent ?
  For he, that once hath missed the right way,
The further he doth goe, the further he doth stray.

Then do no further goe, no further stray,
  But here lie downe, and to thy rest betake,
  Th'ill to preuent, that life ensewen may.
  For what hath life, that may it loued make,
  And giues not rather cause it to forsake ?
  Feare, sicknesse, age, losse, labour, sorrow, strife,
  Paine, hunger, cold, that makes the hart to
    quake ;
  And euer fickle fortune rageth rife,
All which, and thousands mo do make a loathsome
    life.

      ensewen] to follow.   mo] more.

Thou wretched man, of death hast greatest need,
  If in true ballance thou wilt weigh thy state:
  For neuer knight, that dared warlike deede,
  More lucklesse disauentures did amate:
  Witnesse the dongeon deepe, wherein of late
  Thy life shut vp, for death so oft did call;
  And though good lucke prolonged hath thy
      date,
  Yet death then, would the like mishaps forestall,
Into the which hereafter thou maiest happen
  fall.

Why then doest thou, O man of sin, desire
  To draw thy dayes forth to their last degree?
  Is not the measure of thy sinfull hire
  High heaped vp with huge iniquitie,
  Against the day of wrath, to burden thee?
  Is not enough, that to this Ladie milde
  Thou falsed hast thy faith with periurie,
  And sold thy selfe to serue *Duessa* vilde,
With whom in all abuse thou hast thy selfe defilde?

Is not he iust, that all this doth behold
  From highest heauen, and beares an equall eye?
  Shall he thy sins vp in his knowledge fold,
  And guiltie be of thine impietie?
  Is not his law, Let euery sinner die:
  Die shall all flesh? what then must needs be
      donne,
  Is it not better to doe willinglie,
  Then linger, till the glasse be all out ronne?
Death is the end of woes: die soone, O faeries
  sonne.

  disauentures] mishaps, misfortunes.   amate] dismay,
daunt.   vilde] vile.

The knight was much enmoued with his speach,
　　That as a swords point through his hart did
　　　perse,
　　And in his conscience made a secret breach,
　　Well knowing true all, that he did reherse
　　And to his fresh remembrance did reuerse
　　The vgly vew of his deformed crimes,
　　That all his manly powres it did disperse,
　　As he were charmed with inchanted rimes,
That oftentimes he quakt, and fainted oftentimes.

In which amazement, when the Miscreant
　　Perceiued him to wauer weake and fraile,
　　Whiles trembling horror did his conscience dant,
　　And hellish anguish did his soule assaile,
　　To driue him to despaire, and quite to quaile,
　　He shew'd him painted in a table plaine,
　　The damned ghosts, that doe in torments waile,
　　And thousand feends that doe them endlesse
　　　paine
With fire and brimstone, which for euer shall
　　remaine.

The sight whereof so throughly him dismaid,
　　That nought but death before his eyes he saw,
　　And euer burning wrath before him laid,
　　By righteous sentence of th'Almighties law:
　　Then gan the villein him to ouercraw,
　　And brought vnto him swords, ropes, poison, fire,
　　And all that might him to perdition draw;
　　And bad him choose, what death he would desire:
For death was due to him, that had prouokt Gods
　　ire.

　　　　enmoued] moved.　　　prouokt] provoked.

But when as none of them he saw him take,
  He to him raught a dagger sharpe and keene,
  And gaue it him in hand : his hand did quake,
  And tremble like a leafe of Aspin greene,
  And troubled bloud through his pale face was seene
  To come, and goe with tydings from the hart,
  As it a running messenger had beene.
  At last resolu'd to worke his finall smart,
He lifted vp his hand, that backe againe did start.

Which when as *Vna* saw, through euery vaine
  The crudled cold ran to her well of life,
  As in a swowne : but soone reliu'd againe,
  Out of his hand she snatcht the cursed knife,
  And threw it to the ground, enraged rife,
  And to him said, Fie, fie, faint harted knight,
  What meanest thou by this reprochfull strife ?
  Is this the battell, which thou vauntst to fight
With that fire-mouthed Dragon, horrible and bright ?

Come, come away, fraile, feeble, fleshly wight,
  Ne let vaine words bewitch thy manly hart,
  Ne diuelish thoughts dismay thy constant spright.
  In heauenly mercies hast thou not a part ?
  Why shouldst thou then despeire, that chosen art ?
  Where iustice growes, there grows eke greater
    grace,
  The which doth quench the brond of hellish
    smart,
  And that accurst hand-writing doth deface.
Arise, Sir knight arise, and leaue this cursed place.

raught] handed.	crudled] curdled.	swowne] swoon.
reliu'd] revived.	rife] deeply, strongly.	Ne . . . Ne]
neither . . . nor.	diuelish] devilish.	spright] spirit.
brond] brand.		

So vp he rose, and thence amounted streight.
　　Which when the carle beheld, and saw his guest
　　Would safe depart, for all his subtill sleight,
　　He chose an halter from among the rest,
　　And with it hung himselfe, vnbid vnblest.
　　But death he could not worke himselfe thereby;
　　For thousand times he so himselfe had drest,
　　Yet nathelesse it could not doe him die,
Till he should die his last, that is eternally.

(4) *The Knight and Una at the brazen tower wherein
Una's parents are imprisoned by the dragon*

HIGH time now gan it wex for *Vna* faire,
　　To thinke of those her captiue Parents deare,
　　And their forwasted kingdome to repaire :
　　Whereto whenas they now approched neare,
　　With hartie words her knight she gan to cheare,
　　And in her modest manner thus bespake ;
　　Deare knight, as deare, as euer knight was deare,
　　That all these sorrowes suffer for my sake,
High heauen behold the tedious toyle, ye for me
　　take.

Now are we come vnto my natiue soyle,
　　And to the place, where all our perils dwell;
　　Here haunts that feend, and does his dayly spoyle,
　　Therefore henceforth be at your keeping well,
　　And euer ready for your foeman fell.
　　The sparke of noble courage now awake,
　　And striue your excellent selfe to excell;
　　That shall ye euermore renowmed make,
Aboue all knights on earth, that batteill vndertake.

　　amounted] mounted, ascended.　　　　sleight] device,
trickery.　　wex] to wax, grow, become.　　renowmed]
renowned.

And pointing forth, lo yonder is (said she)
   The brasen towre in which my parents deare
   For dread of that huge feend emprisond be,
   Whom I from far see on the walles appeare,
   Whose sight my feeble soule doth greatly cheare :
   And on the top of all I do espye
   The watchman wayting tydings glad to heare,
   That O my parents might I happily
Vnto you bring, to ease you of your misery.

With that they heard a roaring hideous sound,
   That all the ayre with terrour filled wide,
   And seemd vneath to shake the stedfast ground.
   Eftsoones that dreadfull Dragon they espide,
   Where stretcht he lay vpon the sunny side
   Of a great hill, himselfe like a great hill.
   But all so soone, as he from far descride
   Those glistring armes, that heauen with light did
     fill,
He rousd himselfe full blith, and hastned them vntill.

(5) *Defeat and Death of the dragon*

Then freshly vp arose the doughtie knight,
   All healed of his hurts and woundes wide,
   And did himselfe to battell readie dight ;
   Whose early foe awaiting him beside
   To haue deuourd, so soone as day he spyde,
   When now he saw himselfe so freshly reare,
   As if late fight had nought him damnifyde,
   He woxe dismayd, and gan his fate to feare ;
Nathlesse with wonted rage he him aduaunced
   neare.

eftsoones] forthwith.   blith] joyfully.   vntill] unto,
towards.   damnifyde] injured.   woxe] waxed, became,
grew.   nathlesse] nevertheless, none the less.

And in his first encounter, gaping wide,
  He thought attonce him to haue swallowd quight,
  And rusht vpon him with outragious pride ;
  Who him r'encountring fierce, as hauke in flight,
  Perforce rebutted backe. The weapon bright
  Taking aduantage of his open iaw,
  Ran through his mouth with so importune might,
  That deepe emperst his darksome hollow maw,
And back retyrd, his life bloud forth with all did
    draw.

So downe he fell, and forth his life did breath,
  That vanisht into smoke and cloudes swift ;
  So downe he fell, that th'earth him vnderneath
  Did grone, as feeble so great load to lift ;
  So downe he fell, as an huge rockie clift,
  Whose false foundation waues haue washt away,
  With dreadfull poyse is from the mayneland rift,
  And rolling downe, great *Neptune* doth dismay ;
So downe he fell, and like an heaped mountaine lay.

The knight himselfe euen trembled at his fall,
  So huge and horrible a masse it seem'd ;
  And his deare Ladie, that beheld it all,
  Durst not approch for dread, which she mis-
    deem'd,
  But yet at last, when as the direfull feend
  She saw not stirre, off-shaking vaine affright,
  She nigher drew, and saw that ioyous end :
  Then God she praysd, and thankt her faithfull
    knight,
That had atchieu'd so great a conquest by his
    might.

quight] quite.   importune] heavy, severe, grievous.
emperst] penetrated.   misdeem'd] misjudged.

(6) *Betrothal of Una with the Knight*

Then forth he called that his daughter faire,
  The fairest *Vn'* his onely daughter deare,
  His onely daughter, and his onely heyre;
  Who forth proceeding with sad sober cheare,
  As bright as doth the morning starre appeare
  Out of the East, with flaming lockes bedight,
  To tell that dawning day is drawing neare,
And to the world does bring long wished light;
So faire and fresh that Lady shewd her selfe in sight.

So faire and fresh, as freshest flowre in May;
  For she had layd her mournefull stole aside,
  And widow-like sad wimple throwne away,
  Wherewith her heauenly beautie she did hide,
  Whiles on her wearie iourney she did ride;
  And on her now a garment she did weare,
  All lilly white, withoutten spot, or pride,
That seemd like silke and siluer wouen neare,
But neither silke nor siluer therein did appeare.

The blazing brightnesse of her beauties beame,
  And glorious light of her sunshyny face
  To tell, were as to striue against the streame.
  My ragged rimes are all too rude and bace,
  Her heauenly lineaments for to enchace.
  Ne wonder; for her owne deare loued knight,
  All were she dayly with himselfe in place,
  Did wonder much at her celestiall sight:
Oft had he seene her faire, but neuer so faire dight.

*   *   *   *   *   *   *   *

Vn'] Una.   heyre] heir.   cheare] countenance.
bedight] adorned.   wimple] covering of linen worn by
women on the head, cheeks, and neck.   bace] low.
enchace] to set, serve as a setting for.

His owne two hands the holy knots did knit,
    That none but death for euer can deuide ;
    His owne two hands, for such a turne mosᵗ fit,
    The housling fire did kindle and prouide,
    And holy water theron sprinckled wide ;
    At which the bushy Teade a groome did light,
    And sacred lampe in secret chamber hide,
    Where it should not be quenched day nor
        night,
For feare of euill fates, but burnen euer bright.

Then gan they sprinckle all the posts with wine,
    And made great feast to solemnize that day ;
    They all perfumde with frankencense diuine,
    And precious odours fetcht from far away,
    That all the house did sweat with great aray :
    And all the while sweete Musicke did apply
    Her curious skill, the warbling notes to play,
    To driue away the dull Melancholy ;
The whiles one sung a song of loue and iollity.

During the which there was an heauenly noise
    Heard sound through all the Pallace pleasantly,
    Like as it had bene many an Angels voice,
    Singing before th'eternall maiesty,
    In their trinall triplicities on hye ;
    Yet wist no creature, whence that heauenly
        sweet
    Proceeded, yet each one felt secretly
    Himselfe thereby reft of his sences meet,
And rauished with rare impression in his sprite.

---

    deuide] divide.   housling] sacramental (*transf.*).
Teade] torch.   trinall] threefold.   triplicities] trinities,
triads.   sprite] spirit.

Great ioy was made that day of young and old,
    And solemne feast proclaimd throughout the
      land,
  That their exceeding merth may not be told :
  Suffice it heare by signes to vnderstand
  The vsual ioyes at knitting of loues band.
  Thrise happy man the knight himselfe did hold,
  Possessed of his Ladies hart and hand,
  And euer, when his eye did her behold,
His heart did seeme to melt in pleasures manifold.

Her ioyous presence and sweet company
  In full content he there did long enioy,
  Ne wicked enuie, ne vile gealosy
  His deare delights were able to annoy :
  Yet swimming in that sea of blisfull ioy,
  He nought forgot, how he whilome had sworne,
  In case he could that monstrous beast destroy,
  Vnto his Farie Queene backe to returne :
The which he shortly did, and *Vna* left to mourne.

Now strike your sailes ye iolly Mariners,
  For we be come vnto a quiet rode,
  Where we must land some of our passengers,
  And light this wearie vessell of her lode.
  Here she a while may make her safe abode,
  Till she repaired haue her tackles spent,
  And wants supplide. And then againe abroad
  On the long voyage whereto she is bent :
Well may she speede and fairely finish her intent.

ne . . . ne] neither . . . nor.   whilome] formerly,
once.

THE MASQUE OF CUPID

FOR round about, the wals yclothed were
  With goodly arras of great maiesty,
  Wouen with gold and silke so close and nere,
  That the rich metall lurked priuily,
  As faining to be hid from enuious eye ;
  Yet here, and there, and euery where vnwares
  It shewd it selfe, and shone vnwillingly ;
  Like a discolourd Snake, whose hidden snares
Through the greene gras his long bright burnisht
    backe declares.

And in those Tapets weren fashioned
  Many faire pourtraicts, and many a faire feate,
  And all of loue, and all of lusty-hed,
  As seemed by their semblaunt did entreat ;
  And eke all *Cupids* warres they did repeate,
  And cruell battels, which he whilome fought
  Gainst all the Gods, to make his empire great ;
  Besides the huge massacres, which he wrought
On mighty kings and kesars, into thraldome brought.

Therein was writ, how often thundring *Ioue*
  Had felt the point of his hart-percing dart,
  And leauing heauens kingdome, here did roue
  In straunge disguize, to slake his scalding smart ;
  Now like a Ram, faire *Helle* to peruart,
  Now like a Bull, *Europa* to withdraw :
  Ah, how the fearefull Ladies tender hart

faining] feigning, pretending.   vnwares] unexpectedly, suddenly.   Tapets] tapestries, figured cloths.   feate] action, deed.   lusty-hed] pleasure.   semblaunt] semblance, resemblance.   whilome] formerly once. kesars] kaisers, emperors.

Did liuely seeme to tremble, when she saw
The huge seas vnder her t'obay her seruaunts law.

Soone after that into a golden showre
    Him selfe he chaung'd faire *Danaë* to vew,
    And through the roofe of her strong brasen towre
    Did raine into her lap an hony dew,
    The whiles her foolish garde, that little knew
    Of such deceipt, kept th'yron dore fast bard,
    And watcht, that none should enter nor issew ;
    Vaine was the watch, and bootlesse all the ward,
Whenas the God to golden hew him selfe transfard.

Then was he turnd into a snowy Swan,
    To win faire *Leda* to his louely trade :
    O wondrous skill, and sweet wit of the man,
    That her in daffadillies sleeping made,
    From scorching heat her daintie limbes to shade :
    Whiles the proud Bird ruffing his fethers wyde,
    And brushing his faire brest, did her inuade ;
    She slept, yet twixt her eyelids closely spyde,
How towards her he rusht, and smiled at his pryde.

Then shewd it, how the *Thebane Semelee*
    Deceiu'd of gealous *Iuno*, did require
    To see him in his soueraigne maiestee,
    Armd with his thunderbolts and lightning fire,
    Whence dearely she with death bought her
        desire.
    But faire *Alcmena* better match did make,
    Ioying his loue in likenesse more entire ;
    Three nights in one, they say, that for her sake
He then did put, her pleasures lenger to partake.

th'yron] the iron.

Twise was he seene in soaring Eagles shape,
    And with wide wings to beat the buxome ayre,
    Once, when he with *Asterie* did scape,
    Againe, when as the *Troiane* boy so faire
    He snatcht from *Ida* hill, and with him bare:
    Wondrous delight it was, there to behould,
    How the rude Shepheards after him did stare,
    Trembling through feare, least down he fallen
        should,
And often to him calling, to take surer hould.

In *Satyres* shape *Antiopa* he snatcht:
    And like a fire, when he *Aegin'* assayd:
    A shepheard, when *Mnemosyne* he catcht:
    And like a Serpent to the *Thracian* mayd.
    Whiles thus on earth great *Ioue* these pageaunts
        playd,
    The winged boy did thrust into his throne,
    And scoffing, thus vnto his mother sayd,
    Lo now the heauens obey to me alone,
And take me for their *Ioue*, whiles *Ioue* to earth is
    gone.

And thou, faire *Phœbus*, in thy colours bright
    Wast there enwouen, and the sad distresse,
    In which that boy thee plonged, for despight,
    That thou bewray'dst his mothers wantonnesse,
    When she with *Mars* was meynt in ioyfulnesse:
    For thy he thrild thee with a leaden dart,
    To loue faire *Daphne*, which thee loued lesse:
    Lesse she thee lou'd, then was thy iust desart,
Yet was thy loue her death, and her death was thy
    smart.

plonged] plunged.   meynt] joined in marriage.   .for thy] therefore, on that account.   thrild] pierced.

So louedst thou the lusty *Hyacinct,*
   So louedst thou the faire *Coronis* deare :
Yet both are of thy haplesse hand extinct,
   Yet both in flowres do liue, and loue thee beare,
The one a Paunce, the other a sweet breare :
   For griefe whereof, ye mote haue liuely seene
The God himselfe rending his golden heare,
   And breaking quite his gyrlond euer greene,
With other signes of sorrow and impatient teene.

Both for those two, and for his owne deare sonne,
   The sonne of *Climene* he did repent,
Who bold to guide the charet of the Sunne,
   Himselfe in thousand peeces fondly rent,
And all the world with flashing fier brent ;
   So like, that all the walles did seeme to flame.
Yet cruell *Cupid,* not herewith content,
   Forst him eftsoones to follow other game,
And loue a Shepheards daughter for his dearest
     Dame.

He loued *Isse* for his dearest Dàme,
   And for her sake her cattell fed a while.
And for her sake a cowheard vile became,
   The seruant of *Admetus* cowheard vile,
Whiles that from heauen he suffered exile.
   Long were to tell each other louely fit,
Now like a Lyon, hunting after spoile,
   Now like a Stag, now like a faulcon flit :
All which in that faire arras was most liuely
     writ.

Paunce] pansy.   breare] briar.   mote] might.
heare] hair.   gyrlond] garland.   teene] grief, sorrow.
charet] chariot.   brent] burnt.   forst] forced.   eft-
soones] forthwith.   flit] swift, fleet.

Next vnto him was *Neptune* pictured,
  In his diuine resemblance wondrous lyke :
His face was rugged, and his hoarie hed
  Dropped with brackish deaw ; his three-forkt
    Pyke
He stearnly shooke, and therewith fierce did
    stryke
The raging billowes, that on euery syde
Theytremblingstood,andmadealongbroaddyke,
That his swift charet might haue passage wyde,
Which foure great *Hippodames* did draw in teme-
    wise tyde.

His sea-horses did seeme to snort amayne,
  And from their nosethrilles blow the brynie
    streame,
Thatmade the sparcklingwaues to smoke agayne,
  And flame with gold, but the white fomy creame,
Did shine with siluer, and shoot forth his beame.
  The God himselfe did pensiue seeme and sad,
And hong adowne his head, as he did dreame :
  For priuy loue his brest empierced had,
Ne ought but deare *Bisaltis* ay could make himglad.

He loued eke *Iphimedia* deare,
  And *Aeolus* faire daughter *Arne* hight,
For whom he turnd him selfe into a Steare,
  And fed on fodder, to beguile her sight.
Also to win *Deucalions* daughter bright,
  He turnd him selfe into a Dolphin fayre ;
And like a winged horse he tooke his flight,
  To snaky-locke *Medusa* to repayre,
On whom he got faire *Pegasus*, that flitteth in the
    ayre.

    Hippodames] sea-horses.   ne] nor, not.

Next *Saturne* was, (but who would euer weene,
  That sullein *Saturne* euer weend to loue?
Yet loue is sullein, and *Saturnlike* seene,
  As he did for *Erigone* it proue,)
  That to a *Centaure* did him selfe transmoue.
So proou'd it eke that gracious God of wine,
  When for to compasse *Philliras* hard loue,
He turnd himselfe into a fruitfull vine,
And into her faire bosome made his grapes decline.

Long were to tell the amorous assayes,
  And gentle pangues, with which he maked meeke
The mighty *Mars*, to learne his wanton playes:
  How oft for *Venus*, and how often eek
  For many other Nymphes he sore did shreek,
  With womanish teares, and with vnwarlike
    smarts,
  Priuily moystening his horrid cheek.
  There was he painted full of burning darts,
And many wide woundes launched through his
    inner parts.

Ne did he spare (so cruell was the Elfe)
  His owne deare mother, (ah why should he so?)
Ne did he spare sometime to pricke himselfe,
  That he might tast the sweet consuming woe,
  Which he had wrought to many others moe.
  But to declare the mournfull Tragedyes,
  And spoiles, wherewith he all the ground did
    strow,
  More eath to number, with how many eyes
High heauen beholds sad louers nightly theeueryes.

weene] suppose, think.   eke] also.   eath] easy.
theeueryes] thefts.

Kings Queenes, Lords Ladies, Knights and Damzels
    gent
  Were heap'd together with the vulgar sort,
  And mingled with the raskall rablement,
  Without respect of person or of port,
  To shew Dan *Cupids* powre and great effort:
  And round about a border was entrayld,
  Of broken bowes and arrowes shiuered short,
  And a long bloudy riuer through them rayld,
So liuely and so like, that liuing sence it fayld.

And at the vpper end of that faire rowme,
  There was an Altar built of pretious stone,
  Of passing valew, and of great renowme,
  On which there stood an Image all alone,
  Of massy gold, which with his owne light shone;
  And wings it had with sundry colours dight,
  More sundry colours, then the proud *Pauone*
  Beares in his boasted fan, or *Iris* bright,
When her discoloured bow she spreds through
    heauen bright.

Blindfold he was, and in his cruell fist
  A mortall bow and arrowes keene did hold,
  With which he shot at randon, when him list,
  Some headed with sad lead, some with pure gold;
  (Ah man beware, how thou those darts behold)
  A wounded Dragon vnder him did ly,
  Whose hideous tayle his left foot did enfold,
  And with a shaft was shot through either eye,
That no man forth might draw, ne no man remedye.

---

gent] gentle.   port] carriage, bearing.   Dan (*for*
Dominus) lord, sir, a title of respect.   entrailed] entwined, interlaced.   rayld] flowed.   Pauone] peacock.
him list] he liked.

And vnderneath his feet was written thus,
  Vnto the Victor of the Gods this bee :
And all the people in that ample hous
Did to that image bow their humble knee,
And oft committed fowle Idolatree.
That wondrous sight faire *Britomart* amazed,
Ne seeing could her wonder satisfie,
But euermore and more vpon it gazed,
The whiles the passing brightnes her fraile sences
    dazed.

Tho as she backward cast her busie eye,
  To search each secret of that goodly sted,
Ouer the dore thus written she did spye
Be bold : she oft and oft it ouer-red,
Yet could not find what sence it figured :
But what so were therein or writ or ment,
She was no whit thereby discouraged
From prosecuting of her first intent,
But forward with bold steps into the next roome
    went.

Much fairer, then the former, was that roome,
  And richlier by many partes arayd :
For not with arras made in painefull loome,
But with pure gold it all was ouerlayd,
Wrought with wilde Antickes, which their follies
  playd,
In the rich metall, as they liuing were.
A thousand monstrous formes therein were made,
Such as false loue doth oft vpon him weare,
For loue in thousand monstrous formes doth oft
    appeare.

    sted] place, situation.   ouer-red] over-read.

And all about, the glistring walles were hong
  With warlike spoiles, and with victorious prayes
  Of mighty Conquerours and Captaines strong,
  Which were whilome captiued in their dayes
  To cruell loue, and wrought their owne decayes
  Their swerds and speres were broke, and
      hauberques rent;
  And their proud girlonds of tryumphant bayes
  Troden in dust with fury insolent,
To shew the victors might and mercilesse intent.

The warlike Mayde beholding earnestly
  The goodly ordinance of this rich place,
  Did greatly wonder, ne could satisfie
  Her greedy eyes with gazing a long space,
  But more she meruaild that no footings trace,
  Nor wight appear'd, but wastefull emptinesse,
  And solemne silence ouer all that place:
  Straunge thing it seem'd, that none was to
      possesse
So rich purueyance, ne them keepe with carefull
    nesse.

And as she lookt about, she did behold,
  How ouer that same dore was likewise writ,
  Be bold, be bold, and euery where *Be bold,*
  That much she muz'd, yet could not construe i
  By any ridling skill, or commune wit.
  At last she spyde at that roomes vpper end,
  Another yron dore, on which was writ,
  Be not too bold; whereto though she did bend
Her earnest mind, yet wist not what it migh
    intend.

prayes] preys.   hauberques] coats of mail.   gir
londs] garlands.   meruaild] marvelled.

Thus she there waited vntil euentyde,
  Yet liuing creature none she saw appeare :
  And now sad shadowes gan the world to hyde,
  From mortall vew, and wrap in darkenesse
    dreare ;
  Yet nould she d'off her weary armes, for feare
  Of secret daunger, ne let sleepe oppresse
  Her heauy eyes with natures burdein deare,
  But drew her selfe aside in sickernesse,
And her welpointed weapons did about her dresse.

Tho when as chearelesse Night ycouered had
  Faire heauen with an vniuersall cloud,
  That euery wight dismayd with darknesse sad,
  In silence and in sleepe themselues did shroud,
  She heard a shrilling Trompet sound aloud,
  Signe of nigh battell, or got victory ;
  Nought therewith daunted was her courage
    proud,
  But rather stird to cruell enmity,
Expecting euer, when some foe she might descry.

With that, an hideous storme of winde arose,
  With dreadfull thunder and lightning atwixt,
  And an earth-quake, as if it streight would
    lose
  The worlds foundations from his centre fixt ;
  A direfull stench of smoke and sulphure mixt
  Ensewd, whose noyance fild the fearefull sted,
  From the fourth houre of night vntill the sixt ;
  Yet the bold *Britonesse* was nought ydred,
Though much emmou'd, but stedfast still per-
    seuered.

nould] would not.   lose] loosen.   emmou'd] moved.

All suddenly a stormy whirlwind blew
   Throughout the house, that clapped euery
      dore,
   With which that yron wicket open flew,
   As it with mightie leuers had bene tore:
   And forth issewd, as on the ready flore
   Of some Theatre, a graue personage,
   That in his hand a branch of laurell bore,
   With comely haueour and count'nance sage,
Yclad in costly garments, fit for tragicke Stage.

Proceeding to the midst, he still did stand,
   As if in mind he somewhat had to say,
   And to the vulgar beckning with his hand,
   In signe of silence, as to heare a play,
   By liuely actions he gan bewray
   Some argument of matter passioned;
   Which doen, he backe retyred soft away,
   And passing by, his name discouered,
Ease, on his robe in golden letters cyphered.

The noble Mayd, still standing all this vewd,
   And merueild at his strange intendiment;
   With that a ioyous fellowship issewd
   Of Minstrals, making goodly meriment,
   With wanton Bardes, and Rymers impudent,
   All which together sung full chearefully
   A lay of loues delight, with sweet concent:
   After whom marcht a iolly company,
In manner of a maske, enranged orderly.

    clapped] shut, slammed.   haueour] deportment, be-
haviour.   doen] done.   merueild] marvelled.
intendiment] knowledge, understanding.

The whiles a most delitious harmony,
  In full straunge notes was sweetly heard to sound,
  That the rare sweetnesse of the melody
  The feeble senses wholly did confound,
  And the fraile soule in deepe delight nigh dround:
  And when it ceast, shrill trompets loud did bray,
  That their report did farre away rebound,
  And when they ceast, it gan againe to play,
The whiles the maskers marched forth in trim
    aray.

The first was *Fancy*, like a louely boy,
  Of rare aspect, and beautie without peare;
  Matchable either to that ympe of *Troy*,
  Whom *Ioue* did loue, and chose his cup to beare,
  Or that same daintie lad, which was so deare
  To great *Alcides*, that when as he dyde,
  He wailed womanlike with many a teare,
  And euery wood, and euery valley wyde
He fild with *Hylas* name; the Nymphes eke *Hylas*
    cryde.

His garment neither was of silke nor say,
  But painted plumes, in goodly order dight,
  Like as the sunburnt *Indians* do aray
  Their towney bodies, in their proudest plight:
  As those same plumes, so seemd he vaine and
    light,
  That by his gate might easily appeare;
  For still he far'd as dauncing in delight,
  And in his hand a windy fan did beare,
That in the idle aire he mou'd still here and there.

peare] peer, equal.   ympe] child, offspring.   say]
cloth of fine texture, resembling serge.

And him beside marcht amorous *Desyre*,
 Who seemd of riper yeares, then th' other Swaine,
 Yet was that other swayne this elders syre,
 And gaue him being, commune to them twaine:
 His garment was disguised very vaine,
 And his embrodered Bonet sat awry;
 Twixt both his hands few sparkes he close did
  straine,
Which still he blew, and kindled busily,
That soone they life conceiu'd, and forth in flames
  did fly.

Next after him went *Doubt*, who was yclad
 In a discolour'd cote, of straunge disguyse,
 That at his backe a brode Capuccio had,
 And sleeues dependant *Albanese*-wyse:
 He lookt askew with his mistrustfull eyes,
 And nicely trode, as thornes lay in his way,
 Or that the flore to shrinke he did auyse,
 And on a broken reed he still did stay
His feeble steps, which shrunke, when hard theron
  he lay.

With him went *Daunger*, cloth'd in ragged weed,
 Made of Beares skin, that him more dreadfull
  made,
 Yet his owne face was dreadfull, ne did need
 Straunge horrour, to deforme his griesly shade;
 A net in th'one hand, and a rustie blade
 In th'other was, this Mischiefe, that Mishap;
 With th'one his foes he threatned to inuade,
 With th'other he his friends ment to enwrap:
For whom he could not kill, he practizd to entrap.

Capuccio] hood of a cloak.   Albanese-wyse] after the
manner of the Albanese (Albanians?).   auyse] to perceiue, notice.

Next him was *Feare,* all arm'd from top to toe,
  Yet thought himselfe not safe enough thereby,
  But feard each shadow mouing to and fro,
  And his owne armes when glittering he did spy,
  Or clashing heard, he fast away did fly,
  As ashes pale of hew, and wingyheeld ;
  And euermore on daunger fixt his eye,
  Gainst whom he alwaies bent a brasen shield,
Which his right hand vnarmed fearefully did wield.

With him went *Hope* in rancke, a handsome Mayd,
  Of chearefull looke and louely to behold ;
  In silken samite she was light arayd,
  And her faire lockes were wouen vp in gold ;
  She alway smyld, and in her hand did hold
  An holy water Sprinckle, dipt in deowe,
  With which she sprinckled fauours manifold,
  On whom she list, and did great liking sheowe,
Great liking vnto many, but true loue to feowe.

And after them *Dissemblance,* and *Suspect*
  Marcht in one rancke, yet an vnequall paire :
  For she was gentle, and of milde aspect,
  Courteous to all, and seeming debonaire,
  Goodly adorned, and exceeding faire :
  Yet was that all but painted, and purloynd,
  And her bright browes were deckt with borrowed
    haire :
  Her deedes were forged, and her words false
    coynd,
And alwaies in her hand two clewes of silke she
  twynd.

samite] rich silk fabric.   holy water Sprinckle]=
aspergillum or brush for sprinkling holy water.   deowe]
lew.   clewes] balls (of silk).

But he was foule, ill fauoured, and grim,
  Vnder his eyebrowes looking still askaunce ;
  And euer as *Dissemblance* laught on him,
  He lowrd on her with daungerous eyeglaunce ;
  Shewing his nature in his countenance ;
  His rolling eyes did neuer rest in place,
  But walkt each where, for feare of hid mis-
      chaunce,
  Holding a lattice still before his face,
Through which he still did peepe, as forward he
      did pace.

Next him went *Griefe,* and *Fury* matcht yfere ;
  Griefe all in sable sorrowfully clad,
  Downe hanging his dull head with heauy chere,
  Yet inly being more, then seeming sad :
  A paire of Pincers in his hand he had,
  With which he pinched people to the hart,
  That from thenceforth a wretched life they lad,
  In wilfull languor and consuming smart,
Dying each day with inward wounds of dolours dart.

But *Fury* was full ill appareiled
  In rags, that naked nigh she did appeare,
  With ghastly lookes and dreadfull drerihed ;
  For from her backe her garments she did teare,
  And from her head oft rent her snarled heare :
  In her right hand a firebrand she did tosse
  About her head, still roming here and there ;
  As a dismayed Deare in chace embost,
Forgetfull of his safety, hath his right way lost.

  yfere] together, in company with.   chere] countenance.   lad] led.   drerihed] dismalness, gloom.   snarled
heare] twisted, tangled hair.   embost] hard pressed (of
a hunted animal).

After them went *Displeasure* and *Pleasance*,
  He looking lompish and full sullein sad,
  And hanging downe his heauy countenance;
  She chearefull fresh and full of ioyance glad,
  As if no sorrow she ne felt ne drad;
  That euill matched paire they seemd to bee:
  An angry Waspe th'one in a viall had
  Th'other in hers an hony-lady Bee;
Thus marched these sixe couples forth in faire
  degree.

After all these there marcht a most faire Dame,
  Led of two grysie villeins, th'one *Despight*,
  The other cleped *Cruelty* by name:
  She dolefull Lady, like a dreary Spright,
  Cald by strong charmes out of eternall night,
  Had deathes owne image figurd in her face,
  Full of sad signes, fearefull to liuing sight;
  Yet in that horror shewd a seemely grace,
And with her feeble feet did moue a comely pace.

Her brest all naked, as net iuory,
  Without adorne of gold or siluer bright,
  Wherewith the Craftesman wonts it beautify,
  Of her dew honour was despoyled quight,
  And a wide wound therein (O ruefull sight)
  Entrenched deepe with knife accursed keene,
  Yet freshly bleeding forth her fainting spright,
  (The worke of cruell hand) was to be seene,
That dyde in sanguine red her skin all snowy cleene.

---

ne ... ne] neither ... nor.   drad] dreaded, feared.
grysie] horrible, grim, grisly.   cleped] called.   Spright]
spirit.   net] pure, clean.   wonts] is accustomed.
dew] due.   quight] quite.

At that wide orifice her trembling hart
   Was drawne forth, and in siluer basin layd,
   Quite through transfixed with a deadly dart,
   And in her bloud yet steeming fresh embayd :
   And those two villeins, which her steps vpstayd,
   When her weake feete could scarcely her sustaine,
   And fading vitall powers gan to fade,
   Her forward still with torture did constraine,
And euermore encreased her consuming paine.

Next after her the winged God himselfe
   Came riding on a Lion rauenous,
   Taught to obay the menage of that Elfe,
   That man and beast with powre imperious
   Subdeweth to his kingdome tyrannous :
   His blindfold eyes he bad a while vnbind,
   That his proud spoyle of that same dolorous
   Faire Dame he might behold in perfect kind ;
Which seene, he much reioyced in his cruell
   mind.

Of which full proud, himselfe vp rearing hye,
   He looked round about with sterne disdaine ;
   And did suruay his goodly company :
   And marshalling the euill ordered traine,
   With that the darts which his right hand did
      straine,
   Full dreadfully he shooke that all did quake,
   And clapt on hie his coulourd winges twaine,
   That all his many it affraide did make :
Tho blinding him againe, his way he forth did
   take.

vpstayd] supported.   menage] handling, control.
suruay] survey.

Behinde him was *Reproch, Repentance, Shame*;
  Reproch the first, *Shame* next, *Repent* behind:
  Repentance feeble, sorrowfull, and lame:
  Reproch despightfull, carelesse, and vnkind;
  Shame most ill fauourd, bestiall, and blind:
  Shame lowrd, *Repentance* sigh'd, *Reproch* did
    scould;
  Reproch sharpe stings, *Repentance* whips entwind,
  Shame burning brond-yrons in her hand did hold:
All three to each vnlike, yet all made in one mould.

And after them a rude confused rout
  Of persons flockt, whose names is hard to read:
  Emongst them was sterne *Strife*, and *Anger* stout,
  Vnquiet *Care*, and fond *Vnthriftihead*,
  Lewd *Losse of Time*, and *Sorrow* seeming dead,
  Inconstant *Chaunge*, and false *Disloyaltie*,
  Consuming *Riotise*, and guilty *Dread*
  Of heauenly vengeance, faint *Infirmitie*,
Vile *Pouertie*, and lastly *Death* with infamie.

There were full many moe like maladies,
  Whose names and natures I note readen well;
  So many moe, as there be phantasies
  In wauering wemens wit, that none can tell,
  Or paines in loue, or punishments in hell;
  All which disguized marcht in masking wise,
  About the chamber with that Damozell,
  And then returned, hauing marched thrise,
Into the inner roome, from whence they first did
  rise.

Repent] Repentance.   lowrd] loured.   'brond-
yrons] swords.   Vnthriftihead] unthriftiness.   Riotise]
riotous life, conduct.   note] could not.   readen] to
describe.

The Pageant of the Seasons and the Months

So, forth issew'd the Seasons of the yeare ;
  First, lusty *Spring*, all dight in leaues of flowres
  That freshly budded and new bloosmes did beare
  (In which a thousand birds had built their bowres
  That sweetly sung, to call forth Paramours) :
  And in his hand a iauelin he did beare,
  And on his head (as fit for warlike stoures)
  A guilt engrauen morion he did weare ;
That as some did him loue, so others did him feare.

Then came the iolly *Sommer*, being dight
  In a thin silken cassock coloured greene,
  That was vnlyned all, to be more light :
  And on his head a girlond well bescene
  He wore, from which as he had chauffed been
  The sweat did drop ; and in his hand he bore
  A boawe and shaftes, as he in forrest greene
  Had hunted late the Libbard or the Bore,
And now would bathe his limbes, with labor heated
    sore.

Then came the *Autumne* all in yellow clad,
  As though he ioyed in his plentious store,
  Laden with fruits that made him laugh, full glad
  That he had banisht hunger, which to-fore
  Had by the belly oft him pinched sore.
  Vpon his head a wreath that was enrold
  With eares of corne, of euery sort he bore :
  And in his hand a sickle he did holde,
To reape the ripened fruits the which the earth
    had yold.

dight] decked, adorned.   stoures] tumults, conflicts.
morion] a kind of helmet, without beaver or visor, worn by
soldiers in the 16th and 17th c.   chauffed] rubbed.
Libbard] leopard.   Bore] boar.   yold] yielded.

Lastly, came *Winter* cloathed all in frize,
  Chattering his teeth for cold that did him chill,
  Whil'st on his hoary beard his breath did freese;
  And the dull drops that from his purpled bill
  As from a limbeck did adown distill.
  In his right hand a tipped staffe he held,
  With which his feeble steps he stayed still:
  For, he was faint with cold, and weak with eld;
That scarse his loosed limbes he hable was to weld.

These, marching softly, thus in order went,
  And after them, the Monthes all riding came;
  First, sturdy *March* with brows full sternly bent,
  And armed strongly, rode vpon a Ram,
  The same which ouer *Hellespontus* swam:
  Yet in his hand a spade he also hent,
  And in a bag all sorts of seeds ysame,
  Which on the earth he strowed as he went,
And fild her womb with fruitfull hope of nourishment.

Next came fresh *Aprill* full of lustyhed,
  And wanton as a Kid whose horne new buds:
  Vpon a Bull he rode, the same which led
  Europa floting through th'*Argolick* fluds:
  His hornes were gilden all with golden studs
  And garnished with garlonds goodly dight
  Of all the fairest flowres and freshest buds
  Which th'earth brings forth, and wet he seem'd
    in sight
With waues, through which he waded for his loues
    delight.

frize] frieze, coarse woollen cloth.   limbeck] alembic,
retort.   eld] age.   hable] able, powerful.   weld]
govern, control.   hent] took, seized.   ysame] together.
lustyhed] lustiness, energy, vigour.   floting] floating.
fluds] floods.

Then came faire *May*, the fayrest mayd on ground,
  Deckt all with dainties of her seasons pryde,
  And throwing flowres out of her lap around :
  Vpon two brethrens shoulders she did ride,
  The twinnes of *Leda* ; which on eyther side
  Supported her like to their soueraine Queene.
  Lord ! how all creatures laught, when her they spide,
  And leapt and daunc't as they had rauisht beene !
And *Cupid* selfe about her fluttred all in greene.

And after her, came iolly *Iune*, arrayd
  All in greene leaues, as he a Player were ;
  Yet in his time, he wrought as well as playd,
  That by his plough-yrons mote right well appeare :
  Vpon a Crab he rode, that him did beare
  With crooked crawling steps an vncouth pase,
  And backward yode, as Bargemen wont to fare
  Bending their force contrary to their face,
Like that vngracious crew which faines demurest grace.

Then came hot *Iuly* boyling like to fire,
  That all his garments he had cast away :
  Vpon a Lyon raging yet with ire
  He boldly rode and made him to obay :
  It was the beast that whylome did forray
  The Nemæan forrest, till th'*Amphytrionide*
  Him slew, and with his hide did him array ;
  Behinde his back a sithe, and by his side
Vnder his belt he bore a sickle circling wide.

plough-yrons] coulter and share of a plough.   mote] might.   pase] pace.   yode] went.

The sixt was *August*, being rich arrayd
  In garment all of gold downe to the ground
  Yet rode he not, but led a louely Mayd
  Forth by the lilly hand, the which was cround
  With eares of corne, and full her hand was found;
  That was the righteous Virgin, which of old
  Liv'd here on earth, and plenty made abound;
  But, after Wrong was lov'd and Iustice solde,
She left th'vnrighteous world and was to heauen
    extold

Next him, *September* marched eeke on foote;
  Yet was he heauy laden with the spoyle
  Of haruests riches, which he made his boot,
  And him enricht with bounty of the soyle:
  In his one hand, as fit for haruests toyle,
  He held a knife-hook; and in th'other hand
  A paire of waights, with which he did assoyle
  Both more and lesse, where it in doubt did
    stand,
And equall gaue to each as Iustice duly scann'd.

Then came *October* full of merry glee:
  For, yet his noule was totty of the must,
  Which he was treading in the wine-fats see,
  And of the ioyous oyle, whose gentle gust
  Made him so frollick and so full of lust.
  Vpon a dreadfull Scorpion he did ride,
  The same which by *Dianaes* doom vniust
  Slew great *Orion*: and eeke by his side
He had his ploughing share, and coulter ready tyde.

---

    assoyle] to absolve, free, release.   noule] head.
totty] unsteady, dizzy.   must] new wine.   wine-
fats] vats of wine.

Next was *Nouember*, he full grosse and fat,
 As fed with lard, and that right well might seeme;
 For, he had been a fatting hogs of late,
 That yet his browes with sweat, did reek and
  steem,
 And yet the season was full sharp and breem ;
 In planting eeke he took no small delight :
 Whereon he rode, not easie was to deeme ;
 For it a dreadfull *Centaure* was in sight,
The seed of *Saturne*, and faire *Nais*, *Chiron* hight.

And after him, came next the chill *December* :
 Yet he through merry feasting which he made,
 And great bonfires, did not the cold remember ;
 His Sauiours birth his mind so much did glad :
 Vpon a shaggy-bearded Goat he rode,
 The same wherewith *Dan Ioue* in tender yeares,
 They say, was nourisht by th'*Idæan* mayd ;
 And in his hand a broad deepe boawle he beares ;
Of which, he freely drinks an health to all his
  peeres.

Then came old *Ianuary*, wrapped well
 In many weeds to keep the cold away ;
 Yet did he quake and quiuer like to quell,
 And blowe his nayles to warme them if he may :
 For, they were numbd with holding all the day
 An hatchet keene, with which he felled wood,
 And from the trees did lop the needlesse spray :
 Vpon an huge great Earth-pot steane he stood ;
From whose wide mouth, there flowed forth the
  Romane floud.

breem] cold, chill, rough, harsh.   deeme] to think,
consider. s⁺eane] stone.

And lastly, came cold *February*, sitting
   In an old wagon, for he could not ride ;
   Drawne of two fishes for the season fitting,
   Which through the flood before did softly slyde
   And swim away : yet had he by his side
   His plough and harnesse fit to till the ground,
   And tooles to prune the trees, before the pride
   Of hasting Prime did make them burgein round :
So past the twelue Months forth, and their dew
   places found.

THE SHEPHERD'S CALENDER

Perigot and Willye's Roundelay

Perigot. It fell vpon a holly eue,
Willye.   hey ho hollidaye,
Per. When holly fathers wont to shrieue :
Wil.   now gynneth this roundelay.
Per. Sitting vpon a hill so hye
Wil.   hey ho the high hyll,
Per. The while my flocke did feede thereby,
Wil.   the while the shepheard selfe did spill :
Per. I saw the bouncing Bellibone,
Wil.   hey ho Bonibell,
Per. Tripping ouer the dale alone,
Wil.   she can trippe it very well :
Per. Well decked in a frocke of gray,
Wil.   hey ho gray is greete,
Per. And in a Kirtle of greene saye,
Wil.   the greene is for maydens meete :

Prime] spring, spring-time.   burgein] to bud.
holly eue] holy eve.   wont] were accustomed.   to
shrieue] to confess.   Bellibone] fair maid, country lass.
greete] weeping, lamentation.   saye] cloth of fine
texture.

Per. A chapelet on her head she wore,

Wil.   hey ho chapelet,

Per. Of sweete Violets therein was store,

Wil.   she sweeter then the Violet.

Per. My sheepe did leaue theyr wonted foode,

Wil.   hey ho seely sheepe,

Per. And gazd on her, as they were wood,

Wil.   woode as he, that did them keepe.

Per. As the bonilasse passed bye,

Wil.   hey ho bonilasse,

Per. She roude at me with glauncing eye,

Wil.   as cleare as the christall glasse :

Per. All as the Sunnye beame to bright,

Wil.   hey ho the Sunne beame,

Per. Glaunceth from *Phœbus* face forthright,

Wil.   so loue into thy hart did streame :

Per. Or as the thonder cleaues the cloudes,

Wil.   hey ho the Thonder,

Per. Wherein the lightsome leuin shroudes,

Wil.   so cleaues thy soule a sonder :

Per. Or as Dame *Cynthias* siluer raye

Wil.   hey ho the Moonelight,

Per. Vpon the glyttering waue doth playe :

Wil.   such play is a pitteous plight.

Per. The glaunce into my heart did glide,

Wil.   hey ho the glyder,

Per. Therewith my soule was sharply gryde,

Wil.   such woundes soone wexen wider.

Per. Hasting to raunch the arrow out,

Wil.   hey ho Perigot.

wood] mad.   bonilasse] a beautiful girl.   roude] *pret. of* roue, to shoot with arrows (*fig.*).   leuin] lightning. gryde] pierced.   wexen] grow, become.   raunch] to pull, pluck.

Per. I left the head in my hart roote :
Wil.   it was a desperate shot.
Per. There itranckleth ay more and more,
Wil.   hey ho the arrowe,
Per. Ne can I find salue for my sore :
Wil.   loue is a curelesse sorrowe.
Per. And though my bale with death I bought,
Wil.   hey ho heauie cheere,
Per. Yet should thilk lasse not from my thought :
Wil.   so you may buye gold to deare.
Per. But whether in paynefull loue I pyne,
Wil.   hey ho pinching payne,
Per. Or thriue in welth, she shalbe mine.
Wil.   but if thou can her obteine.
Per. And if for gracelesse greefe I dye,
Wil.   hey ho gracelesse griefe,
Per. Witnesse, shee slewe me with her eye,
Wil.   let thy follye be the priefe.
Per. And you, that sawe it, simple shepe,
Wil.   hey ho the fayre flocke,
Per. For priefe thereof, my death shall weepe,
Wil.   and mone with many a mocke.
Per. So learnd I loue on a hollye eue,
Wil.   hey ho holidaye,
Per. That euer since my hart did greue.
Wil.   now endeth our roundelay.

priefe] proof.

PROTHALAMION

CALME was the day, and through the trembling
　　　ayre,
Sweete breathing *Zephyrus* did softly play
A gentle spirit, that lightly did delay
Hot *Titans* beames, which then did glyster fayre:
When I whom sullein care,
Through discontent of my long fruitlesse stay
In Princes Court, and expectation vayne
Of idle hopes, which still doe fly away,
Like empty shaddowes, did aflict my brayne,
Walkt forth to ease my payne
Along the shoare of siluer streaming *Themmes*,
Whose rutty Bancke, the which his Riuer hemmes,
Was paynted all with variable flowers,
And all the meades adornd with daintie gemmes,
Fit to decke maydens bowres,
And crowne their Paramours,
Against the Brydale day, which is not long:
　　Sweete *Themmes* runne softly, till I end my Song.

There, in a Meadow, by the Riuers side,
A Flocke of *Nymphes* I chaunced to espy,
All louely Daughters of the Flood thereby,
With goodly greenish locks all lose vntyde,
As each had bene a Bryde,
And each one had a little wicker basket,
Made of fine twigs entrayled curiously,
In which they gathered flowers to fill their flasket:
And with fine Fingers, cropt full feateously
The tender stalkes on hye.

　　glyster] to glitter, shine.　　　　　rutty] full of ruts.
entrayled] entwined, interlaced.　　flasket] a long shallow
basket.　　　feateously] dexterously.

Of euery sort, which in that Meadow grew,
They gathered some ; the Violet pallid blew,
The little Dazie, that at euening closes,
The virgin Lillie, and the Primrose trew,
With store of vermeil Roses,
To decke their Bridegromes posies,
Against the Brydale day, which was not long :
   Sweete *Themmes* runne softly, till I end my Song.

With that, I saw two Swannes of goodly hewe,
Come softly swimming downe along the Lee ;
Two fairer Birds I yet did neuer see :
The snow which doth the top of *Pindus* strew,
Did neuer whiter shew,
Nor *Ioue* himselfe when he a Swan would be
For loue of *Leda*, whiter did appeare :
Yet *Leda* was they say as white as he,
Yet not so white as these, nor nothing neare ;
So purely white they were,
That euen the gentle streame, the which them bare,
Seem'd foule to them, and bad his billowes spare
To wet their silken feathers, least they might
Soyle their fayre plumes with water not so fayre
And marre their beauties bright,
That shone as heauens light,
Against their Brydale day, which was not long :
   Sweete *Themmes* runne softly, till I end my Song.

Eftsoones the *Nymphes*, which now had Flowers
    their fill,
Ran all in haste, to see that siluer brood,
As they came floating on the Christal Flood.
Whom when they sawe, they stood amazed still,
Their wondring eyes to fill,

        vermeil] vermilion.   least] lest.

Them seem'd they neuer saw a sight so fayre,
Of Fowles so louely, that they sure did deeme
Them heauenly borne, or to be that same payre
Which through the Skie draw *Venus* siluer Teeme,
For sure they did not seeme
To be begot of any earthly Seede,
But rather Angels or of Angels breede:
Yet were they bred of *Somers-heat* they say,
In sweetest Season, when each Flower and weede
The earth did fresh aray,
Euen as their Brydale day, which was not long:
   Sweete *Themmes* runne softly, till I end my Song.

Then forth they all out of their baskets drew,
Great store of Flowers, the honour of the field,
That to the sense did fragrant odours yeild,
All which vpon those goodly Birds they threw,
And all the Waues did strew,
That like old *Peneus* Waters they did seeme,
When downe along by pleasant *Tempes* shore
Scattred with Flowres, through *Thessaly* they
    streeme,
That they appeare through Lillies plenteous store,
Like a Brydes Chamber flore:
Two of those *Nymphes*, meane while, two Garlands
    bound,
Of freshest Flowres which in that Mead they found,
The which presenting all in trim Array,
Their snowie Foreheads therewithall they crownd,
Whil'st one did sing this Lay,
Prepar'd against that Day,
Against their Brydale day, which was not long:
   Sweete *Themmes* runne softly, till I end my Song.

Ye gentle Birdes, the worlds faire ornament,
And heauens glorie, whom this happie hower
Doth leade vnto your louers blisfull bower,
Ioy may you haue and gentle hearts content
Of your loues couplement:
And let faire *Venus*, that is Queene of loue,
With her heart-quelling Sonne vpon you smile,
Whose smile they say, hath vertue to remoue
All Loues dislike, and friendships faultie guile
For euer to assoile.
Let endlesse Peace your steadfast hearts accord,
And blessed Plentie wait vpon your bord,
And let your bed with pleasures chast abound,
That fruitfull issue may to you afford,
Which may your foes confound,
And make your ioyes redound,
Vpon your Brydale day, which is not long:
  Sweete *Themmes* run softlie, till I end my Song.

So ended she; and all the rest around
To her redoubled that her vndersong,
Which said, their bridale daye should not be long.
And gentle Eccho from the neighbour ground,
Their accents did resound.
So forth those ioyous Birdes did passe along,
Adowne the Lee, that to them murmurde low,
As he would speake, but that he lackt a tong
Yeat did by signes his glad affection show,
Making his streame run slow.
And all the foule which in his flood did dwell
Gan flock about these twaine, that did excell
The rest, so far, as *Cynthia* doth shend
The lesser starres. So they enranged well,

assoile] to absolve, free, release.   shend] to surpass.

Did on those two attend,
And their best seruice lend,
Against their wedding day, which was not long:
  Sweete *Themmes* run softly, till I end my Song.

At length they all to mery *London* came,
To mery *London*, my most kyndly Nurse,
That to me gaue this Lifes first natiue sourse:
Though from another place I take my name,
An house of auncient fame.
There when they came, whereas those bricky
      towres,
The which on *Themmes* brode aged backe doe ryde,
Where now the studious Lawyers haue their bowers,
There whylome wont the Templer Knights to byde,
Till they decayd through pride:
Next whereunto there standes a stately place,
Where oft I gayned giftes and goodly grace
Of that great Lord, which therein wont to dwell,
Whose want too well now feeles my freendles case:
But Ah here fits not well
Olde woes but ioyes to tell
Against the Brydale daye, which is not long:
  Sweete *Themmes* runne softly, till I end my Song.

Yet therein now doth lodge a noble Peer,
Great *Englands* glory and the Worlds wide wonder,
Whose dreadfull name, late through all *Spaine* did
      thunder,
And *Hercules* two pillors standing neere,
Did make to quake and feare:
Faire branch of Honor, flower of Cheualrie,
That fillest *England* with thy triumphs fame,
Ioy haue thou of thy noble victorie,

And endlesse happinesse of thine owne name
That promiseth the same :
That through thy prowesse and victorious armes,
Thy country may be freed from forraine harmes :
And great *Elisaes* glorious name may ring
Through al the world, fil'd with thy wide Alarmes,
Which some braue muse may sing
To ages following,
Vpon the Brydale day, which is not long :
  Sweete *Themmes* runne softly, till I end my Song.

From those high Towers, this noble Lord issuing,
Like Radiant *Hesper* when his golden hayre
In th'*Ocean* billowes he hath Bathed fayre,
Descended to the Riuers open vewing,
With a great traine ensuing.
Aboue the rest were goodly to bee seene
Two gentle Knights of louely face and feature
Beseeming well the bower of anie Queen,
With gifts of wit and ornaments of nature,
Fit for so goodly stature :
That like the twins of *Ioue* they seem'd in sight,
Which decke the Bauldricke of the Heauens bright.
They two forth pacing to the Riuers side,
Receiued those two faire Brides, their Loues delight,
Which at th'appointed tyde,
Each one did make his Bryde,
Against their Brydale day, which is not long :
  Sweete *Themmes* runne softly, till I end my Song.

      Bauldricke] belt, girdle.

EPITHALAMION

YE learned sisters which haue oftentimes
Beene to me ayding, others to adorne :
Whom ye thought worthy of your gracefull rymes,
That euen the greatest did not greatly scorne
To heare theyr names sung in your simple layes,
But ioyed in theyr prayse.
And when ye list your owne mishaps to mourne,
Which death, or loue, or fortunes wreck did rayse,
Your string could soone to sadder tenor turne,
And teach the woods and waters to lament
Your dolefull dreriment.
Now lay those sorrowfull complaints aside,
And hauing all your heads with girland crownd,
Helpe me mine owne loues prayses to resound,
Ne let the same of any be enuide :
So Orpheus did for his owne bride,
So I vnto my selfe alone will sing,
The woods shall to me answer and my Eccho ring.

EARLY before the worlds light giuing lampe,
His golden beame vpon the hils doth spred,
Hauing disperst the nights vnchearefull dampe,
Doe ye awake, and with fresh lusty hed,
Go to the bowre of my beloued loue,
My truest turtle doue,
Bid her awake ; for Hymen is awake,
And long since ready forth his maske to moue,
With his bright Tead that flames with many a flake,
And many a bachelor to waite on him,
In theyr fresh garments trim.

dreriment] dreariness, grief, sorrow. lusty hed] lustiness,
energy, vigour.   Tead] torch.

Bid her awake therefore and soone her dight,
For lo the wished day is come at last,
That shall for al the paynes and sorrowes past,
Pay to her vsury of long delight:
And whylest she doth her dight,
Doe ye to her of ioy and solace sing,
That all the woods may answer and your eccho ring.

BRING with you all the Nymphes that you can
      heare
Both of the riuers and the forrests greene :
And of the sea that neighbours to her neare,
Al with gay girlands goodly wel beseene.
And let them also with them bring in hand,
Another gay girland
For my fayre loue of lillyes and of roses,
Bound trueloue wize with a blew silke riband.
And let them make great store of bridale poses,
And let them eeke bring store of other flowers
To deck the bridale bowers.
And let the ground whereas her foot shall tread,
For feare the stones her tender foot should wrong
Be strewed with fragrant flowers all along,
And diapred lyke the discolored mead.
Which done, doe at her chamber dore awayt,
For she will waken strayt,
The whiles doe ye this song vnto her sing,
The woods shall to you answer and your Eccho ring.

YE Nymphes of Mulla which with carefull heed,
The siluer scaly trouts doe tend full well,
And greedy pikes which vse therein to feed,
(Those trouts and pikes all others doo excell)

    dight] to deck, adorn.   diapred] variegated (with
flowers).   discolored] variously coloured.

And ye likewise which keepe the rushy lake,
Where none doo fishes take,
Bynd vp the locks the which hang scatterd light,
And in his waters which your mirror make,
Behold your faces as the christall bright,
That when you come whereas my loue doth lie,
No blemish she may spie.
And eke ye lightfoot mayds which keepe the deere,
That on the hoary mountayne vse to towre,
And the wylde wolues which seeke them to deuoure,
With your steele darts doo chace from comming neer
Be also present heere,
To helpe to decke her and to help to sing,
That all the woods may answer and your eccho ring.

WAKE, now my loue, awake; for it is time,
The Rosy Morne long since left Tithones bed,
All ready to her siluer coche to clyme,
And Phœbus gins to shew his glorious hed.
Hark how the cheerefull birds do chaunt theyr laies
And carroll of loues praise.
The merry Larke hir mattins sings aloft,
The thrush replyes, the Mauis descant playes,
The Ouzell shrills, the Ruddock warbles soft,
So goodly all agree with sweet consent,
To this dayes merriment.
Ah my deere loue why doe ye sleepe thus long,
When meeter were that ye should now awake,
T'awayt the comming of your ioyous make,
And hearken to the birds louelearned song,
The deawy leaues among.
For they of ioy and pleasance to you sing,
That all the woods them answer and theyr eccho
    ring.

make] companion, mate.

My loue is now awake out of her dreame,
And her fayre eyes like stars that dimmed were
With darksome cloud, now shew theyr goodly
      beams
More bright then Hesperus his head doth rere.
Come now ye damzels, daughters of delight,
Helpe quickly her to dight,
But first come ye fayre houres which were begot
In Ioues sweet paradice, of Day and Night,
Which doe the seasons of the yeare allot,
And al that euer in this world is fayre
Doe make and still repayre.
And ye three handmayds of the Cyprian Queene,
The which doe still adorne her beauties pride,
Helpe to addorne my beautifullest bride :
And as ye her array, still throw betweene
Some graces to be seene,
And as ye vse to Venus, to her sing,
The whiles the woods shal answer and your eccho
      ring.

Now is my loue all ready forth to come,
Let all the virgins therefore well awayt,
And ye fresh boyes that tend vpon her groome
Prepare your selues ; for he is comming strayt.
Set all your things in seemely good aray
Fit for so ioyfull day,
The ioyfulst day that euer sunne did see.
Faire Sun, shew forth thy fauourable ray,
And let thy lifull heat not feruent be
For feare of burning her sunshyny face,
Her beauty to disgrace.
O fayrest Phœbus, father of the Muse,

lifull] giving or bestowing life.

If euer I did honour thee aright,
Or sing the thing, that mote thy mind delight,
Doe not thy seruants simple boone refuse,
But let this day, let this one day, be myne,
Let all the rest be thine.
Then I thy souerayne prayses loud wil sing,
That all the woods shal answer and theyr eccho ring.

HARKE how the Minstrels gin to shrill aloud
Their merry Musick that resounds from far,
The pipe, the tabor, and the trembling Croud,
That well agree withouten breach or iar.
But most of all the Damzels doe delite,
When they their tymbrels smyte,
And thereunto doe daunce and carrol sweet,
That all the sences they doe rauish quite,
The whyles the boyes run vp and downe the street,
Crying aloud with strong confused noyce,
As if it were one voyce.
Hymen io Hymen, Hymen they do shout,
That euen to the heauens theyr shouting shrill
Doth reach, and all the firmament doth fill,
To which the people standing all about,
As in approuance doe thereto applaud
And loud aduaunce her laud,
And euermore they Hymen Hymen sing,
That al the woods them answer and theyr eccho ring.

LOE where she comes along with portly pace
Lyke Phœbe from her chamber of the East,
Arysing forth to run her mighty race,
Clad all in white, that seemes a virgin best.
So well it her beseemes that ye would weene
Some angell she had beene.

Croud] fiddle or viol.

Her long loose yellow locks lyke golden wyre,
Sprinckled with perle, and perling flowres a tweene,
Doe lyke a golden mantle her attyre,
And being crowned with a girland greene,
Seeme lyke some mayden Queene.
Her modest eyes abashed to behold
So many gazers, as on her do stare,
Vpon the lowly ground affixed are.
Ne dare lift vp her countenance too bold,
But blush to heare her prayses sung so loud,
So farre from being proud.
Nathlesse doe ye still loud her prayses sing.
That all the woods may answer and your eccho
   ring.

TELL me ye merchants daughters did ye see
So fayre a creature in your towne before,
So sweet, so louely, and so mild as she,
Adornd with beautyes grace and vertues store,
Her goodly eyes lyke Saphyres shining bright,
Her forehead yuory white,
Her cheekes lyke apples which the sun hath rudded,
Her lips lyke cherryes charming men to byte,
Her brest like to a bowle of creame vncrudded,
Her paps lyke lyllies budded,
Her snowie necke lyke to a marble towre,
And all her body like a pallace fayre,
Ascending vppe with many a stately stayre,
To honors seat and chastities sweet bowre.
Why stand ye still ye virgins in amaze,
Vpon her so to gaze,
Whiles ye forget your former lay to sing,
To which the woods did answer and your eccho ring.

vncrudded] uncurdled.

But if ye saw that which no eyes can see,
The inward beauty of her liuely spright,
Garnisht with heauenly guifts of high degree,
Much more then would ye wonder at that sight,
And stand astonisht lyke to those which red
Medusaes mazeful hed.
There dwels sweet loue and constant chastity,
Vnspotted fayth and comely womanhood,
Regard of honour and mild modesty,
There vertue raynes as Queene in royal throne,
And giueth lawes alone.
The which the base affections doe obay,
And yeeld theyr seruices vnto her will,
Ne thought of thing vncomely euer may
Thereto approch to tempt her mind to ill.
Had ye once seene these her celestial threasures,
And vnreuealed pleasures,
Then would ye wonder and her prayses sing,
That al the woods should answer and your eccho
 ring.

Open the temple gates vnto my loue,
Open them wide that she may enter in,
And all the postes adorne as doth behoue,
And all the pillours deck with girlands trim,
For to recyue this Saynt with honour dew,
That commeth in to you.
With trembling steps and humble reuerence,
She commeth in, before th'almighties vew,
Of her ye virgins learne obedience,
When so ye come into those holy places,
To humble your proud faces :
Bring her vp to th'high altar, that she may

threasures] treasures.

The sacred ceremonies there partake,
The which do endlesse matrimony make,
And let the roring Organs loudly play
The praises of the Lord in liuely notes,
The whiles with hollow throates
The Choristers the ioyous Antheme sing,
That al the woods may answere and their eccho
    ring.

BEHOLD whiles she before the altar stands
Hearing the holy priest that to her speakes
And blesseth her with his two happy hands,
How the red roses flush vp in her cheekes,
And the pure snow with goodly vermill stayne,
Like crimsin dyde in grayne,
That euen th'Angels which continually,
About the sacred Altare doe remaine,
Forget their seruice and about her fly,
Ofte peeping in her face that seemes more fayre,
The more they on it stare.
But her sad eyes still fastened on the ground,
Are gouerned with goodly modesty,
That suffers not one looke to glaunce awry,
Which may let in a little thought vnsownd.
Why blush ye loue to giue to me your hand,
The pledge of all our band?
Sing ye sweet Angels, Alleluya sing,
That all the woods may answere and your eccho
    ring.

Now al is done; bring home the bride againe,
Bring home the triumph of our victory,
Bring home with you the glory of her gaine,
With ioyance bring her and with iollity.
Neuer had man more ioyfull day then this,

Whom heauen would heape with blis.
Make feast therefore now all this liue long day,
This day for euer to me holy is,
Poure out the wine without restraint or stay,
Poure not by cups, but by the belly full,
Poure out to all that wull,
And sprinkle all the postes and wals with wine,
That they may sweat, and drunken be withall.
Crowne ye God Bacchus with a coronall,
And Hymen also crowne with wreathes of vine,
And let the Graces daunce vnto the rest;
For they can doo it best:
The whiles the maydens doe theyr carroll sing,
To which the woods shal answer and theyr eccho
 ring.

Ring ye the bels, ye yong men of the towne,
And leaue your wonted labors for this day:
This day is holy; doe ye write it downe,
That ye for euer it remember may.
This day the sunne is in his chiefest hight,
With Barnaby the bright,
From whence declining daily by degrees,
He somewhat loseth of his heat and light,
When once the Crab behind his back he sees.
But for this time it ill ordained was,
To chose the longest day in all the yeare,
And shortest night, when longest fitter weare:
Yet neuer day so long, but late would passe.
Ring ye the bels, to make it weare away,
And bonefiers make all day,
And daunce about them, and about them sing:
that all the woods may answer, and your eccho ring.

wull] will.   bonefiers] bonfires.

Ah when will this long weary day haue end,
And lende me leaue to come vnto my loue ?
How slowly do the houres theyr numbers spend ?
How slowly does sad Time his feathers moue ?
Hast thee O fayrest Planet to thy home
Within the Westerne fome :
Thy tyred steedes long since haue need of rest.
Long though it be, at last I see it gloome,
And the bright euening star with golden creast
Appeare out of the East.
Fayre childe of beauty, glorious lampe of loue
That all the host of heauen in rankes doost lead,
And guydest louers through the nightes dread,
How chearefully thou lookest from aboue,
And seemst to laugh atweene thy twinkling light
As ioying in the sight
Of these glad many which for ioy doe sing,
That all the woods them answer and their echo ring.

Now ceasse ye damsels your delights forepast ;
Enough is it, that all the day was youres :
Now day is doen, and night is nighing fast :
Now bring the Bryde into the brydall boures.
Now night is come, now soone her disaray,
And in her bed her lay ;
Lay her in lillies and in violets,
And silken courteins ouer her display,
And odourd sheetes, and Arras couerlets.
Behold how goodly my faire loue does ly
In proud humility ;
Like vnto Maia, when as Ioue her tooke,
In Tempe, lying on the flowry gras,
Twixt sleepe and wake, after she weary was,

gloome] to gloom, become dusk.

With bathing in the Acidalian brooke.
Now it is night, ye damsels may be gon,
And leaue my loue alone,
And leaue likewise your former lay to sing :
The woods no more shal answere, nor your echo
    ring.

Now welcome night, thou night so long expected,
That long daies labour doest at last defray,
And all my cares, which cruell loue collected,
Hast sumd in one, and cancelled for aye :
Spread thy broad wing ouer my loue and me,
That no man may vs see,
And in thy sable mantle vs enwrap,
From feare of perrill and foule horror free.
Let no false treason seeke vs to entrap,
Nor any dread disquiet once annoy
The safety of our ioy :
But let the night be calme and quietsome,
Without tempestuous storms or sad afray :
Lyke as when Ioue with fayre Alcmena lay,
When he begot the great Tirynthian groome :
Or lyke as when he with thy selfe did lie,
And begot Maiesty.
And let the mayds and yongmen cease to sing :
Ne let the woods them answer, nor theyr eccho ring.

Let no lamenting cryes, nor dolefull teares,
Be heard all night within nor yet without :
Ne let false whispers, breeding hidden feares,
Breake gentle sleepe with misconceiued dout.
Let no deluding dreames, nor dreadful sights
Make sudden sad affrights ;
Ne let housefyres, nor lightnings helpelesse harmes,

Ne let the Pouke, nor other euill sprights,
Ne let mischiuous witches with theyr charmes,
Ne let hob Goblins, names whose sence we see not,
Fray vs with things that be not.
Let not the shriech Oule, nor the Storke be heard:
Nor the night Rauen that still deadly yels,
Nor damned ghosts cald vp with mighty spels,
Nor griesly vultures make vs once affeard:
Ne let th'unpleasant Quyre of Frogs still croking
Make vs to wish theyr choking.
Let none of these theyr drery accents sing;
Ne let the woods them answer, nor theyr eccho ring.

But let stil Silence trew night watches keepe,
That sacred peace may in assurance rayne,
And tymely sleep, when it is tyme to sleepe,
May poure his limbs forth on your pleasant playne,
The whiles an hundred little winged loues,
Like diuers fethered doues,
Shall fly and flutter round about your bed,
And in the secret darke, that none reproues,
Their prety stealthes shal worke, and snares shal
     spread
To filch away sweet snatches of delight,
Conceal'd through couert night.
Ye sonnes of Venus, play your sports at will,
For greedy pleasure, carelesse of your toyes,
Thinks more vpon her paradise of ioyes,
Then what ye do, albe it good or ill.
All night therefore attend your merry play,
For it will soone be day:
Now none doth hinder you, that say or sing,
Ne will the woods now answer, nor your Eccho ring.

Pouke] Puck.

Who is the same, which at my window peepes ?
Or whose is that faire face, that shines so bright,
Is it not Cinthia, she that neuer sleepes,
But walkes about high heauen al the night ?
O fayrest goddesse, do thou not enuy
My loue with me to spy :
For thou likewise didst loue, though now vnthought,
And for a fleece of woll, which priuily,
The Latmian shephard once vnto thee brought,
His pleasures with thee wrought.
Therefore to vs be fauorable now ;
And sith of wemens labours thou hast charge,
And generation goodly dost enlarge,
Encline thy will t'effect our wishfull vow,
And the chast wombe informe with timely seed,
That may our comfort breed :
Till which we cease our hopefull hap to sing,
Ne let the woods vs answere, nor our Eccho ring.

And thou great Iuno, which with awful might
The lawes of wedlock still dost patronize,
And the religion of the faith first plight
With sacred rites hast taught to solemnize :
And eeke for comfort often called art
Of women in their smart,
Eternally bind thou this louely band,
And all thy blessings vnto vs impart.
And thou glad Genius, in whose gentle hand,
The bridale bowre and geniall bed remaine,
Without blemish or staine,
And the sweet pleasures of theyr loues delight
With secret ayde doest succour and supply,
Till they bring forth the fruitfull progeny,

sith] since.

Send vs the timely fruit of this same night.
And thou fayre Hebe, and thou Hymen free,
Grant that it may so be.
Til which we cease your further prayse to sing,
Ne any woods shal answer, nor your Eccho ring.

AND ye high heauens, the temple of the gods,
In which a thousand torches flaming bright
Doe burne, that to vs wretched earthly clods,
In dreadful darknesse lend desired light;
And all ye powers which in the same remayne,
More then we men can fayne,
Poure out your blessing on vs plentiously,
And happy influence vpon vs raine,
That we may raise a large posterity,
Which from the earth, which they may long
    possesse,
With lasting happinesse,
Vp to your haughty pallaces may mount,
And for the guerdon of theyr glorious merit
May heauenly tabernacles there inherit,
Of blessed Saints for to increase the count.
So let vs rest, sweet loue, in hope of this,
And cease till then our tymely ioyes to sing,
The woods no more vs answer, nor our eccho ring.

SONG made in lieu of many ornaments,
With which my loue should duly haue bene dect,
Which cutting off through hasty accidents,
Ye would not stay your dew time to expect,
But promist both to recompens,
Be vnto her a goodly ornament,
And for short time an endlesse moniment.

SONNETS FROM *AMORETTI*

(1)

IN that proud port, which her so goodly graceth,
　whiles her faire face she reares vp to the skie :
　and to the ground her eie lids low embaseth,
　most goodly temperature ye may descry,
Myld humblesse mixt with awfull maiesty.
　For looking on the earth whence she was borne,
　her minde remembreth her mortalitie,
　what so is fayrest shall to earth returne.
But that same lofty countenance seemes to scorne
　base thing, and thinke how she to heauen may
　　clime :
　treading downe earth as lothsome and forlorne,
　that hinders heauenly thoughts with drossy
　　slime.
Yet lowly still vouchsafe to looke on me,
　such lowlinesse shall make you lofty be.

(2)

WHAT guyle is this, that those her golden tresses,
　She doth attyre vnder a net of gold :
　and with sly skill so cunningly them dresses,
　that which is gold or heare, may scarse be told ?
Is it that mens frayle eyes, which gaze too bold,
　she may entangle in that golden snare :
　and being caught may craftily enfold,
　theyr weaker harts, which are not wel aware ?
Take heed therefore, myne eyes, how ye doe stare
　henceforth too rashly on that guilefull net,
　in which if euer ye entrapped are,
　out of her bands ye by no meanes shall get.
Fondnesse it were for any being free,
　to couet fetters, though they golden bee.

(3)

THE merry Cuckow, messenger of Spring,
  His trompet shrill hath thrise already sounded:
  that warnes al louers wayt vpon their king,
  who now is comming forth with girland crouned.
With noyse whereof the quyre of Byrds resounded
  their anthemes sweet devized of loues prayse,
  that all the woods theyr ecchoes back rebounded,
  as if they knew the meaning of their layes.
But mongst them all, which did Loues honor rayse
  no word was heard of her that most it ought,
  but she his precept proudly disobayes,
  and doth his ydle message set at nought.
Therefore O loue, vnlesse she turne to thee
  ere Cuckow end, let her a rebell be.

(4)

EASTER MORNING

MOST glorious Lord of lyfe, that on this day,
  Didst make thy triumph ouer death and sin:
  and hauing harrowd hell, didst bring away
  captiuity thence captiue vs to win:
This ioyous day, deare Lord, with ioy begin,
  and grant that we for whom thou diddest dye
  being with thy deare blood clene washt from sin,
  may liue for euer in felicity.
And that thy loue we weighing worthily,
  may likewise loue thee for the same againe:
  and for thy sake that all lyke deare didst buy,
  with loue may one another entertayne.
So let vs loue, deare loue, lyke as we ought,
  loue is the lesson which the Lord vs taught.

THE BUTTERFLY

(From *Muiopotmos*)

THERE he arriuing, round about doth flie,
From bed to bed, from one to other border,
And takes suruey with curious busie eye,
Of euerie flowre and herbe there set in order ;
Now this, now that he tasteth tenderly,
Yet none of them he rudely doth-disorder,
Ne with his feete their silken leaues deface ;
But pastures on the pleasures of each place.

And euermore with most varietie,
And change of sweetnesse (for all change is sweete)
He casts his glutton sense to satisfie,
Now sucking of the sap of herbe most meete,
Or of the deaw, which yet on them does lie,
Now in the same bathing his tender feete :
And then he pearcheth on some braunch thereby,
To weather him, and his moyst wings to dry.

THE DEATH OF ASTROPHEL

SHEPHEARDS that wont on pipes of oaten reed,
Oft times to plaine your loues concealed smart :
And with your piteous layes haue learnd to breed
Compassion in a countrey lasses hart.
Hearken ye gentle shepheards to my song,
And place my dolefull plaint your plaints emong.

To you alone I sing this mournfull verse,
The mournfulst verse that euer man heard tell :
To you whose softened hearts it may empierse,
With dolours dart for death of *Astrophel*.
To you I sing and to none other wight,
For well I wot my rymes bene rudely dight.

bene rudely dight] are composed in homely manner.

Yet as they been, if any nycer wit
Shall hap to heare, or couet them to read:
Thinke he, that such are for such ones most fit,
Made not to please the liuing but the dead.
And if in him found pity euer place,
Let him be moov'd to pity such a case.

AN HYMN OF HEAVENLY LOVE

Loue, lift me vp vpon thy golden wings,
From this base world vnto thy heauens hight,
Where I may see those admirable things,
Which there thou workest by thy soueraine might,
Farre aboue feeble reach of earthly sight,
That I thereof an heauenly Hymne may sing
Vnto the god of Loue, high heauens king.

Many lewd layes (ah woe is me the more)
In praise of that mad fit, which fooles call loue,
I haue in th'heat of youth made heretofore,
That in light wits did loose affection moue.
But all those follies now I do reproue,
And turned haue the tenor of my string,
The heauenly prayses of true loue to sing.

And ye that wont with greedy vaine desire
To reade my fault, and wondring at my flame,
To warme your selues at my wide sparckling fire,
Sith now that heat is quenched, quench my blame,
And in her ashes shrowd my dying shame:
For who my passed follies now pursewes,
Beginnes his owne, and my old fault renewes.

BEFORE this worlds great frame, in which al things
Are now contain'd, found any being place
Ere flitting Time could wag his eyas wings
About that mightie bound, which doth embrace
The rolling Spheres, and parts their houres by
    space
That high eternall powre, which now doth moue
In all these things, mou'd in it selfe by loue.

It lou'd it selfe, because it selfe was faire ;
(For faire is lou'd ;) and of it selfe begot
Like to it selfe his eldest sonne and heire,
Eternall, pure,. and voide of sinfull blot,
The firstling of his ioy, in whom no iot
Of loues dislike, or pride was to be found,
Whom he therefore with equall honour crownd.

With him he raignd, before all time prescribed,
In endlesse glorie and immortall might,
Together with that third from them deriued,
Most wise, most holy, most almightie Spright,
Whose kingdomes throne no thought of earthly
    wight
Can comprehend, much lesse my trembling verse
With equall words can hope it to reherse.

Yet O most blessed Spirit, pure lampe of light,
Eternall spring of grace and wisedome trew,
Vouchsafe to shed into my barren spright,
Some little drop of thy celestiall dew,
That may my rymes with sweet infuse embrew,
And giue me words equall vnto my thought,
To tell the marueiles by thy mercie wrought.

eyas] new-fledged.   Spright] Spirit.   infuse embrew]
colour with infusion.

Yet being pregnant still with powrefull grace,
And full of fruitfull loue, that loues to get
Things like himselfe, and to enlarge his race,
His second brood though not in powre so great,
Yet full of beautie, next he did beget
An infinite increase of Angels bright,
All glistring glorious in their Makers light.

To them the heauens illimitable hight,
Not this round heauen, which we from hence behold,
Adornd with thousand lamps of burning light,
And with ten thousand gemmes of shyning gold,
He gaue as their inheritance to hold,
That they might serue him in eternall blis,
And be partakers of those ioyes of his.

There they in their trinall triplicities
About him wait, and on his will depend,
Either with nimble wings to cut the skies,
When he them on his messages doth send,
Or on his owne dread presence to attend,
Where they behold the glorie of his light,
And caroll Hymnes of loue both day and night.

Both day and night is vnto them all one,
For he his beames doth still to them extend,
That darknesse there appeareth neuer none,
Ne hath their day, ne hath their blisse an end,
But there their termelesse time in pleasure spend,
Ne euer should their happinesse decay,
Had not they dar'd their Lord to disobay.

But pride impatient of long resting peace;
Did puffe them vp with greedy bold ambition,
That they gan cast their state how to increase

trinall] threefold.   triplicities] trinities, triads.

Aboue the fortune of their first condition,
And sit in Gods owne seat without commission :
The brightest Angell, euen the Child of light,
Drew millions more against their God to fight.

Th'Almighty seeing their so bold assay,
Kindled the flame of his consuming yre,
And with his onely breath them blew away
From heauens hight, to which they did aspyre,
To deepest hell, and lake of damned fyre ;
Where they in darknesse and dread horror dwel
Hating the happie light from which they fell.

So that next off-spring of the Makers loue,
Next to himselfe in glorious degree,
Degendering to hate, fell from aboue
Through pride ; (for pride and loue may ill agree
And now of sinne to all ensample bee :
How then can sinfull flesh it selfe assure,
Sith purest Angels fell to be impure ?

But that eternall fount of loue and grace,
Still flowing forth his goodnesse vnto all,
Now seeing left a waste and emptie place
In his wyde Pallace, through those Angels fall,
Cast to supply the same, and to enstall
A new vnknowen Colony therein,
Whose root from earths base groundworke shol
  begin.

Therefore of clay, base, vile, and next to nought
Yet form'd by wondrous skill, and by his might
According to an heauenly patterne wrought,

Degendering] degenerating.

Which he had fashiond in his wise foresight,
He man did make, and breathd a liuing spright
Into his face most beautifull and fayre,
Endewd with wisedomes riches, heauenly, rare.

Such he him made, that he resemble might
Himselfe, as mortall thing immortall could ;
Him to be Lord of euery liuing wight,
He made by loue out of his owne like mould,
In whom he might his mightie selfe behould :
For loue doth loue the thing belou'd to see,
That like it selfe in louely shape may bee.

But man forgetfull of his makers grace,
No lesse than Angels, whom he did ensew,
Fell from the hope of promist heauenly place,
Into the mouth of death, to sinners dew,
And all his off-spring into thraldome threw :
Where they for euer should in bonds remaine,
Of neuer dead, yet euer dying paine.

Till that great Lord of Loue, which him at first
Made of meere loue, and after liked well,
Seeing him lie like creature long accurst,
In that deepe horror of despeyred hell,
Him wretch in doole would let no lenger dwell,
But cast out of that bondage to redeeme,
And pay the price, all were his debt extreme.

Out of the bosome of eternall blisse,
In which he reigned with his glorious syre,
He downe descended, like a most demisse

ensew] follow after.   doole] sorrow.   cast] con-
sidered how.   all were] although it were.   demisse]
submissive.

And abiect thrall, in fleshes fraile attyre,
That he for him might pay sinnes deadly hyre,
And him restore vnto that happie state,
In which he stood before his haplesse fate.

In flesh at first the guilt committed was,
Therefore in flesh it must be satisfyde :
Nor spirit, nor Angell, though they man surpas,
Could make amends to God for mans misguyde,
But onely man himselfe, who selfe did slyde.
So taking flesh of sacred virgins wombe,
For mans deare sake he did a man become.

And that most blessed bodie, which was borne
Without all blemish or reprochfull blame,
He freely gaue to be both rent and torne
Of cruell hands, who with despightfull shame
Reuyling him, that them most vile became,
At length him nayled on a gallow tree,
And slew the iust, by most vniust decree.

O huge and most vnspeakeable impression
Of loues deepe wound, that pierst the piteous hart
Of that deare Lord with so entyre affection,
And sharply launching euery inner part,
Dolours of death into his soule did dart ;
Doing him die, that neuer it deserued,
To free his foes, that from his heast had swerued.

What hart can feele least touch of so sore launch,
Or thought can think the depth of so deare wound ?
Whose bleeding sourse their streames yet neuer
    staunch,

misguyde] sin.   became] suited.   launching] lancing,
piercing.   heast] command.

But stil do flow, and freshly still redound,
To heale the sores of sinfull soules vnsound,
And clense the guilt of that infected cryme,
Which was enrooted in all fleshly slyme.

O blessed well of loue, O floure of grace,
O glorious Morning starre, O lampe of light,
Most liuely image of thy fathers face,
Eternall King of glorie, Lord of might,
Meeke lambe of God before all worlds behight,
How can we thee requite for all this good?
Or what can prize that thy most precious blood?

Yet nought thou ask'st in lieu of all this loue,
But loue of vs for guerdon of thy paine.
Ay me; what can vs lesse then that behoue?
Had he required life of vs againe,
Had it beene wrong to aske his owne with gaine?
He gaue vs life, he it restored lost;
Then life were least, that vs so litle cost.

But he our life hath left vnto vs free,
Free that was thrall, and blessed that was band;
Ne ought demaunds, but that we louing bee,
As he himselfe hath lou'd vs afore hand,
And bound therto with an eternall band,
Him first to loue, that vs so dearely bought,
And next, our brethren to his image wrought.

Him first to loue, great right and reason is,
Who first to vs our life and being gaue;
And after when we fared had amisse,
Vs wretches from the second death did saue;

redound] flow freely.   behight] ordained.   prize}
equal in value.   behoue] profit.

And last the food of life, which now we haue,
Euen himselfe in his deare sacrament,
To feede our hungry soules vnto vs lent.

Then next to loue our brethren, that were made
Of that selfe mould, and that selfe makers hand,
That we, and to the same againe shall fade,
Where they shall haue like heritage of land,
How euer here on higher steps we stand ;
Which also were with selfe same price redeemed
That we, how euer of vs light esteemed.

And were they not, yet since that louing Lord
Commaunded vs to loue them for his sake,
Euen for his sake, and for his sacred word,
Which in his last bequest he to vs spake,
We should them loue, and with their needs partake ;
Knowing that whatsoere to them we giue,
We giue to him, by whom we all doe liue.

Such mercy he by his most holy reede
Vnto vs taught, and to approue it trew,
Ensampled it by his most righteous deede,
Shewing vs mercie, miserable crew,
That we the like should to the wretches shew,
And loue our brethren ; thereby to approue,
How much himselfe that loued vs, we loue.

Then rouze thy selfe, O earth, out of thy soyle,
In which thou wallowest like to filthy swyne
And doest thy mynd in durty pleasures moyle,
Vnmindfull of that dearest Lord of thyne ;
Lift vp to him thy heauie clouded eyne,
That thou his soueraine bountie mayst behold,
And read through loue his mercies manifold.

   That we [were].   land] the grave.   reede] counsel.
moyle] defile.

Beginne from first, where he encradled was
In simple cratch, wrapt in a wad of hay,
Betweene the toylefull Oxe and humble Asse,
And in what rags, and in how base aray,
The glory of our heauenly riches lay,
When him the silly Shepheards came to see,
Whom greatest Princes sought on lowest knee.

From thence reade on the storie of his life,
His humble carriage, his vnfaulty wayes,
His cancred foes, his fights, his toyle, his strife,
His paines, his pouertie, his sharpe assayes,
Through which he past his miserable dayes,
Offending none, and doing good to all,
Yet being malist both of great and small.

And looke at last how of most wretched wights,
He taken was, betrayd, and false accused,
How with most scornefull taunts, and fell despights
He was reuyld, disgrast, and foule abused,
How scourgd, how crownd, how buffeted, how
    brused;
And lastly how twixt robbers crucifyde,
With bitter wounds through hands, through feet
    and syde.

Then let thy flinty hart that feeles no paine,
Empierced be with pittifull remorse,
And let thy bowels bleede in euery vaine,
At sight of his most sacred heauenly corse,
So torne and mangled with malicious forse,
And let thy soule, whose sins his sorrows wrought,
Melt into teares, and grone in grieued thought.

    cratch] manger.   silly] simple.   cancred] venemous,
corrupt, malignant.   malist] evilly regarded.

With sence whereof whilest so thy softened
    spirit
Is inly toucht, and humbled with meeke zeale,
Through meditation of his endlesse merit,
Lift vp thy mind to th'author of thy weale,
And to his soueraine mercie doe appeale ;
Learne him to loue, that loued thee so deare,
And in thy brest his blessed image beare.

With all thy hart, with all thy soule and mind,
Thou must him loue, and his beheasts embrace ;
All other loues, with which the world doth
    blind
Weake fancies, and stirre vp affections base,
Thou must renounce, and vtterly displace,
And giue thy selfe vnto him full and free,
That full and freely gaue himselfe to thee.

Then shalt thou feele thy spirit so possest,
And rauisht with deuouring great desire
Of his deare selfe, that shall thy feeble brest
Inflame with loue, and set thee all on fire
With burning zeale, through euery part entire,
That in no earthly thing thou shalt delight,
But in his sweet and amiable sight.

Thenceforth all worlds desire will in thee dye,
And all earthes glorie on which men do gaze,
Seeme durt and drosse in thy pure sighted eye,
Compar'd to that celestiall beauties blaze,
Whose glorious beames all fleshly sense doth
    daze
With admiration of their passing light,
Blinding the eyes and lumining the spright.

Then shall thy rauisht soule inspired bee
With heauenly thoughts, farre aboue humane skil,
And thy bright radiant eyes shall plainely see
Th'Idee of his pure glorie, present still
Before thy face, that all thy spirits shall fill
With sweete enragement of celestiall loue,
Kindled through sight of those faire things aboue.

JOHN LYLY

1553–1606

TO WELCOME IN THE SPRING

What Bird so sings yet so dos wayle ?
O 'ts the rauishd Nightingale.
Iug, Iug, Iug, Iug, tereu, shee cryes,
And still her woes at Midnight rise.
Braue prick song ! who is't now we heare ?
None but the Larke so shrill and cleare ;
How at heauen's gates she claps her wings,
The Morne not waking till shee sings.
Heark, heark, with what a pretty throat
Poore Robin red-breast tunes his note ;
Heark how the iolly Cuckoes sing
Cuckoe, to welcome in the spring,
Cuckoe, to welcome in the spring.

PAN'S SONG

Pan's Syrinx was a girle indeed,
Though now shee's turn'd into a reed,
From that deare Reed Pan's pipe does come,
A Pipe that strikes Apollo dumbe ;

enragement] rapture.
wayle] wail.   prick song] song of which notes are
written down, not extempore.

Nor Flute, nor Lute, nor Gitterne can
So chant it, as the pipe of Pan ;
Cross-gartrd swains, and Dairie girls,
With faces smug and round as Pearles,
When Pan's shrill pipe begins to play,
With dancing weare out night and day :
The bag-pipes drone his Hum laes by,
When Pan sounds vp his minstrelsie.
His minstrelsie ! O Base ! This Quill
Which at my mouth with winde I fill,
Puts me in minde, though Her I misse,
That still my Syrinx lips I kisse.

CUPID AND CAMPASPE

Cvpid and my Campaspe playd
At Cardes for kisses, Cupid payd ;
He stakes his Quiuer, Bow, and arrows,
His Mothers doues, and teeme of sparrows ;
Looses them too ; then, downe he throwes
The corrall of his lippe, the rose
Growing on 's cheek (but none knows how),
With these, the cristall of his Brow,
And then the dimple of his chinne :
All these did my Campaspe winne.
At last, hee set her both his eyes ;
Shee won, and Cupid blind did rise.
    O Loue ! has shee done this to Thee ?
    What shall (Alas !) become of mee ?

      cristall] crystal, fairness.

ANTHONY MUNDAY (SHEPHERD TONY)

1553–1633

BEAUTY BATHING

England's Helicon

BEAUTIE sate bathing by a Spring,
    where fairest shades did hide her.
The windes blew calme, the birds did sing,
    the coole streames ranne beside her.
My wanton thoughts entic'd mine eye,
    to see what was forbidden :
But better Memory said, fie,
    so, vaine Desire was chidden.
      Hey nonnie, nonnie O
      Hey nonnie, nonnie.

Into a slumber then I fell,
    when fond imagination
Seemed to see, but could not tell
    her feature or her fashion.
But euen as Babes in dreames doe smile,
    and sometime fall a weeping :
So I awakt, as wise this while,
    as when I fell a sleeping.
      Hey nonnie, nonnie, &c.

THE WOOD-MAN'S WALK

THROUGH a faire Forrest as I went
    vpon a Summers day,
I met a Wood-man quaint and gent ;
    yet in a strange aray.

fashion] shape.   this while] this time.
gent] refined, neat.

I maruail'd much at his disguise,
    whom I did know so well :
But thus in tearmes both graue and wise,
    his minde he gan to tell.
Friend, muse not at this fond aray,
    but list a while to me :
For it hath holpe me to suruay
    what I shall shew to thee.
Long liu'd I in this Forrest faire,
    till wearie of my weale,
Abroad in walkes I would repaire,
    as now I will reueale.
My first dayes walke was to the Court,
    where beautie fed mine eyes ;
Yet found I that the Courtly sport,
    did maske in slie disguise.
For falsehood sate in fairest lookes,
    and friend to friend was coy :
Court fauour fill'd but emptie bookes,
    and there I found no ioy.
Desert went naked in the colde,
    when crouching craft was fed :
Sweet words were cheaply bought and solde,
    but none that stood in sted.
Wit was imployed for each mans owne,
    plaine meaning came too short :
All these deuises seene and knowne,
    made me forsake the Court.
Vnto the Cittie next I went,
    in hope of better hap :
Where liberally I lanch'd and spent,
    as set on Fortunes lap.

maruail'd] marvelled.   fond] foolish.   hap] lot,
fortune, fate.

The little stock I had in store,
    Me thought would nere be done :
Friends flockt about me more and more,
    as quickely lost as wone.
For when I spent, then they were kinde,
    but when my purse did faile,
The foremost man came last behinde,
    thus loue with wealth doth quaile.
Once more for footing yet I stroue,
    although the world did frowne :
But they before that held me vp,
    together troad me downe.
And least once more I should arise,
    they sought my quite decay :
Then got I into this disguise,
    and thence I stole away.
And in my minde (me thought) I said,
    Lord blesse mee from the Cittie :
Where simplenes is thus betraide,
    and no remorce or pittie.
Yet would I not giue ouer so,
    but once more trie my fate :
And to the Country than I goe,
    to liue in quiet state.
There did appeare no subtile showes,
    but yea and nay went smoothly :
But Lord how Country-folkes can glose,
    when they speake most vntruely ?
More craft was in a buttond cap,
    and in old wiues saile :

---

quaile] fade, wither.   least] lest.   blesse] defend.
glose] flatter, lie.   buttond cap] button cap (country
fashion).   saile] coarse cloth.

Then in my life it was my hap,
 to see on Downe, or Dale.
There was no open forgerie,
 but vnder-handed-gleaning :
Which they call Countrie pollicie,
 but hath a worser meaning,
Some good bold-face beares out the wrong,
 because he gaines thereby :
The poore mans backe is crakt ere long,
 yet there he lets him lie.
And no degree among them all,
 but had such close intending,
That I vpon my knees did fall,
 and prayed for their amending.
Back to the woods I got againe,
 in minde perplexed sore :
Where I found ease of all this paine,
 and meane to stray no more.
There, Citty, Court, nor Country to,
 can any way annoy me :
But as a wood-man ought to doe,
 I freely may imploy me.
There liue I quietly alone,
 and none to trip my talke :
Wherefore when I am dead and gone,
 thinke on the Wood-mans walke.

forgerie] deceit, artifice

SIR PHILIP SIDNEY

1554–1585

SONNETS FROM *ASTROPHEL AND STELLA*

(1)

LOUING in truth, and faine in verse my loue to
    show,
    That she (deare she) might take some pleasure
      of my paine :
    Pleasure might cause her reade, reading might
      make her know,
    Knowledge might pitie win, and pitie grace
      obtaine,

I sought fit words to paint the blackest face of woe,
    Studying inuentions fine, her wits to entertaine :
    Oft turning others leaues, to see if thence would
      flow
    Some fresh and fruitfull showers vpon my sunne-
      burn'd braine.

But words came halting forth, wanting Inuention's
    stay,
    Invention Natures child, fled step-dame Studies
      blowes,
    And others feete still seem'd but strangers in
      my way.

Thus, great with child to speake, and helplesse in
    my throwes,
    Biting my trewand pen, beating my selfe for spite.
    Foole, said my Muse to me, looke in thy heart
      and write.

        trewand] truant.

(2)

THE curious wits, seeing dull pensiuenesse
  Bewray it selfe in my long setled eyes,
  Whence those same fumes of melancholy rise,
  With idle paines, and missing ayme, do guesse.

Some that know how my spring I did addresse,
  Deeme that my Muse some fruit of knowledge
    plies :
  Others, because the Prince my seruice tries,
  Thinke that I thinke state errours to redresse.

But harder Iudges iudge ambitions rage,
  Scourge of it selfe, still climing slipprie place,
  Holds my young braine captiu'd in golden cage.

O fooles, or ouer-wise, alas the race
  Of all my thoughts hath neither stop nor start,
  But only *Stellas* eyes, and *Stellas* heart.

(3)

WITH how sad steps, ô Moone, thou climb'st the
    skies,
  How silently, and with how wanne a face,
  What may it be, that euen in heauenly place
  That busie archer his sharpe arrowes tries ?

Sure if that long with *Loue* acquainted eyes
  Can iudge of *Loue*, thou feel'st a Louers case ;
  I reade it in thy lookes, thy languisht grace,
  To me that feele the like, thy state descries.

Then ev'n of fellowship, ô Moone, tell me,
  Is constant *Loue* deem'd there but want of wit?
  Are Beauties there as proud as here they be?

Do they above *loue* to be lou'd, and yet
  Those Louers scorne whom that *Loue* doth
    possesse?
  Do they call *Vertue* there vngratefulnesse.

(4)

You that do search for euerie purling spring,
  Which from the ribs of old Parnassus flowes,
  And euerie floure not sweet perhaps, which
    growes
  Neare thereabouts, into your Poesie wring.

You that do Dictionaries methode bring
  Into your rimes, running in ratling rowes:
  You that poore *Petrarchs* long deceased woes,
  With new-borne sighes and denisend wit do
    sing.

You take wrong waies those far-fet helpes be such,
  As do bewray a want of inward tuch:
  And sure at length stolne goods do come to
    light.

But if (both for your loue and skill) your name
  You seeke to nurse at fullest breasts of Fame,
  Stella behold, and then begin to endite.

far-fet] far-fetched.

(5)

O HAPPIE Tems, that didst my *Stella* beare,
   I saw thy selfe with many a smiling line
   Vpon thy cheereful face, ioyes livery weare :
While those faire planets on thy streames did
    shine.

The bote for ioy could not to daunce forbeare,
   While wanton winds with beauties so deuine
   Ravisht, staid not, till in her golden haire
They did themselves (ô sweetest prison) twine.

And faine those Æols youth there would their stay
   Have made, but, forst by Nature still to flie,
   First did with puffing kisse those lockes display :

She so discheveld, blusht : from window I
   With sight thereof cride out ; ô faire disgrace,
   Let honor selfe to thee graunt highest place.

(6)

COME sleepe, ô sleepe, the certaine knot of peace,
   The baiting place of wit, the balme of woe,
   The poore mans wealth, the prisoners release,
   Th'indifferent Iudge betweene the high and low ;

With shield of proofe shield me from out the prease
   Of those fierce darts, dispaire at me doth throw :
   O make in me those ciuill warres to cease ;
   I will good tribute pay if thou do so.

    Tems] Thames.   deuine] divine.   prease] press.

Take thou of me smooth pillowes, sweetest bed,
 A chamber deafe to noise, and blind to light :
 A rosie garland, and a wearie hed :

And if these things, as being thine in right,
 Move not thy heavy grace, thou shalt in me,
 Livelier than else-where *Stellas* image see.

(7)

O IOY, too high for my low stile to show :
 O blisse, fit for a nobler state then me :
 Enuie, put out thine eyes, least thou do see
What oceans of delight in me do flow.

My friend, that oft saw through all maskes my wo,
 Come, come, and let me powre my selfe on thee ;
 Gone is the winter of my miserie,
My spring appeares, ô see what here doth grow.

For *Stella* hath with words where faith doth shine,
 Of her high heart giu'n me the monarchie :
 I, I, ô I may say, that she is mine.

And though she giue but thus conditionly
 This realme of blisse, while vertuous course
  I take,
 No kings be crown'd, but they some couenants
  make.

hed] head. enuie] envy. least] lest. powre] pour.

(8)

Stella since thou so right a Princesse art
    Of all the powers which life bestowes on me,
    That ere by them ought vndertaken be,
    They first resort vnto that soueraigne part;

Sweete for a while giue respite to my hart,
    Which pants as though it still should leape to
        thee ;
    And on my thoughts giue thy Lieftenancy
    To this great cause, which needs both vse and art.

And as a Queene, who from her presence sends
    Whom she imployes, dismisse from thee my wit,
    Till it haue wrought what thy owne will attends.

On seruants shame oft Maisters blame doth sit;
    O let not fooles in me thy workes reproue
    And scorning say, see what it is to loue.

SONGS FROM *ASTROPHEL AND STELLA*

FIRST SONG

DOUBT you to whom my Muse these notes entendeth
Which now my breast ore charg'd to Musicke
        lendeth ;
To you, to you, all song of praise is due,
Only in you my song begins and endeth.

Who hath the eyes which marrie state with pleasure,
Who keepes the key of Natures chiefest treasure :
To you, to you, all song of praise is due,
Only for you the heau'n forgate all measure.

Who has lips, where wit in fairenesse raigneth,
Who womankind at once both deckes and stayneth:
To you, to you, all song of praise is due,
Onely by you *Cupid* his crowne maintaineth.

Who hath the feet, whose step of sweetnesse
 planteth,
Who else for whom *Fame* worthy trumpets wanteth:
To you, to you, all song of praise is due,
Onely to you her Scepter *Venus* granteth.

Who hath the breast, whose milke doth passions
 nourish,
Whose grace is such, that when it chides doth
 cherish,
To you, to you, all song of praise is due,
Onelie through you the tree of life doth flourish.

Who hath the hand which without stroke subdueth,
Who long dead beautie with increase reneweth:
To you, to you, all song of praise is due,
Onely at you all enuie hopelesse rueth.

Who hath the haire which loosest fastest tieth,
VVho makes a man liue then glad when he dieth:
To you, to you, all song of praise is due:
Only of you the flatterer neuer lieth.

Who hath the voyce, which soule from sences
 sunders,
Whose force but yours the bolts of beautie thunders:
To you, to you, all song of praise is due:
Only with you not miracles are wonders.

 stayneth] to stain here means to take out colour.

Doubt you to whom my Muse these notes entendeth,
Which now my breast orecharg'd to Musicke
　　lendeth :
To you, to you, all song of praise is due :
Only in you my song begins and endeth.

ELEVENTH SONG

VVho is it that this darke night,
Vnderneath my window playneth ?
It is one who from the sight,
Being (ah) exild, disdayneth
Euery other vulgar light.

VVhy alas, and are you he ?
Be not yet those fancies changed ?
Deere when you find change in me,
Though from me you be estranged,
Let my chaunge to ruine be.

Well in absence this will dy,
Leaue to see, and leaue to wonder :
Absence sure will helpe, if I
Can learne, how my selfe to sunder
From what in my hart doth ly.

But time will these thoughts remoue :
Time doth worke what no man knoweth,
Time doth as the subiect proue,
With time still the affection groweth
In the faithfull Turtle doue.

What if you new beauties see,
Will not they stir new affection ?
I will thinke th[e]y pictures be,
(Image like of Saints perfection)
Poorely counterfeting thee.

But your reasons purest light,
Bids you leaue such minds to nourish ?
Deere, do reason no such spite,
Neuer doth thy beauty florish
More, then in my reasons sight.

But the wrongs loue beares, will make
Loue at length leaue vndertaking ;
No the more fooles it do shake,
In a ground of so forme making,
Deeper still they driue the stake.

Peace, I thinke that some giue eare :
Come no more, least I get anger.
Blisse, I will my blisse forbeare,
Fearing (sweete) you to endanger,
But my soule shall harbour thee.

VVell, be gone, be gone, I say,
Lest that *Argus* eyes perceiue you,
O vniust fortunes sway,
VVhich can make me thus to leaue you,
And from lowts to run away.

SPLENDIDIS LONGUM VALEDICO NUGIS

Leaue me ô Loue, which reachest but to dust,
And thou my mind aspire to higher things :
Grow rich in that which neuer taketh rust :
What euer fades, but fading pleasure brings.

Draw in thy beames, and humble all thy might
To that sweet yoke, where lasting freedomes be :
Which breakes the clowdes and opens forth the
    light.
That doth both shine and giue vs sight to see.

O take fast hold, let that light be thy guide
In this small course which birth drawes out to
    death,
And thinke how euill becommeth him to slide,
Who seeketh heau'n, and comes of heau'nly breath.
    Then farewell world, thy vttermost I see,
    Eternall Loue maintaine thy life in me.

THE BARGAIN

My true loue hath my hart, and I haue his,
By iust exchange, one for another giu'ne.
I hold his deare, and myne he cannot misse:
There neuer was a better bargaine driu'ne.

His hart in me, keepes me and him in one,
My hart in him, his thoughts and senses guides:
He loues my hart, for once it was his owne:
I cherish his because in me it bides.

His hart his wound receiued from my sight:
My hart was wounded, with his wounded hart,
For as from me, on him his hurt did light,
So still me thought in me his hurt did smart:
    Both equall hurt, in this change sought our blisse:
    My true loue hath my hart and I haue his.

            euill] evil.
            giu'ne] given.   driu'ne] driven.

DIRGE

RING out your belles, let mourning shewes be
    spread ;
  For loue is dead :
    All Loue is dead, infected
    With plague of deepe disdaine :
    Worth as nought worth reiected,
    And Faith faire scorne doth gaine.
      From so vngrateful fancie,
      From such a femall franzie,
      From them that vse men thus,
      Good Lord deliver vs.

Weepe neighbours, weepe, do you not heare it said,
  That Loue is dead :
    His death-bed peacocks follie,
    His winding sheete is shame,
    His will false-seeming holie,
    His sole exectour blame.
      From so vngrateful fancie,
      From such a femall franzie,
      From them that vse men thus,
      Good Lord deliver vs.

Let Dirge be sung, and Trentals rightly read,
  For Loue is dead :
    Sir vvrong his tombe ordaineth :
    My mistresse Marble-heart,
    Which Epitaph containeth,
    Her eyes were once his dart.

---

  femall franzie] female frenzy. **holie**] wholly. **Trentals**]
(sets of) thirty masses for the dead.

From so vngrateful fancie,
From such a femall franzie,
From them that vse men thus,
Good Lord deliver vs.

Alas, I lie : rage hath this errour bred,
Loue is not dead.
   Loue is not dead, but sleepeth
   In her vnmatched mind :
   Where she his counsell keepeth,
   Till due desert she find.
     Therefore, from so vile fancie
     To call such wit a franzie,
     Who loue can temper thus,
     Good Lord deliver vs.

PHILOMELA

THE Nightingale as soone as Aprill bringeth
Vnto her rested sense a perfect waking,
While late bare earth, proud of new clothing
   springeth,
Sings out her woes, a thorne her song-booke making;
  And mournfully bewailing,
  Her throate in tunes expresseth
  What griefe her breast oppresseth,
  For Thereus force on her chaste will prevailing.

   O *Philomela* faire, ô take some gladnesse,
   That here is iuster cause of plaintful sadnesse ;
   Thine earth now springs, mine fadeth,
   Thy thorne without, my thorne my heart
    inuadeth.

Alas she hath no other cause of anguish
But *Thereus* loue, on her by strong hand wrokne,
Wherein she suffring all her spirits languish,
Full womanlike complaines her will was brokne.
  But I who dayly crauing,
  Cannot haue to content me,
  Haue more cause to lament me,
  Since wanting is more woe then too much hauing.

  O *Philomela* faire, ô take some gladnesse,
  That here is iuster cause of plaintfull sadnesse :
  Thine earth now springs, mine fadeth :
  Thy thorne without, my thorne my heart
    inuadeth.

THE HIGHWAY

Highway since you my chief *Pernassus* be,
And that my Muse to some eares not vnsweet,
Tempers her words to trampling horses feet
More oft then to a chamber melodie.

Now blessed you, beare onward blessed me
To her, where I my heart safeleft shall meet,
My Muse and I must you of dutie greet
With thankes and wishes, wishing thankfully.

Be you still faire, honourd by publike heed,
By no encrochment wrongd, nor time forgot :
Nor blam'd for bloud, nor sham'd for sinfull deed.

And that you know, I enuy you no lot
  Of highest wish, I wish you so much blisse,
  Hundreds of yeares you *Stellas* feet may kisse.

EPITHALAMIUM

LET mother earth now decke her selfe in flowers,
To see her ofspring seeke a good increase,
Where justest love doth vanquish *Cupids* powers
And ware of thoughts is swallow'd up in peace
    Which neuer may decrease
    But like the turtells faire
    Live one in two, a well united paire,
    Which that no chaunce may staine,
    O *Himen* long their coupled joyes maintaine.

O heav'n awake shewe forth thy stately face,
Let not these slumbring clowds thy beawties hide,
But with thy cheerefull presence helpe to grace
The honest Bridegroome, and the bashfull Bride,
    Whose loves may ever bide,
    Like to the Elme and Vyne,
    With mutuall embracements them to twyne:
    In which delightfull paine,
    O *Himen* long their coupled joyes maintaine.

Yee Muses all which chaste affects allow,
And have to *Thyrsis* shewd your secret skill,
To this chaste love your sacred favours bow,
And so to him and her your giftes distill,
    That they all vice may kill:
    And like to lillies pure
    May please all eyes, and spotlesse may endure.
    Where that all blisse may raigne,
    O *Himen* long their coupled joyes maintaine.

ware] war.

Yee Nymphes which in the waters empire have,
Since *Thyrsis* musick oft doth yeeld you praise,
Graunt to the thing which we for *Thyrsis* crave.
Let one time (but long first) close up their daies,
 One grave their bodies seaze :
 And like two rivers sweete,
 When they though divers do together meete :
 One streame both streames containe,
 O *Himen* long their coupled joyes maintaine.

Pan, father *Pan*, the god of silly sheepe,
Whose care is cause that they in number growe,
Have much more care of them that them do keepe,
Since from these good the others good doth flowe,
 And make their issue showe
 In number like the hearde
 Of yonglings, which thy selfe with love hast rearde.
 Or like the drops of raine.
 O *Himen* long their coupled joyes maintaine.

Vertue (if not a God) yet Gods chiefe parte,
Be thou the knot of this their open vowe,
That still he be her head, she be his harte,
He leane to her, she unto him do bow :
 Each other still allow :
 Like Oke and Mistletoe.
 Her strength from him, his praise from her do
  growe.
 In which most lovely traine,
 O *Himen* long their coupled joyes maintaine.

But thou foule *Cupid* syre to lawlesse lust,
Be thou farre hence with thy empoyson'd darte,
Which though of glittring golde, shall heere take rust
Where simple love, which chastnesse doth imparte,

   divers] diverse. silly] simple.

Avoydes thy hurtfull arte,
Not needing charming skill,
Such mindes with sweet affections for to fill,
Which being pure and plaine,
O *Himen* long their coupled joyes maintaine.

All churlish wordes, shrewd answeres, crabbed
    lookes,
All privatenes, selfe-seeking, inward spite,
All waywardnes, which nothing kindly brookes,
All strife for toyes, and clayming masters right :
    Be hence aye put to flight,
    All sturring husbands hate
    Gainst neighbors good for womanish debate
    Be fled as things most vaine,
    O *Himen* long their coupled joyes maintaine.

All peacock pride, and fruites of peacocks
    pride
Longing to be with losse of substance gay
With retchlesnes what may thy house betide,
So that you may on hyer slippers stay
    For ever hence awaye :
    Yet let not sluttery,
    The sinke of filth, be counted huswifery :
    But keeping holesome meane,
    O *Himen* long their coupled joyes maintaine.

But above all away vile jealousie,
The evill of evils just cause to be unjust,
(How can he love suspecting treacherie ?
How can she love where love cannot win trust ?)
    Goe snake hide thee in dust,

retchlesnes] recklessness.

Ne dare once shew thy face,
Where open hartes do holde so constant place,
That they thy sting restraine,
O *Himen* long their coupled joyes maintaine.

The earth is deckt with flowers, the heav'ns displaid,
Muses graunt guiftes, Nymphes long and joyned life,
Pan store of babes, vertue their thoughts well staid,
Cupids lust gone, and gone is bitter strife,
    Happy man, happy wife.
    No pride shall them oppresse,
    Nor yet shall yeeld to loathsome sluttishnes,
    And jealousie is slaine :
For *Himen* will their coupled joyes maintaine.

FULKE GREVILLE, LORD BROOKE

1554–1628

CHORUS OF PRIESTS

Oh wearisome Condition of Humanity !
Borne vnder one Law, to another bound :
Vainely begot, and yet forbidden vanity,
Created sicke, commanded to be sound :
What meaneth Nature by these diuerse Lawes ?
Passion and Reason, selfe-diuision cause :
Is it the marke, or Maiesty of Power,
To make offences that it may forgiue ?
Nature herselfe, doth her owne selfe defloure,
To hate those errors she her-selfe doth giue.
For how should man thinke that, he may not doe
If Nature did not faile, and punish too ?
Tyrant to others, to her selfe vniust,
Onely commands things difficult and hard.

          ne] nor.
          defloure] deflower.

Forbids vs all things, which it knowes is lust,
Makes easie paines, vnpossible reward.
If Nature did not take delight in blood,
She would haue made more easie waies to good,
We that are bound by vowes, and by Promotion,
With pompe of holy Sacrifice and rites,
To teach beleefe in good and still deuotion,
To preach of Heauens wonders, and delights :
Yet when each of vs, in his owne heart lookes,
He finds the God there, farre vnlike his Bookes.

JUSTICE AND MERCY

Solyman. If Mercie be so large, where's Iustice place?
Camœna. Where Loue despaires, and where Gods
    promise ends.
For Mercie is the highest reach of wit,
A safety vnto them that saue with it :
Borne out of God, and vnto humane eyes,
Like God, not seene, till fleshly passion dies.
Solyman. God may forgiue, whose being, and
    whose harmes
Are farre remou'd from reach of fleshly armes :
But if God Equalls, or Successors had ;
Euen God, of safe reuenges would be glad.
While he is yet aliue, he may be slaine ;
But *from the dead no flesh comes backe againe.*
Solyman. While he remaines aliue, I liue in feare.
Camœna. Though he were dead, that doubt still
    liuing were.
Solyman. None hath the power to end what he
    begunne.
Camœna. The same occasion followes euery Sonne.

is lust (line 1) should probably read *we lust.*   still
deuotion] instil devotion.

Solyman. Their Greatnesse, or their Worth is not
    so much.
Camœna. And shall the best be slaine, for being
    such ?
Solyman. Thy Mother, or thy Brother are amisse :
I am betray'd, and one of them it is.
Camœna. My Mother, if shee erres erres vertuously :
And let her erre, ere *Mustapha* should die.
*Kings, for their safetie, must not blame mistrust ;
Nor, for surmises, sacrifice the iust.*
Solyman. Well : deare *Camœna* ! keepe this secretly.
I will be well aduis'd before he die.

MYRA

I WITH whose colors Myra dresst her head,
I, that ware posies of her owne hand making,
I, that mine owne name in the chimnies read
By Myra finely wrought ere I was waking :
    Must I looke on ? in hope time comming may
    With change bring backe my turne againe to
      play.

I, that on Sunday at the Church-stile found,
A Garland sweet, with true-loue knots in flowers,
Which I to weare about mine arme was bound,
That each of vs might know that all was ours :
    Must I lead now an idle life in wishes ?
    And follow *Cupid* for his loaues, and fishes ?

I, that did weare the ring her Mother left,
I, for whose loue she gloried to be blamed,
I, with whose eyes her eyes committed theft,
I, who did make her blush when I was named ;

  chimnies] *cheminées*, chimney pieces of tapestry work.

Must I lose ring, flowers, blush, theft and go
    naked,
Watching with sighs, till dead loue be awaked?

I, that when drowsie *Argus* fell asleep,
Like Iealousie o'rewatched with desire,
Was euer warned modestie to keepe,
While her breath speaking kindled Natures fire :
    Must I looke on a-cold, while others warme
        them ?
    Doe *Vulcans* brothers in such fine nets arm
        them ?

Was it for this that I might *Myra* see ?
Washing the water with her beauties, white,
Yet would she neuer write her loue to me ;
Thinks wit of change while thoughts are in delight ?
    Mad Girles must safely loue, as they may leaue,
    No man can print a kisse, lines may deceiue.

THOMAS LODGE

1556(?)–1625

ROSALYNDE'S DESCRIPTION

LIKE to the cleere in higest spheare
Where all imperiall glorie shines,
Of selfe same colour is her haire
Whether vnfolded or in twines :
    Heigh ho faire *Rosalynde* !
Her eyes are Saphires set in snow,
Refining heauen by euerie winke ;
The Gods doo feare when as they glow,
And I doo tremble when I thinke.
    Heigh ho, would she were mine.

Her cheekes are like the blushing clowde
That beautefies *Auroraes* face,
Or like the siluer crimson shrowde
That *Phœbus* smiling lookes doth grace.
    Heigh ho, faire *Rosalynde*.
Her lippes are like two budded roses
Whom rankes of lillies neighbour nie,
Within which bounds she balme incloses,
Apt to intice a Deitie :
    Heigh ho, would she were mine.

Her necke like to a stately towre,
Where Loue himselfe imprisoned lies,
To watch for glaunces euerie howre,
From her deuine and sacred eyes,
    Heigh ho, fair *Rosalynde*.
Her pappes are centers of delight,
Her breasts are orbes of heauenlie frame,
Where Nature moldes the deaw of light
To feede perfection with the same :
    Heigh ho, would she were mine.

With orient pearle, with rubie red,
With marble white, with saphire blew,
Her bodie euerie way is fed ;
Yet soft in touch, and sweete in view :
    Heigh ho, faire *Rosalynde*.
Nature her selfe her shape admires,
The Gods are wounded in her sight,
And Loue forsakes his heauenly fires,
And at her eyes his brand doth light :
    Heigh ho, would she were mine.

euerie howre] every hour.   moldes the deaw]
moulds the dew.

Then muse not Nymphes though I bemoane
The absence of faire *Rosalynde* :
Since for her faire there is fairer none,
Nor for her vertues so deuine.
　　Heigh ho faire *Rosalynde* :
　Heigh ho my heart, would God that she were
　　mine.

ROSALYNDE'S MADRIGAL

Loue in my bosome like a Bee
　　doth sucke his sweete :
Now with his wings he playes with me,
　　now with his feete.
Within mine eies he makes his neast,
His bed amidst my tender breast,
My kisses are his daily feast ;
And yet he robs me of my rest.
　　Ah wanton, will ye ?

And if I sleepe, then pearcheth he
　　with prettie flight,
And makes his pillow of my knee
　　the liuelong night.
Strike I my lute, he tunes the string ;
He musicke playes if so I sing,
He lends me euerie louelie thing,
Yet cruell he my heart doth sting.
　　Whist wanton, still ye.

Else I with roses euerie day
　　will whip you hence ;
And binde you when you long to play,
　　for your offence.

deuine] divine.

Ile shut mine eyes to keepe you in,
Ile make you fast it for your sinne,
Ile count your power not worth a pinne ;
Ahlas what hereby shall I winne
    If he gainsay me ?

What if I beate the wanton boy
    with manie a rod ?
He will repay me with annoy,
    because a God.
Then sit thou safely on my knee,
Then let thy bowre my bosome be :
Lurke in mine eyes I like of thee ;
Oh *Cupid* so thou pitie me.
    Spare not but play thee.

PLUCK THE FRUIT AND TASTE THE PLEASURE

PLUCKE the fruite and tast the pleasure
    Youthfull Lordings of delight,
Whil'st occasion giues you seasure,
    Feede your fancies and your sight :
        After death when you are gone,
        Joy and pleasure is there none.

Here on earth nothing is stable,
    Fortunes chaunges well are knowne,
Whil'st as youth doth then enable,
    Let your seedes of ioy be sowne :
        After death when you are gone,
        Ioy and pleasure is there none.

seasure] **seizure.**

Feast it freely with your Louers,
    Blyth and wanton sweetes doo fade,
Whilst that louely *Cupid* houers
    Round about this louely shade :
        Sport it freely one to one,
        After death is pleasure none.

Now the pleasant spring allureth,
    And both place and time inuites :
But alas, what heart endureth
    To disclaime his sweete delightes ?
        After death when we are gone,
        Joy and pleasure is there none.

                Robert, Second Duke of Normandy, 1591.

GEORGE PEELE
1558(?)–1597

FAIR AND FAIR

Œnone.   FAIRE and fayre and twise so faire,
        As fayre as any may be ;
    The fayrest sheepeherd on our grene,
        A loue for anie Ladie.
Paris.   Faire and faire and twise so fayre,
        As fayre as anie may be ;
    Thy loue is fayre fore thee alone
        And for no other Ladie.
Œnone.   My loue is faire, my loue is gaie,
        As fresh as bine the flowers in May
    And of my loue my roundylaye,
    My merrie merrie merrie roundelaie,
        Concludes with Cupids curse :
    They that do chaunge olde loue for newe
        Pray Gods they chaunge for worse.

Ambo Simul.   They that do chaunge, &c.
     Œnone.   Faire and faire, &c.
      Paris.   Faire and faire, &c.   Thy loue is
                 faire, &c.
     Œnone.   My loue can pype, my loue can sing,
                     My loue can manie a pretie thing,
                     And of his louelie prayses ring
                     My merry merry roundelayes :
                         Amen to Cupids curse :
                         They that do chaunge, &c.
      Paris.   They that do chaunge, &c.
      Ambo.   Faire and fayre, &c.

A FAREWELL TO ARMS

(TO QUEEN ELIZABETH)

His golden locks time hath to siluer turnde,
O time too swift, O swiftnes neuer ceasing,
His youth gainst time & age hath euer spurnd,
But spurnd in vaine, youth waneth by encreasing :
    Beautie, strength, youth are flowers but fading
    seene,
    Duty, Faith, Loue, are roots and euer greene.

His helmet now shall make a hiue for bees,
And louers sonets turne to holy psalmes :
A man at armes must now serue on his knees,
And feed on prayers which are ages almes,
    But though from court to cotage he departe
    His saint is sure of his vnspotted hart.
And when he saddest sits in homely Cell,
Hele teach his swaines this Caroll for a songe,
Blest be the harts that wish my soueraigne well,

Curst be the soule that thinke her any wrong :
　Goddes allow this aged man his right
　To be your beadsman now that was your knight.

A FAREWELL

ENTITULED TO THE FAMOUS AND FORTUNATE
GENERALLS OF OUR ENGLISH FORCES : SIR IOHN
NORRIS & SIR FRAUNCIS DRAKE KNIGHTS, AND ALL
　THEYR BRAUE AND RESOLUTE FOLLOWERS,
　　　　　　　1589

HAUE doone with care my harts, aborde amaine,
With stretching sayles to plowe the swelling waues.
Bid Englands shoare and Albions chalkie clyffes
Farewell : bid statelie Troynouant adiewe,
Where pleasant Thames from Isis siluer head
Begins her quiet glide, and runnes along,
To that braue Bridge the barre that th'warts her
　　course,
Neere neighbour to the auncient stonie Towre,
The glorious hold that *Iulius Caesar* built :
Change Loue for Armes, gyrt to your blades my
　　boyes,
Your Rests and Muskets take, take Helme and
　　Targe,
And let God Mars his consort make you mirth,
The roring Cannon and the brasen Trumpe,
The angry sounding Drum, the whistling Fife,
The shrikes of men, the princelie coursers ney.
Now vaile your bonnets to your freends at home,
Bid all the louelie brittish dames adiewe,

　　　　　aged] agèd.

That vnder many a Standarde well aduaunc'd,
Haue hid the sweete allarmes and braues of loue.
Bid Theaters and proude Tragædians,
Bid *Mahomets Poo*, and mightie *Tamburlaine*,
King *Charlemaine*, *Tom Stukeley* and the rest
Adiewe : to Armes, to Armes, to glorious Armes,
With noble *Norris*, and victorious *Drake*,
Vnder the sanguine Crosse, braue Englands badge,
To propagate religious pietie,
And hewe a passage with your conquering swordes
By lande and Sea : wher euer Phœbus eye
Th' eternall Lampe of Heauen lendes vs light ;
By golden Tagus or the westerne Inde,
Or through the spacious Bay of Portugale,
The welthy Ocean maine, the Terrhen sea,
From great Alcides pyllers braunching foorth,
Euen to the Gulfe that leades to loftie Rome,
There to deface the pryde of Antechrist,
And pull his Paper Walles and popery downe :
A famous enterprise for Englands strength,
To steele your swordes on Auarice triple crowne,
And clense Augeas staules in Italie.
To Armes my fellow Souldiers, Sea and land
Lie open to the voyage you intende :
And sea or land bold Brittons farre or neare,
What euer course your matchles vertue shapes,
Whether to Europes boundes or Asian plaines,
To Affricks shore, or rich America,
Downe to the shades of deepe Auernus cragges,
Sayle on, pursue your honours to your graues :
Heauen is a sacred couering for your heads,
And euery Climat vertues Tabernacle.
To Armes, to Armes, to honourable Armes,
Hoyse sayles, waie Anckers vp, plowe vp the Seas

With flying keeles, plowe up the land with swordes,
In Gods name venture on, and let me say
To you my Mates, as *Caesar* sayd to his
Striuing with Neptunes hils : You beare, quoth he,
Caesar, and *Caesars* fortune in your ships.
You follow them whose swords successful are.
You follow *Drake* by Sea, the scourge of Spayne,
The dreadfull Dragon, terror to your foes.
Victorius in his returne from Inde,
In all his high attempts vnuanquished.
You followe noble *Norris*, whose renowne,
Wonne in the fertile fieldes of Belgia,
Spreades by the gates of Europe, to the Courts
Of Christian Kings and heathen Potentates.
You fight for Christ and Englands peereles Queene,
Elizabeth, the wonder of the worlde.
Ouer whose throne th'enemies of God,
Haue thundred earst their vaine successles braues.
O tenne times treble happy men that fight,
Vnder the Crosse of Christ and Englands Queene,
And follow such as *Drake* and *Norris* are.
All honours doo this cause accompanie,
All glory on these endlesse honours waites :
These honors, and this glory shall he sende :
Whose honour and whose glory you defende.

PEEPING FLOWERS

Not *Iris* in her pride and brauerie,
Adornes her arche with such varietie :
Nor doth the milke white way in frostie night,
Appeare so faire and beautifull in sight :
As done these fieldes, and groues, and sweetest
    bowres,
Bestrewed and deckt with partie collord flowers.
Alonge the bubling brookes & siluer glyde,
That at the bottome doth in sylence slyde,
The waterie flowers and lillies on the bankes,
Like blazing cometes burgen all in rankes :
Vnder the *Hathorne* and the *Poplar* tree,
Where sacred *Phoebe* may delight to be :
The *Primerose* and the purple *Hyacinthe*,
The dayntie *Violet* and the holsome *Minthe* :
The dooble *Daisie*, and the *Couslip* queene
Of sommer floures, do ouer peere the greene :
And rounde about the valley as ye passe,
Ye may ne see for peeping flowers the grasse :
That well the mightie *Iono* and the rest,
May boldlie thinke to be a welcome guest
On *Ida* hills, when to approue the thing,
The queene of flowers prepares a second spring.

Araygnment of Paris.

holsome] wholesome.

ROBERT GREENE

1560–1592

THE PALMER'S ODE

OLDE Menalcas on a day,
As in field this shepheard lay,
Tuning of his oten pipe,
Which he hit with manie a stripe;
Said to Coridon that hee
Once was yong and full of glee,
Blithe and wanton was I then:
Such desires follow men.
As I lay and kept my sheepe,
Came the God that hateth sleepe,
Clad in armour all of fire,
Hand in hand with Queene Desire:
And with a dart that wounded nie,
Pearst my heart as I did lie:
That when I wooke I gan sweare,
Phillis beautie palme did beare.
Up I start, foorth went I,
With hir face to feede mine eye:
Then I saw Desire sit,
That my heart with Love had hit,
Laying foorth bright Beauties hookes,
To intrap my gazing lookes.
Love I did and gan to woe;
Pray and sigh, all would not doe:
Women when they take the toy
Covet to be counted coy.
Coy she was, and I gan court,
She thought Love was but a sport.

to woe] to woo.

Profound Hell was in my thought,
Such a paine Desire had wrought,
That I sued with sighes and teares,
Still ingrate she stopt her eares,
Till my youth I had spent,
Last a passion of Repent,
Tolde me flat that Desire,
Was a brond of Loves fire,
Which consumeth men in thrall,
Vertue, youth, wit, and all.
At this sawe backe I start,
Bet Desire from my hart,
Shooke of Love and made an oth,
To be enemie to both.
Olde I was when thus I fled,
Such fond toyes as cloyde my head.
But this I learn'd at Vertues gate,
The way to good is never late.

THE DESCRIPTION OF A SHEPHERD
AND HIS WIFE

It was neere a thicky shade,
That broad leaves of Beech had made :
Ioyning all their tops so nie,
That scarce Phoebus in could prie,
To see if Lovers in the thicke,
Could dally with a wanton tricke.
Where sate the swaine and his wife,
Sporting in that pleasing life,
That Coridon commendeth so,
All other lives to over-go.

brond] brand. sawe] saying, speech. bet] beat.
of] off.

He and she did sit and keepe
Flocks of kids, and fouldes of sheepe :
He upon his pipe did play,
She tuned voice unto his lay.
And for you might her Huswife knowe,
Voice did sing and fingers sowe :
He was young, his coat was greene,
With welts of white, seamde betweene,
Turned over with a flappe,
That brest and bosome in did wrappe,
Skirts side and plighted free,
Seemingly hanging to his knee.
A whittle with a silver chape,
Cloke was russet, and the cape
Served for a Bonnet oft,
To shrowd him from the wet aloft.
A leather scrip of colour red,
With a button on the head,
A bottle fulle of Country whigge,
By the shepheards side did ligge :
And in a little bush hard by,
There the shepheards dogge did lye,
Who while his Master gan to sleepe,
Well could watch both kiddes and sheep.
The shepheard was a frolicke Swaine,
For though his parell was but plaine,
Yet doone the Authors soothly say,
His colour was both fresh and gay :
And in their writes plaine discusse,
Fairer was not Tytirus,
Nor Menalcas whom they call
The Alderleefest swaine of all.

plighted] pleated.   ligge] lie.   Alderleefest] dearest
of all.

Seeming him was his wife,
Both in line, and in life :
Faire she was as faire might be,
Like the roses on the tree ;
Buxsane, blieth, and young, I weene,
Beautious, like a sommers Queene,
For her cheekes were ruddy hued,
As if Lillies were imbrued,
With drops of bloud to make thee white,
Please the eye with more delight ;
Love did lye within her eyes,
In ambush for some wanton prize.
A leefer Lasse then this had beene,
Coridon had never seene.
Nor was Phillis that faire May,
Halfe so gawdy or so gay :
She wore a chaplet on her head,
Her cassocke was of scarlet red,
Long and large as streight as bent,
Her middle was both small and gent.
A necke as white as whales bone,
Compast with a lace of stone,
Fine she was and faire she was,
Brighter than the brightest glasse.
Such a Shepheards wife as she,
Was not more in Thessaly.

Seeming] 'seeming.　　gent] graceful.

THE SHEPHERD'S WIFE'S SONG

Ah what is love ?   It is a pretty thing,
As sweet unto a shepheard as a king,
    And sweeter too :
For kings have cares that waite upon a Crowne
And cares can make the sweetest love to frowne :
    Ah then, ah then,
If countrie loves such sweet desires gaine,
What Lady would not love a Shepheard Swaine ?

His flockes are foulded, he comes home at night,
As merry as a king in his delight,
    And merrier too :
For kings bethinke them what the state require,
Where Shepheards carelesse Carroll by the fire.
    Ah then, ah then,
If countrie loves such sweet desires gaine,
What Lady would not love a Shepheard Swaine.

He kisseth first, then sits as blyth to eate
His creame and curds, as doth the king his meate ;
    And blyther too :
For kings have often fears when they do sup,
Where Shepheards dread no poyson in their cup.
    Ah then, ah then,
If country loves such sweet desires gaine,
What Lady would not love a Shepheard Swaine.

To bed he goes, as wanton then I weene,
As is a king in dalliance with a Queene ;
    More wanton too :
For Kings have many griefes affects to move,

Where Shepheards have no greater grief then love :
  Ah then, ah then,
If countrie loves such sweet desires gaine,
What Lady would not love a Shepheard Swaine.

Upon his couch of straw he sleeps as sound,
As doth the king upon his bed of downe,
  More sounder too :
For cares cause kings full oft their sleepe to spill,
Where weary Shepheards lye and snort their fill :
  Ah then, ah then,
If country loves such sweet desires gaine,
What Lady would not love a Shepheard Swaine.

Thus with his wife he spends the yeare as blyth,
As doth the king at every tyde or syth ;
  And blyther too :
For kings have warres and broyles to take in hand,
Where Shepheards laugh, and love upon the land.
  Ah then, ah then,
If countrie loves such sweet desires gaine,
What Lady would not love a Shepheard Swaine ?

MAESIA'S SONG

Sweet are the thoughts that sauour of content,
  the quiet mind is richer than a crowne,
Sweet are the nights in carelesse slumber spent,
  the poore estate scornes fortunes angrie frowne.
Such sweete content, such minds, such sleep, such
    blis
  beggers inioy, when Princes oft do mis

        syth] time.
        inioy] enjoy.

The homely house that harbors quiet rest,
   the cottage that affoords no pride nor care,
The meane that 'grees with Countrie musick best,
   the sweet consort of mirth and musicks fare,
Obscured life sets downe a type of blis,
   a minde content both crowne and kingdome is.

SEPHESTIA'S SONG TO HER CHILD

WEEPE not my wanton, smile vpon my knee,
When thou art olde ther 's griefe inough for thee.
   Mothers wagge, pretie boy,
   Fathers sorrow, fathers ioy.
   When thy father first did see
   Such a boy by him and mee,
   He was glad, I was woe,
   Fortune changde made him so,
   When he left his pretie boy,
   Last his sorrowe, first his ioy.
Weepe not my wanton, smile vpon my knee :
When thou art olde ther 's griefe inough for thee.
   Streaming teares that neuer stint,
   Like pearle drops from a flint
   Fell by course from his eyes,
   That one anothers place supplies :
   Thus he grieud in euerie part,
   Teares of bloud fell from his hart,
   When he left his pretie boy,
   Fathers sorrow, fathers ioy.
Weepe not my wanton, smile vpon my knee :
When thou art olde ther 's griefe inough for thee.

changde] changèd.

The wanton smilde, father wept :
Mother cride, babie lept :
More he crowde, more we cried ;
Nature could not sorowe hide.
He must goe, he must kisse
Childe and mother, babie blisse :
For he left his pretie boy,
Fathers sorowe, fathers ioy,
Weepe not my wanton, smile vpon my knee :
When thou art olde ther's griefe inough for thee.

DORON'S DESCRIPTION OF SAMELA

LIKE to Diana in her Summer weede
Girt with a crimson roabe of brightest die,
                    goes faire Samela.
Whiter than be the flockes that straggling feede,
When washt by Arethusa's Fount they lie :
                    is faire Samela.
As faire Aurora in her morning gray
Deckt with the ruddie glister of her loue,
                    is faire Samela.
Like louelie Thetis on a calmed day,
Whenas her brightnesse Neptunes fancie moue,
                    shines faire Samela.
Her tresses gold, her eyes like glassie streames,
Her teeth are pearle, the breasts are yuorie
                    of faire Samela.
Her cheekes like rose and lilly yeeld foorth gleames,
Her browes bright arches framde of ebonie :
                    Thus faire Samela.

whenas] when.   moue] move.   yuorie] ivory.

Passeth faire Venus in her brauest hiew,
And Iuno in the shew of maiestie,
               for she 's Samela.
Pallas in wit, all three if you well view,
For beautie, wit, and matchlesse dignitie
               yeeld to Samela.

ALEXANDER HUME

1560–1609

A SUMMER DAY

O PERFITE Light, quhilk schaid away,
   The darkenes from the light,
And set a ruler ou'r the day,
   Ane vther ou'r the night.

Thy glorie when the day foorth flies,
   Mair vively dois appeare,
Nor at midday vnto our eyes
   The shining sun is cleare.

The shaddow of the earth anon,
   Remooves and drawes by,
Sine in the East, when it is gon,
   Appeares a clearer sky.

Quhilk Sunne perceaves the little larka,
   The lapwing and the snyp,
And tunes their sangs like nature's clarks,
   Ou'r midow, mure, and stryp.

hiew] hue.
perfite] perfect.   quhilk] which.   schaid] parted.
Ane vther ou'r] another o'er.   midow, mure, and stryp]
meadow, muir, and rill.

Bot euerie bail'd nocturnall beast,
 Na langer may abide
They hy alway baith maist and least,
 Them selues in house to hide.

They dread the day fra thay it see,
 And from the sight of men.
To saits, and couars fast they flee,
 And Lyons to their den.

Oure Hemisphere is poleist clein,
 And lightened more and more,
While everie thing be clearely sein
 Quhilk seemed dim before.

Except the glistering astres bright,
 Which all the night were cleere,
Offusked with a greater light,
 Na langer dois appeare.

The golden globe incontinent
 Sets vp his shining head,
And ou'r the earth and firmament,
 Displayes his beims abread.

For ioy the birds with boulden throts,
 Agains his visage shein,
Takes vp their kindelie musicke nots,
 In woods and gardens grein . . .

The passenger from perrels sure,
 Sangs gladly foorth the way :
Breife, euerie liuing creature,
 Takes comfort of the day . . .

Offusked] darkened. boulden] swollen. shein]
bright.

The dew vpon the tender crops,
　　Lyke pearles white and round,
Or like to melted silver drops,
　　Refreshes all the ground.

The mystie rocke, the clouds of raine,
　　From tops of mountaines skails,
Cleare are the highest hils and plaine,
　　The vapors takes the vails . . .

The ample heauen of fabrik sure,
　　In cleannes dois surpas,
The chrystall and the silver pure,
　　Or clearest poleist glas.

The time sa tranquill is and still,
　　That na where sall ye find,
Saife on ane high, and barren hill,
　　Ane aire of peeping wind.

All trees and simples great and small,
　　That balmie leife do beir,
Nor thay were painted on a wall,
　　Na mair they moue or steir.

Calme is the deepe and pourpour se,
　　Yee smuther nor the sand,
The wals that woltring wont to be
　　Are stable like the land.

Sa silent is the cessile air,
　　That euery cry and call,
The hils, and dails, and forrest fair,
　　Againe repeates them all . . .

skails] clears.　　simples] herbs.　　pourpour] purple.
smuther nor] smoother than.　　cessile] yielding, ceasing.

The field, and earthly superfice,
  With verdure greene is spread,
And naturallie but artifice,
  In partie coulours clad.

The flurishes and fragrant flowres,
  Thro *Phœbus* fostring heit,
Refresht with dew and siluer showres,
  Casts vp an odor sweit.

The clogged busie humming beis,
  That neuer thinks to drowne,
On flowers and flourishes of treis
  Collects their liquor browne.

The Sunne maist like a speedie post,
  With ardent course ascends,
The beautie of the heauenly host
  Up to our Zenith tends.

The burning beims downe from his face,
  Sa feruently can beat ;
That man and beast now seekes a place
  To saue them fra the heat.

The brethles flocks drawes to the shade,
  And frechure of their fald,
The startling nolt as they were madde,
  Runnes to the riuers cald.

The heards beneath some leaffie trie,
  Amids the flowers they lie,
The stabill ships vpon the sey,
  Tends vp their sails to drie.

---

  flourishes] blossoms.

The labowrers that timellie raise
　　All wearie faint and weake :
For heate downe to their houses gais,
　　Noone-meate and sleepe to take . . .

With gilted eyes and open wings,
　　The cock his courage shawes,
With claps of ioy his breast he dings,
　　And twentie times he crawes.

The dow with whisling wings sa blew,
　　The winds can fast collect,
Her pourpour pennes turnes mony hew,
　　Against the sunne direct.

Now noone is went, gaine is mid-day
　　The heat dois slake at last,
The sunne descends downe west away,
　　Fra three of clock be past.

A little cule of braithing wind,
　　Now softly can arise,
The warks throw heate that lay behind,
　　Now men may enterprise . . .

The rayons of the Sunne we see,
　　Diminish in their strength,
The schad of euerie towre and tree,
　　Extendit is in length.

Great is the calme for everiequhair,
　　The wind is sitten downe,
The reik thrawes right vp in the air,
　　From everie towre and towne . . .

pennes] pens, quills.　　　everiequhair] everywhere.

The gloming comes, the day is spent,
　　The Sun goes out of sight,
And painted is the occident,
　　With pourpour sanguine bright.

The Skarlet nor the golden threid,
　　Who would their beawtie trie,
Are naething like the colour reid,
　　And beautie of the sky.

Our West Horizon circuler
　　Fra time the Sunne be set
Is all with rubies (as it wer)
　　Or Rosis reid ou'rfret.

What pleasour were to walke and see,
　　Endlang a riuer cleare,
The perfite forme of euerie tree,
　　Within the deepe appeare ? . . .

O : then it were a seemely thing,
　　While all is still and calme,
The praise of God to play and sing,
　　With cornet and with shalme.

Bot now the hirds with mony schout,
　　Cals vther be their name,
Ga, Billie, turne our gude about,
　　Now time is to go hame . . .

All labourers drawes hame at even,
　　And can till vther say,
Thankes to the gracious God of heauen,
　　Quhilk send this summer day.

OF GOD'S OMNIPOTENCIE

O EUERIE liuing warldly wight,
Awake and dres your selfe with speede :
To serue and praise the God of might,
From whome all bountie dois proceede :
For gif ye drift, and still refuse,
The heauens and earth will you accuse.

The brutall beasts but ony stryfe,
They willinglie his voice obay :
The creätures that hes na life,
Sets forth his glorie day by day :
The earth, the aire, the sea, and fire,
Are subiect all to his impire.

The heauen it is his dwelling place,
The earth his littil fute-stule law,
His warks are all before his face :
Of hearts the secreits he dois knaw,
And euerie thing as in a glas,
He sees before it cum to pas.

The swift and actiue fierie spreits,
The *Cherubins* of substance pure,
They walk amang the holie streits,
And makes him daylie seruice sure :
Yea, at all times they readie stand,
To gang and cum at his command . . .

His halie statute to fulfill,
And potent power to declaire,
The massiue earth reposis still,
Suspendid in the cessill eire :

gif] if.   na] no.   fute-stule] foot stool.   fierie
spreits] fiery sprights.   halie] holy.

And at hir dew appointed houres,
Brings forth maist pleasant fruits & floures.

Quhat thing is fiercer nor the sea ?
Mair raging nor the awfull deepe ?
Quhilk back retird at his decrie,
And dois her bounds and marchis keepe :
Syne at his charge apart stude by,
To make his hoste a passage dry.

Without the subtile aire but dout,
Nor plaint nor liuing thing may lest :
Therefore it cleaues the earth about,
And is in euerie place possest,
Then as his godlie wisdome wald,
Decernes the seasons hett and cald . . .

The brimstane and the burning fire,
Maist sudenely from heauen fell downe,
For to consume into this yre,
Baith Sodome, and Gomorrah towne :
Bot in the firie furnace he,
Preserued safe the children three.

The mightie winds blaws to and fra,
From euerie airth be day and night,
We heare them thudding by vs ga,
Yet not conceaues them by our sight :
Bot in a clap the Lord to please,
Their blasts they quietly appease

Quhat] what.   Mair] more.   Quhilk] which.   ga]
go.

Like flocks of fowls the clouds aboue,
Furth flies and couers all the sky :
Againe they suddenly remoove,
We wat not where nor reason why :
Bot till obay his holy law,
They poure out rain, sharpe haile, and snaw . . .

He made the sun a lampe of light,
A woll of heate to shine by day,
He made the moone to guide the night :
And set the starres in good array,
Orion, *Pleiads*, and the *Vrse*,
Obserues their dew prescriued course.

O Poets : paganes impudent,
Quhy worship ye the planets seauen ?
The glore of God be you is spent,
On Idols and the hoste of heauen,
Ye pride your pens mens eares to pleis
With fables and fictitious leis.

Your knowledge is bot ignorance,
Your cunning curiositie :
I finde your facund eloquence,
Repleete with fekles fantasie :
Ye neuer knew the lively rod,
Nor gospell of the sun of God.

He is aboue *Mercurius*
Aboue *Neptunus* on the sea,
The winds they knaw not *Eolus* :
Their is na *Iupiter* but he,
And all your Gods baith great and small,
Are of na force for he is all.

wat not] wot not.   Bot till] but to.   be you] by you.

Bot sonnes of light ye knaw the trueth,
Extoll the Lord with heart and minde,
Remoue all stayes and sluggish sleuth,
Obey his voice for he is kinde :
That heauen and earth may witnes beare,
Ye loue that God which bought you deare.

Hymnes, or Sacred Songs, 1599.

SIMON WASTELL

1560(?)–1635(?)

OF MAN'S MORTALITIE

LIKE as the Damaske Rose you see,
Or like the blossome on the tree,
Or like the daintie flower of May,
Or like the morning to the day,
Or like the Sunne ; or like the shade,
Or like the Gourd which *Ionas* had.
Euen such is man, whose thred is spun,
Drawne out, and cut, and so is done.
The Rose withers, the blossome blasteth,
The flower fades, the morning hasteth.
The Sun sets, the shadow flies,
The Gourd consumes, and man he dyes.

Like to the Grasse thats newly sprung,
Or like a tale thats new begun,
Or like the bird thats here to day,
Or like the pearléd dew of May,
Or like an houre, or like a span
Or like the singing of a Swan.

sleuth] sloth.

Euen such is man, who liues by breath,
Is here, now there, in life, and death :
The Grasse withers, the tale is ended,
The birde is flowne, the dew's ascended,
The houre is short, the span not long,
The Swan's neere death, man's life is done.

Like to the bubble in the brooke,
Or, in a Glasse, much like a looke :
Or like a shuttle in Weauers hand,
Or like the writing on the sand,
Or like a thought, or like a dreame,
Or like the glyding of the streame :
Euen such is man, who liues by breath,
Is heere, now there, in life, and death.
The Bubble's cut, the looke's forgot,
The Shuttle's flung, the writing's blot :
The thought is past, the dreame is gone
The water glides, man's life is done.

Like to an Arrow from the Bow,
Or like swift course of watery flow,
Or like the time twixt flood and ebbe,
Or like the spiders tender webbe,
Or like a race, or like a Goale,
Or like the dealing of a dole.
Euen such is man, whose britle state
Is alwayes subiect unto fate :
The Arrowe's shot, the flood soone spent,
The time no time, the webbe soone rent :
The race soone run, the Goale soone wonne,
The dole soone dealt, man's life first done.

Like to the lightning from the skie,
Or like a Post that quicke doth hie.

Or like a quauer in short song,
Or like a Iourney three dayes long ;
Or like the Snow when Summers' come,
Or like the Peare, or like the Plum :
Euen such is man, who heapes vp sorrow,
Liues but this day, and dyes to morrow.
The Lightning's past, the Post must goe,
The Song is short, the Iourneys' so,
The Peare doth rot, the Plum doth fall,
The Snow dissolues, and so must all.

Microbiblion, 1629.

GEORGE CHAPMAN

1560–1634

FROM THE TRANSLATION OF THE *ILIAD*

i. *Achilles goes forth to battle* (BOOK XIX).

THE host set forth ; and pour'd his steele waues,
    farre out of the fleete
nd as from aire ; the frostie Northwind blowes a
    cold thicke sleete,
hat dazels eyes ; flakes after flakes, incessantly
    descending :
o thicke helmes, curets, ashen darts, and round
    shields, neuer ending,
lowd from the nauies hollow wombe : their
    splendors gaue heauens eye,
is beames againe ; Earth laught to see, her face
    so like the skie.

curet or curets] an old form of cuirass.

Armes shin'd so hote ; and she such clouds, made
    with the dust she cast,

She thunderd ; feete of men and horse, importun'd
    her so fast.

In midst of all ; diuine *Achilles* his faire person
    arm'd ;

His teeth gnasht as he stood ; his eyes, so full of
    fire, they warm'd.

Vnsufferd griefe and anger at, the *Troians* so com-
    bin'd.

His greaues first vsde, his goodly curets on his
    bosome shin'd,

His sword, his shield ; that cast a brightnesse from
    it, like the Moone.

And as from sea, sailers discerne, a harmfull fire, let
    runne

By herdsmens faults, till all their stall, flies vp in
    wrastling flame ;

Which being on hils, is seene farre off ; but being
    alone, none came

To giue it quench ; at shore no neighbours ; and
    at sea, their friends

Driuen off with tempests ; such a fire, from his
    bright shield extends

His ominous radiance ; and in heauen, impress
    his feruent blaze.

His crested helmet, graue and high, had next
    triumphant place,

On his curl'd head : and like a starre, it cast a
    spurry ray ;

About which, a bright thickend bush, of golden
    haire, did play ;

spurry] many-pointed.

Which *Vulcan* forg'd him for his plume. Thus
    compleate arm'd, he tride
How fit they were : and if his motion could with
    ease abide
Their braue instruction ; and so farre, they were
    from hindring it ;
That to it they were nimble wings ; and made so
    light his spirit,
That from the earth, the princely Captaine they
    tooke vp to aire,
Then from his armoury he drew, his lance, his
    fathers speare,
Huge, weightie, firme ; that not a *Greeke*, but he
    himselfe alone
Knew how to shake ; it grew vpon, the mountaine
    Pelion ;
From whose height, *Chiron* hew'd it for his *Sire*,
    and fatall twas
To great-soul'd men. Of *Peleus* and *Pelion*, sur-
    named *Pelias*.
  Then from the stable, their bright horse, *Auto-
    medon* withdrawes,
And *Alcymus*. Put Poitrils on, and cast vpon their
    iawes,
Their bridles ; hurling backe the raines, and hung
    them on the seate,
The fair scourge then *Automedon* takes vp, and vp
    doth get,
To guide the horse. The fights seate last, *Achilles*
    tooke behind ;
Who lookt so arm'd, as if the Sunne, there falne
    from heauen had shin'd.

Poitrils] harness for the breast.   iawes] jaws.

And terribly, thus charg'd his steeds. *Xanthus*
    and *Balius*,

Seed of the Harpye; in the charge, ye vndertake
    of vs;

Discharge it not; as when *Patroclus* ye left dead in
    field.

But when with bloud, for this dayes fast obseru'd,
    reuenge shall yeeld

Our heart sacietie; bring vs off. Thus since
    Achilles spake,

As if his aw'd steeds vnderstood: twas *Iunoes* will
    to make

Vocall the pallat of the one; who shaking his faire
    head,

(Which in his mane (let fall to earth) he almost
    buried)

Thus *Xanthus* spake: Ablest *Achilles* now (at
    least) our care

Shall bring thee off; but not farre hence, the fatall
    minutes are,

Of thy graue ruine. Nor shall we, be then to be
    reprou'd,

But mightiest Fate, and the great God. Nor was
    thy best belou'd

Spoil'd so of armes by our slow pace; or courages
    empaire;

The best of gods, *Latonaes* sonne, that weares the
    golden haire,

Gaue him his deaths wound; though the grace, he
    gaue to *Hectors* hand.

We, like the spirit of the West, that all spirits can
    command

sacietie] satiety.   pallat] palate.   empaire] diminution.

For powre of wing, could runne him off : but thou
    thy selfe must go ;
So Fate ordaines ; God and a man, must giue thee
    ouerthrow.
  This said, the Furies stopt his voice. *Achilles*
    farre in rage,
Thus answered him : It fits not thee, thus proudly
    to presage
My ouerthrow ; I know my selfe it is my fate to
    fall
Thus farre from *Phthia* ; yet that Fate, shall faile
    to vent her gall,
Till mine vent thousands. These words vsde, he
    fell to horrid deeds ;
Gaue dreadfull signall ; and forthright, made flie,
    his one-hou'd steeds.

ii. *The Chariot Race* (BOOK XXIII).

                All leapt to chariot ;
And euery man then for the start, cast in, his
    proper lot.
Achilles drew ; *Antilochus*, the lot set foremost
    foorth ;
Eumelus next ; *Atrides* third ; *Meriones* the
    fourth.
The fifth and last, was *Diomed* ; farre first in
    excellence.
All stood in order, and the lists, *Achilles* fixt farre
    thence
In plaine field ; and a seate ordain'd, fast by. In
    which he set
Renowmed *Phœnix*, that in grace, of *Peleus* was so
    great ;

To see the race, and giue a truth, of all their
  passages.
All start together, scourg'd, and cried; and gaue
  their businesse
Study and order. Through the field, they held a
  winged pace.
Beneath the bosome of their steeds, a dust so
  dim'd the race:
It stood aboue their heads in clowds; or like to
  stormes amaz'd.
Manes flew like ensignes with the wind; the
  chariots sometime graz'd,
And sometimes iumpt vp to the aire; yet still sat
  fast the men:
Their spirits euen panting in their breasts, with
  feruour to obtaine,
But when they turn'd to fleet againe: then all
  men's skils were tride;
Then stretcht the pasternes of their steeds.
  Eumelus horse in pride
Still bore their Soueraigne. After them, came
  Diomeds coursers close,
Still apt to leape their chariot, and ready to
  repose
Vpon the shoulders of the king, their heads. His
  backe euen burn'd
With fire, that from their nostrils flew. And then,
  their Lord had turn'd
The race for him, or giuen it doubt, if *Phœbus* had
  not smit
The scourge out of his hands; and teares, of help-
  lesse wrath with it,
From forth his eyes; to see his horse, for want of
  scourge, made slow,

And th' others (by *Apollos* helpe) with much more
    swiftnesse go.

Apollos spite, *Pallas* discern'd, and flew to
    Tydeus sonne ;

His scourge reacht, and his horse made fresh.
    Then tooke her angry run

At king *Eumelus* ; brake his geres ; his mares on
    both sides flew ;

His draught tree fell to earth ; and him, the tost-vp
    chariot threw

Downe to the earth ; his elbowes torne, his fore-
    head, all his face

Strooke at the center ; his speech lost. And then
    the turnèd race

Fell to *Tydides* : before all, his conquering horse he
    draue :

And first he glitter'd in the race : diuine *Athenia*
    gaue

Strength to his horse, and fame to him. Next him,
    draue *Spartas* king.

Antilochus, his fathers horse, then vrg'd, with all
    his sting

Of scourge and voice. Runne low (said he) stretch
    out your lims,

With *Diomeds* horse, I bid not striue ; nor with
    himselfe striue I.

Athenia wings his horse, and him, renowmes.
    Atrides steeds

Are they ye must not faile but reach ; and soone,
    lest soone succeeds

The blot of all your fames : to yeeld, in swiftnesse
    to a mare :

To femall Æthe. Whats the cause (ye best that
    euer were)

That thus ye faile vs ? Be assur'd, that *Nestors* loue
    ye lose

For euer if ye faile his sonne : through both your
    both sides goes

His hote steele, if ye suffer me, to bring the last
    prise home.

Haste, ouertake them instantly ; we needs must
    ouercome.

This harsh way next vs : this my mind, will take ;
    this I despise

For perill ; this Ile creepe through ; hard, the way
    to honor lies.

And that take I, and that shall yeeld. His horse
    by all this knew

He was not pleasde, and fear'd his voice ; and for
    a while, they flew :

But straite, more cleare, appear'd the streight,
    Antilochus foresaw ;

It was a gaspe the earth gaue, forc't, by humours,
    cold and raw,

Pour'd out of Winters watrie breast ; met there,
    and cleauing deepe

All that neare passage to the lists. This *Nestors*
    sonne would keepe,

And left the rode way, being about ; *Atrides*
    fear'd, and cride :

Antilochus ! thy course is mad ; containe thy
    horse ; we ride

A way most dangerous ; turne head, betime take
    larger field,

We shall be splitted. *Nestors* sonne, with much
    more scourge impeld

His horse, for this ; as if not heard ; and got as
    farre before

As any youth can cast a quoyte ; *Atrides* would no
    more ;
He backe againe, for feare himselfe, his goodly
    chariot,
And horse together, strew'd the dust ; in being so
    dustie hote,
Of thirsted conquest. But he chid, at parting,
    passing sore :   [bore :
Antilochus (said he) a worse, then thee, earth neuer
Farewell ; we neuer thought thee wise, that were
    wise ; but not so
Without othes, shall the wreath (be sure) crowne
    thy mad temples, Go.

A BRAVE SPIRIT

GIUE me a spirit that on this lifes rough sea
Loues t' haue his sailes fild with a lustie winde,
Euen till his sayle-yeardes tremble ; his Masts crack,
And his rapt ship runne on her side so lowe
That shee drinkes water, and her keele plowes ayre ;
There is no danger to a man, that knowes
What life and deathe is : there's not any law,
Exceeds his knowledge ; neither is it lawefull
That he should stoope to any other lawe.
He goes before them, and commands them all,
That to him-selfe is a law rationall.

                       Byron's Conspiracie, 1608.

EPITHALAMION TERATOS

COME come deare night, Loues Mart of kisses,
Sweet close of his ambitious line,
The fruitfull summer of his blisses,
Loues glorie doth in darknes shine.

O come soft rest of Cares, come night,
Come naked vertue's only tire,
The reaped haruest of the light
Bound vp in sheaues of sacred fire.
> *Loue cals to warre,*
> *Sighs his Alarmes,*
> *Lips his swords are,*
> *The field his Armes.*

Come Night and lay thy veluet hand
On glorious Dayes outfacing face;
And all thy crouned flames command,
For Torches to our Nuptiall grace.
> *Loue cals to warre,*
> *Sighes his Alarmes,*
> *Lips his swords are,*
> *The field his Armes.*

No neede haue we of factious Day,
To cast in enuie of thy peace,
Her bals of Discord in thy way:
Here beauties day doth neuer cease,
Day is abstracted here,
And varied in a triple sphere,
Hero, Alcmane, Mya, so outshine thee,
Ere thou come here let Thetis thrice refine **thee.**
> *Loue cals to warre,*
> *Sighs his Alarmes,*
> *Lips his swords are,*
> *The field his Armes.*

reaped] reapèd.   crouned] crownèd.

HERCULEAN SILENCE

BEFORE her flew Affliction, girt in storms,
Gasht all with gushing wounds; and all the formes
Of bane, and miserie, frowning in her face;
Whom Tyrranie, and Iniustice, had in Chace;
Grimme Persecution, Pouertie, and Shame;
Detraction, Enuie, foule Mishap and lame;
Scruple of Conscience; Feare, Deceipt, Despaire;
Slaunder, and Clamor, that rent all the Ayre;
Hate, Warre, and Massacre; vncrowned Toyle;
And Sickenes (t' all the rest, the Base, and Foile)
Crept after; and his deadly weight, trode downe
Wealth, Beautie, and the Glorie of a Crowne.
These vsherd her farre of; as figures giuen,
To showe, these Crosses borne, make peace with
    heauen.
But now (made free from them) next her, before;
Peacefull, and young, Herculean silence bore
His craggie Club; which vp, aloft, hee hild;
With which, and his forefingers charme, hee stild
All soundes in ayre; and left so free, mine eares,
That I might heare, the musique of the Spheres,
And all the Angels, singing, out of heauen;
Whose tunes were solemne (as to Passion giuen)
For now, that Iustice was the Happinesse there
For all the wrongs to Right, inflicted here.
Such was the Passion that Peace now put on;
And on all went.

Euthymiae Raptus, 1609.

THE SIRENS' SONG

Come here, thou, worthy of a world of praise ;
That dost so high, the *Grecian* glory raise ;
Vlysses ! stay thy ship ; and that song heare
That none past euer, but it bent his eare :
But left him ravish'd, and instructed more
By vs, then any, euer heard before.
For we know all things whatsoeuer were
In wide *Troy* labour'd ; whatsoeuer there
The *Grecians* and the *Troians* both sustain'd ;
By those high issues that the Gods ordain'd.
And whatsoeuer, all the earth can show
T'informe a knowledge of desert, we know.

Translation of the Odyssey, Book XII.

AN INVOCATION

I long to know
How my dear mistresse fares ; and be informd
What hand she now holds on the troubled bloud
Of her incensed Lord : me thought the Spirit,
(When he had vtterd his perplext presage)
Threw his chang'd countenance headlong into
    clowdes ;
His forehead bent, as it would hide his face ;
He knockt his chin against his darkned breast,
And strooke a churlish silence through his powrs ;
Terror of darknesse : O thou King of flames,
That with thy Musique-footed horse dost strike
The cleare light out of chrystall, on darke earth ;
And hurlst instructive fire about the world :
Wake, wake the drowsie and enchanted night ;

That sleepes with dead eies in this heauy riddle :
Or thou great Prince of shades where neuer sunne
Stickes his far-darted beames : whose eies are
    made,
To see in darknesse : and see euer best
Where sense is blindest : open now the heart
Of thy abashed oracle : that for feare,
Of some ill it includes, would faine lie hid,
And rise thou with it in thy greater light.

Bussy D'Ambois, v. i.

THE HIGH AND GENERAL CAUSE

Good sir, beleeve that no perticular torture
Can force me from my glad obedience
To any thing the high and generall cause,
To match with his whole Fabricke, hath ordainde,
And know yee all (though farre from all your aymes,
Yet worth them all, and all mens endlesse studies)
That in this one thing, all the discipline
Of manners, and of manhood is contain'd ;
A man to ioyne himselfe with th' Vniuerse,
In his maine sway, and make (in all things fit)
One with that all, and goe on, round as it ;
Not plucking from the whole his wretched part,
And into straites, or into nought reuert,
Wishing the compleate Vniuerse might be
Subiect to such a ragge of it as hee :
But to consider great necessitie
All things as well refract, as voluntarie
Reduceth to the prime celestiall cause,
Which he that yeelds to with a mans applause,

And cheeke, by cheeke, goes; crossing it, no
    breath,
But like Gods Image, followes to the death,
That man is truely wise. . . .

Revenge of Bussy D'Ambois, IV. i.

ROBERT SOUTHWELL

1561–1595

LOOK HOME

RETYRED thoughts enioy their owne delights,
    As beautie doth in selfe beholding eye:
Mans mind a mirrour is of heauenlie sights,
    A briefe wherein all meruailes summed lye.
Of fayrest formes, and sweetest shapes the store,
Most graceful all, yet thought may grace them
    more.

The mind a creature is, yet can create,
    To natures patterns adding higher skill:
Of finest works wit better could the state,
    If force of wit had equall power of will.
Deuise of man in working hath no end,
VVhat thought can think an other thought can
    mend.

Mans soule of endlesse beauties image is,
    Drawne by the worke of endles skill and might,
This skilfull might gaue many sparkes of blisse,
    And to discerne this blisse a natiue light,
To frame Gods image as his worthes requird,
His might, his skill, his word, and will conspird.

Retyred] retirèd.   meruailes summed lye] marvels
summèd lie.   wit better could] i. e. wit could better.
Deuise] device.

All that he had his image should present,
　All that it should present he could afford :
To that he could afford his will was bent,
　His will was followed with performing word.
Let this suffize, by this conceiue the rest,
He should, he could, he would, he did the best.

Saint Peters Complaint.

LEWD LOVE IS LOSS

MISDEEMING eye that stoupest to the lure
　Of mortall worthes not worth so worthy loue :
All beauties base, all graces are impure :
　That do thy erring thoughts from God remoue.
Sparkes to the fire, the beames yeelde to the sunne,
All grace to God from whom all graces runne.

If picture moue, more should the patterne please,
　No shaddow can, with shaddowed things compare,
And fayrest shapes whereon our loues do seaze :
　But seely signes of Gods high beauties are.
Goe steruing sence, feede thou on earthly mast,
True loue in Heau'n, seeke thou thy sweet repast.

Gleane not in barren soyle these offall eares,
　Sith reap thou maiest whole haruests of delight.
Base ioyes with griefes, bad hopes doe end in feares ;
　Lewd loue with losse, euill peace with deadly fight :
Gods loue alone doth end with endlesse ease,
VVhose ioyes in hope, whose hope concludes in peace.

seely] simple.

Let not the luring traine of fansies trap,
 Or gratious features proofes of natures skill,
Lull reasons force asleep in errors lap,
 Or draw thy wit to bent of wanton will;
The fayrest flowers, haue not the sweetest smell,
A seeming heauen, proues oft a damning hell.

Selfe-pleasing soules that play with beauties bayte,
 In shyning shroud may swallow fatall hooke,
VVhere eager sight, or semblant faire doth waite,
 A locke it proues that first was but a looke;
The fish with ease into the Net doth glide,
But to get out the way is not so wide.

So long the flie doth dallie with the flame,
 Vntil his singed wings doe force his fall,
So long the eye doth follow fancies game,
 Till loue hath left the hart in heauie thrall;
Soone may the minde be cast in Cupids Iayle,
But hard it is imprisoned thoughts to bayle.

O loath that loue, whose finall ayme is lust,
 Moth of the mind, eclypse of reasons light,
The graue of grace, the mole of natures rust,
 The wrack of wit, the wrong of euery right;
In summe, an euill whose harmes no tongue can tell,
In which to liue is death, to dye is hell.

Saint Peters Complaint, &c.

singed] singèd.

THE BURNING BABE

As I in hoarie Winters night stood shiuering in the
    snow,
Surpris'd I was with sudden heat, which made my
    heart to glow ;
And lifting vp a fearefull eye, to view what fire
    was neere,
A pretie Babe all burning bright did in the ayre
    appeare ;
Who, scorched with excessiue heate, such floods
    of teares did shed,
As though his floods should quench his flames,
    which with his teares were bred :
' Alas ! ' quoth He, ' but newly born in fiery heats
    I fry,
Yet none approch to warme their hearts, or feele
    my fire but I ;
My faultlesse brest the furnace is, the fuell wound-
    ing thornes :
Loue is the fire, and sighes the smoake, the ashes
    shames and scornes ;
The fuell Iustice layeth on, and mercie blowes the
    coales,
The mettall in this Furnace wrought, are men's
    defiled soules :
For which, as now on fire I am to worke them to
    their good,
So will I melt into a bath, to wash them in my blood.'
With this he vanisht out of sight, and swiftly
    shrunke away,
And straight I called vnto mind, that it was
    Christmasse day.   *Saint Peters Complaint.*

scorched] scorchèd.   defiled] defilèd.   called] callèd.

TIMES GO BY TURNS

The lopped tree in time may grow againe,
Most naked plants renew both fruit and flower :
The soriest wight may finde release of paine,
The dryest soyle sucke in some moystning shower.
Times goe, by turnes, and chaunces chaunge by
    course :
From foule to faire : from better happe, to worse.

The sea of fortune doth not euer flowe,
She drawes her fauours to the lowest ebbe :
Her tydes hath equall times to come and goe,
Her Loome doth weaue the fine and coursest webbe.
No ioy so great, but runneth to an end :
No hap so hard, but may in fine amend.

Not alwaies fall of leafe, nor euer spring,
No endles night, yet not eternall day :
The saddest birds a season find to sing,
The roughest storme a calme may soone alay.
Thus with succeeding turnes God tempereth all :
That man may hope to rise, yet feare to fall.

A chaunce may winne that by mischaunce was lost,
The net that holdes no great, takes little fish ;
In some things all, in all things none are crost,
Fewe, all they neede : but none, haue all they
    wish,
Vnmedled ioyes here to no man befall,
VVho least, hath some, who most, hath neuer all.

Saint Peters Complaint.

lopped] loppèd.   Vnmedled] unmixèd.

NEW PRINCE, NEW POMP

BEHOLD, a silly tender Babe,
  In freezing VVinter night,
In homely Manger trembling lyes ;
  Alas a pitious sight :

The Innes are full, no man will yeeld
  This little Pilgrime bed ;
But forc't he is with silly beasts,
  In Crib to shrowd his head.

Despise him not for lying there :
  First what he is enquire :
An orient pearle is often found
  In depth of dirtie mire.

VVaigh not his Crib, his woodden dish,
  Nor beasts that by him feed :
VVaigh not his Mothers poore attire,
  Nor *Iosephs* simple weed.

This Stable is a Princes Court,
  The Crib his chaire of State :
The Beasts are parcell of his Pompe,
  The woodden dish his plate.

The persons, in that poore attire,
  His royall liueries weare,
The Prince himselfe is com'n from heauen,
  This pompe is prizèd there.

With ioy approach, O Christian wight,
  Doe homage to thy King ;
And highly prayse his humble Pompe,
  Which He from Heauen doth bring.

                              Saint Peters Complaint.

FRANCIS BACON
1561–1626

LIFE

THE world's a bubble, and the life of man
     lesse then a span,
In his conception wretched, from the wombe
     so to the tombe :
Curst from the cradle, and brought vp to yeares,
     with cares and feares.
Who then to fraile mortality shall trust,
But limmes the water, or but writes in dust.

Yet since with sorrow here we liue opprest :
     what life is best ?
Courts are but only superficiall scholes
     to dandle fooles.
The rurall parts are turn'd into a den
     of sauage men.
And wher 's a city from all vice so free,
But may be term'd the worst of all the three ?

Domesticke cares afflict the husbands bed,
     or paines his head :
Those that liue single take it for a curse,
     or doe things worse.
Some would have children, those that have them,
  mone,
       or wish them gone.
What is it then to haue or haue no wife,
But single thraldome, or a double strife ?

limmes] paints.   the three] i. e. the Court, the
Country, and the City. mone] moan.

Our owne affections still at home to please,
                         is a disease,
To crosse the sea to any foreine soyle,
                         perills and toyle.
Warres with their noyse affright vs : when they
    cease,
                              W'are worse in peace.
What then remaines ? but that we still should cry,
Not to be borne, or, being borne, to dye.

Florilegium Epigrammatum Graecorum.

HENRY CONSTABLE

1562(?)–1613(?)

DAMELUS' SONG TO HIS DIAPHENIA

Diaphenia like the Daffadown-dillie,
White as the Sunne, faire as the Lillie,
     heigh hoe, how I doo loue thee ?
I doo loue thee as my Lambs
Are beloued of their Dams,
          how blest were I if thou would'st proue me ?

Diaphenia like the spreading Roses,
That in thy sweetes all sweetes incloses,
          faire sweete, how I doo loue thee ?
I doo loue thee as each flower,
Loues the Sunnes life-giuing power.
          for dead, thy breath to life might moue me.

still at home] continually at home.
     Daffadown-dillie] poetic form of daffodil.   beloued]
beloved.   for dead] i. e. for, were I dead.

Diaphenia like to all things blessed,
When all thy praises are expressed,
    deare Ioy, how I doo loue thee ?
As the birds doo loue the Spring :
Or the Bees their carefull King,
    then in requite, sweet Virgin loue me.

SAMUEL DANIEL

1562–1619

CARE-CHARMER SLEEP

Care-charmer Sleep, sonne of the sable night,
    Brother to death, in silent darknes borne :
    Relieue my languish, and restore the light,
    With darke forgetting of my cares returne.
And let the day be time enough to mourne
    The shipwrack of my ill aduentied youth :
    Let waking eues suffise to waile their scorne,
    Without the torment of the nights vntruth.
Cease dreames, th' Images of day desires,
    To modell forth the passions of the morrow :
    Neuer let rising Sunne approue you liers,
    To adde more griefe to aggrauate my sorrow.
Still let me sleep, imbracing clouds in vaine,
And neuer wake to feele the daies disdaine.

    blessed] blessèd.   expressed] expressèd.
    restore the light] i. e. of unconsciousness. ill aduentied]
ill-adventured.

THE DEATH OF TALBOT

(From the *Civil Wars*)

WHILST *Talbot*, whose fresh spirit hauing got
A meruailous aduantage of his yeeres,
Carries his vnfelt age as if forgot,
Whirling about where any need appeares :
His hand, his eye, his wits all present, wrought
The function of the glorious part he beares :
Now vrging here, now cheering there, he flyes,
Vnlocks the thickest troupes, where most force lyes.

In midst of wrath, of wounds, of blood, and
death,
There is he most, where as he may do best :
And there the closest rankes he severeth,
Driues backe the stoutest powres that forward
prest :
There makes his sword his way, there laboreth
Th'infatigable hands that neuer rest,
Scorning vnto his mortall woundes to yeeld
Till death become best maister of the field.

Then like a sturdie Oke that hauing long
Against the warres of fiercest windes made head,
When with some forst tempestuous rage, more
strong,
His downe-borne top comes over-maistered,
All the neere bordering Trees he stood among,
Crusht with his waightie fall, lie ruined :
So lay his spoyles, all round about him slaine,
T'adorne his death, that could not die in vaine.

meruailous] marvellous.   maister] master.   forst]
forced.

On th' other part, his most all-daring sonne,
(Although the inexperience of his yeeres
Made him lesse skild in what was to be done,
Yet did it thrust him on beyond all feares)
Flying into the maine Battallion,
Neare to the King, amidst the chiefest Peeres,
With thousand wounds, became at length opprest,
As if he scornd to die, but with the best.

Who thus both hauing gaind a glorious end,
Soone ended that great day, that set so red,
As all the purple plaines that wide extend,
A sad tempestious season witnessed :
So much ado had toyling *Fraunce* to rend
From vs, the right so long inherited :
And so hard went we from what we possest,
As with it, went the blood we loued best.

Which blood not lost, but fast layd vp with
heed
In euerlasting fame, is there held deere,
To seale the memorie of this dayes deed,
Th' eternal euidence of what we were :
To which our Fathers, wee, and who succeed,
Doe owe a sigh, for that it toucht vs neere :
Who must not sinne so much as to neglect
The holy thought of such a deere respect.

The Civil Wars, Book **V.**

ULYSSES AND THE SYREN

Syren.   COME worthy Greeke, *Vlisses* come
Possesse these shores with me :
The windes and Seas are troublesome,
And heere we may be free.
    Here may we sit, and view their toile
That trauaile in the deepe,
And ioy the day in mirth the while,
And spend the night in sleepe.

Vlis.   Faire Nimph, if fame, or honor were
To be attaynd with ease
Then would I come, and rest with thee,
And leaue such toyles as these.
    But here it dwels, and here must I
With danger seeke it forth,
To spend the time luxuriously
Becomes not men of worth.

Syr.   *Vlisses*, O be not deceiu'd
With that vnreall name :
This honour is a thing conceiu'd,
And rests on others fame.
    Begotten onely to molest
Our peace, and to beguile
(The best thing of our life) our rest,
And giue vs vp to toile.

Vlis.   Delicious Nimph, suppose there were
Nor honour, nor report,
Yet manlines would scorne to weare
The time in idle sport.

For toyle doth giue a better touch,
To make vs feele our ioy ;
And ease findes tediousnesse as much
As labour yeelds annoy.

Syr. Then pleasure likewise seemes the shore,
Whereto tends all your toyle,
Which you forgo to make it more,
And perish oft the while.
Who may disporte them diuersly
Finde neuer tedious day,
And ease may haue varietie,
As well as action may.

Vlis. But natures of the noblest frame
These toyles, and dangers please,
And they take comfort in the same,
As much as you in ease.
And with the thought of actions past
Are recreated still ;
When pleasure leaues a touch at last,
To shew that it was ill.

Syr. That doth opinion onely cause,
That's out of custome bred,
Which makes vs many other lawes
Then euer Nature did.
No widdowes waile for our delights,
Our sportes are without bloud,
The world we see by warlike wights
Receiues more hurt then good.

Vlis. But yet the state of things require
These motions of vnrest,
And these great Spirits of high desire
Seeme borne to turne them best.

To purge the mischiefes that increase,
And all good order mar :
For oft we see a wicked peace
To be well chang'd for war.

Syr. Well, well *Vlisses* then I see,
I shall not haue thee heere,
And therefore I will come to thee,
And take my fortunes there.
  I must be wonne that cannot win,
Yet lost were I not wonne :
For beauty hath created bin,
T' vndoo, or be vndonne.

A REMINISCENCE OF EARLY LOVE

AH I remember well (and how can I
But euer more remember well) when first
Our flame began, when scarce we knew what was
The flame we felt, when as we sate and sigh'd
And look'd vpon each other, and conceiu'd
Not what we ayld, yet something we did ayle.
And yet were well, and yet we were not well,
And what was our disease we could not tell.
Then would we kisse, then sigh, then looke : and
  thus
In that first garden of our simplenesse
We spent our child-hood : but when yeeres began
To reape the fruite of knowledge ; ah how then
Would she with grauer looks, with sweet stern brow
Check my presumption and my forwardnes,
Yet still would giue me flowers, stil would me shew
What she would haue me, yet not haue me know.

Hymens Trivmph.

TO THE LADY MARGARET, COUNTESS
OF CUMBERLAND

HE that of such a height hath built his minde,
And rear'd the dwelling of his thoughts so strong,
As neither feare nor hope can shake the frame
Of his resolued pow'rs, nor all the winde
Of vanitie or malice pierce to wrong
His setled peace, or to disturbe the same ;
What a faire seate hath he, from whence he may
The boundlesse wastes and weilds of man suruay.

And with how free an eye doth he looke downe
Vpon these lower regions of turmoyle,
Where all the stormes of passions mainly beat
On flesh and bloud, where honour, pow'r, renowne
Are onely gay afflictions, golden toyle,
Where greatnesse stands vpon as feeble feet
As frailty doth, and onely great doth seeme
To little minds, who doe it so esteeme.

He lookes vpon the mightiest Monarchs warres
But onely as on stately robberies,
Where euermore the fortune that preuailes
Must be the right, the ill-succeeding marres
The fairest and the best-fac't enterprize :
Great Pirat *Pompey* lesser Pirats quailes,
Iustice, he sees, as if seduced, still
Conspires with pow'r, whose cause must not be ill.

He sees the face of *Right* t'appeare as manifolde
As are the passions of vncertaine man,
Who puts it in all colours, all attires,
To serue his ends and make his courses holde :

weilds] wilds.   suruay] survey.

He sees, that let Deceit worke what it can,
Plot and contriue base wayes to high desires,
That the all-guiding Prouidence doth yet
All disappoint, and mocks this smoake of wit.

Nor is he mou'd with all the thunder-cracks
Of Tyrants threats, or with the surly brow
Of power, that proudly sits on others crimes,
Charg'd with more crying sinnes then those he
    checks ;
The stormes of sad confusion, that may grow
Vp in the present, for the comming times,
Appall not him, that hath no side at all
But of himselfe, and knowes the worst can fall.

Although his heart so neere allied to earth,
Cannot but pitty the perplexed State
Of troublous and distrest mortalitie,
That thus make way vnto the ougly birth
Of their owne sorrowes, and doe still beget
Affliction vpon imbecillitie :
Yet seeing thus the course of things must runne,
He lookes thereon, not strange : but as foredone.

And whilst distraught Ambition compasses
And is incompast, whil'st as craft deceiues
And is deceiued, whil'st man doth ransacke man,
And builds on bloud, and rises by distresse,
And th' inheritance of desolation leaues
To great expecting hopes, he lookes thereon
As from the shore of peace with vnwet eie,
And beares no venture in impietie.

ougly] ugly.

Thus, Madam, fares the man that hath prepar'd
A rest for his desires, and sees all things
Beneath him, and hath learn'd this booke of man,
Full of the notes of frailty, and compar'd
The best of glory with her sufferings,
By whom I see you labour all you can
To plant your heart, and set your thoughts as neare
His glorious mansion as your pow'rs can beare.

Which, Madam, are so soundly fashioned
By that cleere iudgement that hath carryed you
Beyond the feeble limits of your kinde,
As they can stand against the strongest head
Passion can make, inur'd to any hue
The world can cast, that cannot cast that minde
Out of her forme of goodnesse, that doth see
Both what the best and worst of earth can be.

Which makes, that whatsoeuer here befalles,
You in the region of your selfe remaine,
Where no vaine breath of th' impudent molests,
That hath secur'd within the brasen walles
Of a cleere conscience, that without all staine
Rises in peace, in innocencie rests,
Whilst all what malice from without procures,
Shewes her owne ougly heart, but hurts not yours.

And whereas none reioyce more in reuenge
Then women vse to doe, yet you well know,
That wrong is better checkt by being contemn'd
Then being pursu'd leaving to him t' auenge
To whom it appertaines ; wherein you show
How worthily your cleerenesse hath condemn'd
Base malediction, liuing in the darke,
That at the raies of goodnesse still doth barke.

Knowing the heart of man is set to be
The centre of this world, about the which
These reuolutions of disturbances
Still roule, where all th' aspects of miserie
Predominate, whose strong effects are such
As he must beare, being pow'rlesse to redresse ;
And that vnlesse aboue himselfe he can
Erect himselfe, how poore a thing is man !

And how turmoyl'd they are, that leuell lie
With earth, and cannot lift themselues from thence ;
That neuer are at peace with their desires,
But worke beyond their yeeres, and euen denie
Dotage her rest, and hardly will dispence
With death : that when ability expires,
Desire liues still : so much delight they haue
To carry toyle and trauell to the graue.

Whose ends you see, and what can be the best
They reach vnto, when they haue cast the summe
And reckonings of their glory, and you know
This floting life hath but this Port of rest,
A heart prepar'd that feares no ill to come :
And that mans greatnesse rests but in his show,
The best of all whose dayes consumed are,
Either in warre, or peace conceiuing warre.

This concord, Madame, of a well-tun'd minde
Hath beene so set, by that all-working hand
Of heauen, that though the world hath done his
    worst
To put it out, by discords most vnkinde,

roule] roll.   trauell] travail.

Yet doth it still in perfect vnion stand
With God and man, nor euer will be forc't
From that most sweet accord, but still agree
Equall in Fortunes inequality.

And this note (Madame) of your worthinesse
Remaines recorded in so many hearts,
As time nor malice cannot wrong your right,
In th' inheritance of Fame you must possesse,
You that haue built you by your great deserts,
Out of small meanes, a farre more exquisit
And glorious dwelling for your honoured name
Then all the gold that leaden minds can frame.

THE TREASURE OF OUR TONGUE

Power above powers, O heauenly *Eloquence*,
   That with the strong reine of commanding words,
   Dost manage, guide, and master th' eminence
   Of men's affections, more than all their swords :
   Shall we not offer to thy excellence
   The richest treasure that our wit affoords ?

Thou that canst do much more with one poor pen
   Then all the powers of princes can effect :
   And draw, diuert, dispose, and fashion men
   Better then force or rigour can direct —
   Should we this ornament of glorie then
   As th' vnmateriall fruits of shades neglect ?

Or should we carelesse come behind the rest
   In power of words, that go before in worth,
   When as our accents equall to the best
   Is able greater wonders to bring forth :
   When all that euer hotter spirits exprest
   Comes bettered by the patience of the North ?

And who in time knowes whither we may vent
   The treasure of our tongue, to what strange shores
   This gain of our best glorie shall be sent,
T' inrich vnknoweing Nations with our stores ?
   What worlds in th' yet vnformed Occident
   May come refin'd with th' accents that are ours ?

Or who can tell for what great worke in hand
   The greatnes of our stile is now ordain'd ?
   What powers it shall bring in, what spirits
      command,
   What thoughts let out, what humors keep
      restraind,
   What mischieef it may powerfully withstand,
   And what faire ends may thereby be attain'd ?

LOVE IS A SICKNESS

Loue is a sicknesse full of woes,
   All remedies refusing :
A plant that with most cutting growes,
   Most barren with best using.
          Why so ?
More we enjoy it, more it dyes,
If not enioy'd, it sighing cries,
          Hey ho.

Loue is a torment of the minde,
   A tempest euerlasting ;
And Ioue hath made it of a kinde,
   Not well, nor full nor fasting.
          Why so ?
More we enioy it, more it dyes,
If not enioyd, it sighing cries,
          Hey ho.

SHADOWS

Are they shadowes that we see ?
And can shadowes pleasure giue ?
　Pleasures onely shadowes bee,
　Cast by bodies we conceiue,
　And are made the thinges we deeme,
　In those figures which they seeme.
But these pleasures vanish fast,
Which by shadowes are exprest.
　Pleasures are not, if they last,
　In their passing, is their best.
　Glory is most bright and gay
　In a flash, and so away.
Feed apace then greedy eyes
On the wonder you behold.
　Take it sodaine as it flies
　Though you take it not to hold :
　When your eyes haue done their part,
　Thought must length it in the hart.

sodaine] sudden.

JOSHUA SYLVESTER

1563–1618

SONNET

WERE I as base as is the lowly plaine,
And you (my loue) as high as heau'n aboue,
Yet should the thoughts of me your humble swaine,
Ascend to heau'n, in honour of my loue.
Were I as high as heau'n aboue the plaine,
And you (my loue) as humble and as low
As are the deepest bottoms of the Mayne,
Whereso'ere you were, with you my loue should go,
Were you the earth (dear loue) and I the skies,
My loue should shine on you like to the Sun,
And looke vpon you with ten thousand eyes,
Till heau'n wax't blind, and till the world were dun.

Whereso'ere I am, below, or else aboue you,
Whereso'ere you are, my heart shall truly loue
you.

A CONTENTED MIND

I WAIGH not Fortunes frowne or smile,
I joy not much in earthly Joyes,
I seeke not state, I reake not stile,
I am not fond of fancies Toyes :
I rest so pleas'd with what I have,
I wish no more, no more I crave.

I quake not at the Thunders crack,
I tremble not at noise of warre,
I swound not at the newes of wrack,
I shrink not at a Blazing-Starre ;
I feare not losse, I hope not gaine,
I envie none, I none disdaine.

I see Ambition never pleas'd,
I see some *Tantals* starv'd in store,
I see golds dropsie seldome eas'd,
I see even *Midas* gape for more :
    I neither want, nor yet abound,
    Enough's a Feast, content is crown'd.

I faine not friendship where I hate,
I fawne not on the great (in show),
I prize, I praise a meane estate,
Neither too lofty nor too low :
    This, this is all my choice, my cheere,
    A minde content, a conscience clere.

MICHAEL DRAYTON

1563–1631

AGINCOURT

FAIRE stood the Wind for *France,*
When we our Sayles aduance,
Nor now to proue our chance,
    Longer will tarry ;
But putting to the Mayne,
At *Kaux,* the Mouth of *Sene,*
With all his Martiall Trayne,
    Landed King HARRY.

And taking many a Fort,
Furnish'd in Warlike sort,
Marcheth tow'rds *Agincourt,*
    In happy howre ;
Skirmishing day by day,
With those that stop'd his way,
Where the *French* Gen'rall lay,
    With all his Power.

faine] feign.

Which in his Hight of Pride,
King HENRY to deride,
His Ransome to prouide
    To the King sending.
Which he neglects the while,
As from a Nation vile,
Yet with an angry smile,
    Their fall portending.

And turning to his Men,
Quoth our braue HENRY then,
Though they to one be ten,
    Be not amazed.
Yet haue we well begunne,
Battles so brauely wonne,
Haue euer to the Sonne,
    By Fame beene raysed.

And, for my Selfe (quoth he),
This my full rest shall be,
England ne'r mourne for Me,
    Nor more esteeme me.
Victor I will remaine,
Or on this Earth lie slaine,
Neuer shall Shee sustaine,
    Losse to redeeme me.

Poiters and *Cressy* tell,
When most their Pride did swell,
Vnder our Swords they fell,
    No lesse our skill is,
Than when our Grandsire Great,
Clayming the Regall Seate,
By many a Warlike feate,
    Lop'd the *French* Lillies.

amazed] amazèd.

The Duke of *Yorke* so dread,
The eager Vaward led ;
With the maine, HENRY sped,
    Among'st his Hench-men.
EXCESTER had the Rere,
A Brauer man not there,
O Lord, how hot they were,
    On the false *French-men* !

They now to fight are gone,
Armour on Armour shone,
Drumme now to Drumme did grone,
    To heare, was wonder ;
That with the cryes they make,
The very Earth did shake,
Trumpet to Trumpet spake,
    Thunder to Thunder.

Well it thine Age became,
O Noble ERPINGHAM,
Which didst the Signall ayme,
    To our hid Forces ;
When from a Medow by,
Like a Storme suddenly
The *English* Archery
    Stuck the *French* Horses,

With *Spanish* Ewgh so strong,
Arrowes a Cloth-yard long,
That like to Serpents stung,
    Piercing the Weather ;
None from his fellow starts,
But playing Manly parts,
And like true *English* hearts,
    Stuck close together.

EXCESTER] Exeter.   Ewgh] yew.

When downe their Bowes they threw,
And forth their Bilbowes drew,
And on the French they flew,
　　Not one was tardie ;
Armes were from shoulders sent,
Scalpes to the Teeth were rent,
Downe the *French* Pesants went,
　　Our Men were hardie.

This while our Noble King,
His broad Sword brandishing,
Downe the *French* Hoast did ding,
　　As to o'r-whelme it ;
And many a deepe Wound lent,
His Armes with Bloud besprent,
And many a cruell Dent
　　Bruised his Helmet.

GLOSTER, that Duke so good,
Next of the Royall Blood,
For famous *England* stood,
　　With his braue Brother ;
CLARENCE, in Steele so bright,
Though but a Maiden Knight,
Yet in that furious Fight,
　　Scarce such another.

WARWICK in Bloud did wade,
OXFORD the Foe inuade,
And cruell slaughter made,
　　Still as they ran vp ;
SVFFOLKE his Axe did ply,
BEAVMONT and WILLOVGHBY
Bare them right doughtily,
　　FERRERS and FANHOPE.

Bilbowes] swords from Bilboa.　**Bruised]** bruised.

Vpon Saint CRISPIN's day
Fought was this Noble Fray,
Which Fame did not delay,
  To *England* to carry ;
O, when shall *English* Men
With such Acts fill a Pen,
Or *England* breed againe,
  Such a King HARRY ?

LOVE'S FAREWELL

SINCE there 's no helpe, Come let vs kisse and part,
Nay, I haue done : You get no more of Me,
And I am glad, yea glad withall my heart,
That thus so cleanly, I my Selfe can free,
Shake hands for euer, Cancell all our Vowes,
And when we meet at any time againe,
Be it not seene in either of our Browes,
That We one iot of former Loue reteyne ;
Now at the last gaspe of Loues latest Breath,
When his Pulse fayling, Passion speechlesse lies,
When Faith is kneeling by his bed of Death,
And Innocence is closing vp his Eyes,
    Now if thou would'st, when all haue giuen him
      ouer,
    From Death to Life, thou might'st him yet
      recouer.

cleanly] entirely.   reteyne] retain.

DAFFODIL

BATTE. *Gorbo*, as thou cam'st this waye
By yonder little hill,
Or as thou through the fields didst straye
Sawst thou my *Daffadill* ?

Shee's in a frock of Lincolne greene
The colour maides delight
And neuer hath her beauty seen
But through a vale of white.

Then Roses richer to behold
That trim vp louers bowers,
The Pansy and the Marigould
Tho *Phœbus* Paramours.

GORBO. Thou well describ'st the Daffadill.
It is not full an hower
Since by the spring neare yonder hill
I saw that louely flower.

BATTE. Yet my faire flower thou didst not meet,
Nor news of her didst bring,
And yet my Daffadill more sweete,
Then that by yonder spring.

GORBO. I saw a shepheard that doth keepe
In yonder field of Lillies,
Was making (as he fed his sheepe)
A wreathe of Daffadillies.

BATTE. Yet *Gorbo* thou delud'st me stil
My flower thou didst not see,
For know my pretie *Daffadill*
Is worne of none but me.

To shew it selfe but neare her seate,
No Lilly is so bould,
Except to shade her from the heate,
Or keepe her from the colde:

GORBO.   Through yonder vale as I did passe,
Descending from the hill,
I met a smerking bony lasse,
They call her *Daffadill*:

Whose presence as along she went,
The prety flowers did greet,
As though their heads they downward
    bent,
With homage to her feete.

And all the shepheards that were nie,
From toppe of euery hille,
Vnto the vallies lowe did crie,
There goes sweet *Daffadill*.

BATTE.   I gentle shepheard, now with joy
Thou all my flockes dost fill,
That's she alone kind shepheards boy,
Let vs to *Daffadill*.

QUEEN MAB VISITS PIGWIGGEN, THE FAIRY KNIGHT

HER Chariot ready straight is made,
Each thing therein is fitting layde,
That she by nothing might be stayde,
    For naught must be her letting,
Foure nimble Gnats the Horses were,
Their Harnesses of Gossamere,
Flye Cranion her Chariottere,
    Vpon the Coach-box getting.

Her Chariot of a Snayles fine shell,
Which for the colours did excell :
The faire Queene *Mab*, becomming well,
  So liuely was the limming :
The seate the soft wool of the Bee ;
The couer, (gallantly to see)
The wing of a pyde Butterflee
  I trowe t'was simple trimming.

The wheeles compos'd of Crickets bones,
And daintily made for the nonce,
For feare of rattling on the stones,
  With Thistle-downe they shod it ;
For all her Maydens much did feare,
If *Oberon* had chanc'd to heare,
That *Mab* his Queene should haue bin there,
  He would not haue aboad it.

She mounts her Chariot with a trice,
Nor would she stay for no advice,
Vntill her Maydes that were so nice,
  To wayte on her were fitted,
But ranne her selfe away alone ;
Which when they heard there was not one,
But hasted after to be gone,
  As she had been diswitted.

Hop, and *Mop*, and *Drop* so cleare,
Pip, and *Trip*, and *Skip* that were,
To *Mab* their Soueraigne euer deare :
  Her speciall Maydes of Honour ;
Fib, and *Tib*, and *Pinck*, and *Pin*,
Tick, and *Quick*, and *Iill*, and *Iin*,
Tit, and *Nit*, and *Wap*, and *Win*,
  The Trayne that wayte vpon her.

Vpon a Grasshopper they got,
And what with Amble, and with Trot,
For hedge nor ditch they spared not,
   But after her they hie them.
A Cobweb ouer them they throw,
To shield the winde if it should blowe,
Themselues they wisely could bestow,
   Lest any should espie them.

Nimphidia, or the Court of Fayris.

PIGWIGGEN PREPARES FOR THE FIGHT
WITH KING OBERON

[HE] quickly Armes him for the Field,
A little Cockle-shell his Shield,
Which he could very brauely wield :
   Yet could it not be pierced :
His Speare a Bent both stiffe and strong,
And well-neere of two Inches long ;
The Pyle was of a Horse-flyes tongue,
   Whose sharpnesse nought reuersed.

And puts him on a coat of Male,
Which was of a Fishes scale,
That when his Foe should him assaile,
   No poynt should be preuayling ;
His Rapier was a Hornets sting,
It was a very dangerous thing :
For if he chanc'd to hurt the King,
   It would be long in healing.

His Helmet was a Bettles head,
Most horrible and full of dread,
That able was to strike one dead,
   Yet it did well become him :

Bettles] beetle's.

And for a plume, a horses hayre,
Which being tossed with the ayre,
Had force to strike his Foe with feare,
    And turne his weapon from him.

Himselfe he on an Earewig set,
Yet scarce he on his back could get,
So oft and high did he coruet,
    Ere he himself could settle :
He made him turne, and stop, and bound,
To gallop, and to trot the Round,
He scarce could stand on any ground,
        He was so full of mettle.

Nimphidia, or the Court of Fayrie.

TO THE VIRGINIAN VOYAGE

You braue Heroique minds,
Worthy your Countries Name ;
    That Honour still pursue,
    Goe, and subdue,
Whilst loyt'ring Hinds
Lurke here at home, with shame.

Britans, you stay too long,
Quickly aboard bestow you,
    And with a merry Gale
    Swell your stretch'd Sayle,
With Vowes as strong,
As the Winds that blow you.

Your Course securely steere,
West and by South forth keepe,
    Rocks, Lee-shores, nor Sholes,
    When EOLUS scowles,
You need not feare,
So absolute the Deepe.

And cheerefully at Sea,
Successe you still intice,
    To get the Pearle and Gold,
    And ours to hold,
VIRGINIA,
Earth's onely Paradise.

Where Nature hath in store
Fowle, Venison, and Fish,
    And the Fruitfull'st Soyle,
    Without your Toyle,
Three Haruests more,
All greater then your Wish.

And the ambitious Vine
Crownes with his purple Masse,
    The cedar reaching hie
    To kisse the Sky.
The Cypresse, Pine
And vse-full Sassafras.

To whome, the golden Age
Still Natures lawes doth give
    No other Cares that tend,
    But Them to defend
From Winters rage,
That long there doth not liue.

When as the Lushious smell
Of that delicious Land,
    Aboue the Seas that flowes,
    The cleere Wind throwes,
Your Hearts to swell
Approaching the deare Strande.

In kenning of the Shore
(Thanks to God first giuen,)
   O you the happy'st men,
    Be Frolike then,
Let Cannons roare,
Frighting the wide Heauen.

And in Regions farre
Such Heroes bring yee foorth,
   As those from whom We came,
    And plant Our name,
Vnder that Starre
Not knowne vnto our North.

And as there Plenty growes
Of Lawrell euery where,
   APOLLO's Sacred tree,
    You may it see,
A Poets Browes
To crowne, that may sing there.

Thy Voyages attend,
Industrious HACKLVIT,
   Whose Reading shall inflame
    Men to seeke Fame,
And much commend
To after-Times thy Wit.

     Hacklvit] Hakluyt.

LOVE'S PROVERBS

As Loue and I, late harbour'd in one Inne,
With Prouerbs thus each other intertaine :
In Loue there is no lack, thus I begin,
Faire words make Fooles, replyeth he againe :
Who sparcs to speake, doth spare to speed (quoth I)
As well (sayth he) too forward, as too slow ;
Fortune assists the boldest, I reply,
A hastie Man (quoth he) ne'r wanted Woe ;
Labour is light, where Loue (quoth I) doth pay,
(Saith he) Light Burthen's heauy, if farre borne ;
(Quoth I) The Maine lost, cast the By away ;
You haue spunne a faire Thred, he replyes in scorne.
   And hauing thus awhile each other thwarted,
   Fooles as we met, so Fooles againe we parted.

SIRENA

Neare to the Siluer *Trent,*
  Sirena dwelleth :
Shee to whom Nature lent
  All that excelleth :
By which the *Muses* late,
  And the neate *Graces,*
Haue for their greater state
  Taken their places :
Twisting an *Anadem,*
  Wherewith to Crowne her,
As it belong'd to them
  Most to renowne her.
Chorus. On thy Bancke,
  In a Rancke,
Let the swanes sing her,
  And with their Musick,
Along let them bring her.

swanes] swans.

Tagus and *Pactolus*
   Are to thee Debter,
Nor for their gould to vs
   Are they the better:
Henceforth of all the rest,
   Be thou the Riuer,
Which as the daintiest,
   Puts them downe euer,
For as my precious one,
   O'r thee doth trauell,
She to Pearl Parragon
   Turneth thy grauell.
     Chorus.

Our mournefull *Philomell*,
   That rarest Tuner,
Henceforth in *Aperill*
   Shall wake the sooner,
And to her shall complaine
   From the thicke Couer,
Redoubling euery straine
   Ouer and ouer:
For when my Loue too long
   Her Chamber keepeth;
As though it suffered wrong,
   The Morning weepeth.
     Chorus.

Oft have I seene the Sunne
   To doe her honour.
Fix himselfe at his noone,
   To look vpon her,
And hath guilt every Groue,
   Euery Hill neare her,

With his flames from aboue,
  Striuing to cheere her,
And when shee from his sight
  Hath her selfe turned,
He as it had beene night
  In Cloudes hath mourned,
    Chorus.

The Verdant Meades are seene,
  When she doth view them,
In fresh and gallant Greene,
  Straight to renewe them,
And euery little Grasse
  Broad it selfe spreadeth,
Proud that this bonny Lasse
  Vpon it treadeth :
Nor flower is so sweete
  In this large Cincture
But it upon her feete
  Leaueth some Tincture.
    Chorus.

The Fishes in the Flood,
  When she doth Angle,
For the Hooke striue a good
  Them to intangle ;
And leaping on the Land
  From the cleare water,
Their Scales vpon the sand,
  Lauishly scatter ;
Therewith to paue the mould
  Whereon she passes,
So her selfe to behold,
  As in her glasses.
    Chorus.

turned] turnèd.   mourned] mournèd.

When shee lookes out by night,
　The Starres stand gazing,
Like Commets to our sight
　Fearefully blazing,
As wondring at her eyes
　With their much brightnesse,
Which to amaze the skies,
　Dimming their lightnesse,
The raging Tempests are calme,
　When shee speaketh,
Such most delightsome balme
　From her lips breaketh.
　　　Chorus.

In all our *Brittany*,
　Ther's not a fayrer,
Nor can you fitt any :
　Should you compare her.
Angels her eye-lids keepe
　All harts surprizing,
Which looke whilst she doth sleepe
　Like the Sunnes rising :
She alone of her kinde
　Knoweth true measure
And her vnmatched mind
　Is Heauens treasure :
　　　Chorus.

Fayre *Dove* and *Darwine* cleere
　Boast yee your beauties,
To *Trent* your Mistres here
　Yet pay your duties,
My Loue was higher borne
　Tow'rds the full Fountaines,
　　vnmatched] unmatchèd.

Yet she doth *Moorland* scorne,
  And the *Peake* Mountaines;
Nor would she none should dreame,
  Where she abideth,
Humble as is the streame,
  Which by her slydeth,
    Chorus.

Yet my poore Rusticke *Muse*,
  Nothing can moue her,
Nor the means I can vse,
  Though her true Louer:
Many a long Winters night,
  Haue I wak'd for her,
Yet this my piteous plight,
  Nothing can stirre her.
All thy Sands Siluer *Trent*
  Down to the *Humber*,
The sighes I haue spent,
  Neuer can number.
    Chorus.

UPON A BANK

VPPON a bank with roses set about
where pretty turtles ioyning bil to bil,
and gentle springs steale softly murmuring out
washing the foote of pleasures sacred hill:
  there little love sore wounded lyes,
  his bowe and arrowes broken
  bedewd with teares from Venus eyes
  oh greeuous to be spoken.

                greeuous] grievous.

Beare him my hart slaine with her scornefull eye
where sticks the arrowe that poore hart did kill
with whose sharp pile request him ere he die,
about the same to write his latest will,
    and bid him send it back to me
    at instant of his dying,
    that cruell cruell shee may see
    my faith and her denying.

His chapell be a mournefule Cypresse shade
and for a chauntry Philomels sweet lay
where prayers shall continually be made
by pilgrim louers passing by that way.
    with Nymphes and shepheards yearly moane
    his timeles death beweeping,
    in telling that my hart alone
    hath his last will in keeping.

CHRISTOPHER MARLOWE

1564–1593

THE PASSIONATE SHEPHERD TO HIS LOVE

Come liue with mee and be my loue,
And we will all the pleasures proue,
That hills and valleys, dales and fields,
And all the craggy mountain yeeldes.

There we will sit vpon the Rocks,
And see the sheepheards feede theyr flocks
By shallow riuers, to whose falls
Melodious byrds sing Madrigalls.

And I will make thee beds of Roses,
And a thousand fragrant poesies,
A cap of flowers, and a kirtle,
Imbroydered all with leaues of Mirtle.

A gowne made of the finest wooll,
Which from our pretty Lambes we pull,
Fayre lined slippers for the cold,
With buckles of the purest gold.

A belt of straw and Iuie buds,
With Corall clasps and Amber studs,
And if these pleasures may thee moue,
Come liue with mee, and be my loue.

The sheepheard swains shall daunce and sing
For thy delight each May-morning.
If these delights thy minde may moue,
Then liue with mee, and be my loue.

THE POET'S PEN

If all the pens that euer poets held,
Had fed the feeling of their maisters thoughts,
And euery sweetnes that inspir'd their harts,
Their minds, and muses on admyred theames :
If all the heauenly Quintessence they still
From their immortall flowers of Poesy,
Wherein as in a myrrour we perceiue
The highest reaches of a humaine wit.
If these had made one Poems period
And all combin'd in Beauties worthiness,
Yet should ther houer in their restlesse heads,
One thought, one grace, one wonder at the least,
Which into words no vertue can digest.

1 Tamburlaine the Great, **v.** i.

Fayre lined] fair-linèd.   Iuie] ivy.
admyred] admirèd.   still] 'still.   houer] hover.

PRECIOUS STONES

THE wealthy Moore, that in the Easterne rockes,
Without controule can picke his riches vp,
And in his house heape pearle like pibble-stones;
Receiue them free, and sell them by the weight,
Bags of fiery *Opals*, *Saphires*, *Amatists*,
Iacints, hard *Topas*, grass-greene *Emeraulds*,
Beauteous *Rubyes*, sparkling *Diamonds*,
And seildsene costly stones of so great price,
As one of them indifferently rated,
And of a Carrect of this quantity,
May serue in peril of calamity
To ransome great Kings from captiuity.
This is the ware wherein consists my wealth:
And thus me thinkes should men of iudgement
     frame
Their meanes of traffique from the vulgar trade,
And as their wealth increaseth, so inclose
Infinite riches in a little room.

The Jew of Malta, I. i.

CLIMBING AFTER KNOWLEDGE

NATURE that fram'd vs of foure Elements,
Warring within our breasts for regiment,
Doth teach vs all to haue aspyring minds:
Our soules, whose faculties can comprehend
The wondrous Architecture of the world:
And measure euery wandring plannets course,

Amatists] amethysts.   seildsene] seld-seen.   Carrect]
carat.
    regiment] rule.

Still climing after knowledge infinite,
And alwaies mouing as the restles Spheares,
Wils vs to weare our selues and neuer rest,
Vntill we reach the ripest fruit of all,
That perfect blisse and sole felicitie
The sweet fruition of an earthly crowne.

1 Tamburlaine, II. vii.

HELEN OF TROY

Faustus. Was this the face that lancht a
    thousand shippes ?
And burnt the toplesse Towres of Ilium ?
Sweet *Helen*, make me immortall with a kisse :
[*Kisses her.*
Her lips sucke forth my soule, see where it flies :
Come *Helen*, come giue me my soule againe.
Here wil I dwel, for heauen be in these lips,
And all is drosse that is not *Helena* :
I wil be *Paris*, and for loue of thee,
Insteede of *Troy* shal *Wertenberge* be sackt,
And I wil combate with weake *Menelaus*,
And weare thy colours on my plumed Crest :
Yes I wil wound *Achillis* in the heele,
And then returne to *Helen* for a kisse.
O thou art fairer then the euening aire,
Clad in the beauty of a thousand starres,
Brighter art thou then flaming Iupiter,
When he appeard to haplesse Semele,
More louely then the monarke of the skie
In wanton Arethusaes azurde armes,
And none but thou shalt be my paramour.

Faustus, sc. xiv.

alwaies mouing] always moving.

LOVE AT FIRST SIGHT

It lies not in our power to loue, or hate,
For will in vs is ouer-rul'd by fate.
When two are stript long ere the course begin,
We wish that one should loose, the other win ;
And one especiallie doe we affect
Of two gold Ingots like in each respect.
The reason no man knowes, let it suffise,
What we behold is censur'd by our eies.
Where both deliberat, the loue is slight,
Who euer lov'd, that lou'd not at first sight ?

Hero and Leander.

WILLIAM SHAKESPEARE

1564–1616

THIS ENGLAND

This England never did, nor never shall,
Lie at the proud foot of a conqueror,
But when it first did help to wound itself.
Now these her princes are come home again,
Come the three corners of the world in arms,
And we shall shock them. Nought shall make
    us rue,
If England to itself do rest but true.

King John, v. vii.

[loose] lose.

THIS ROYAL THRONE OF KINGS

John of Gaunt's dying Speech

METHINKS I am a prophet new inspir'd,
And thus expiring do foretell of him:
His rash fierce blaze of riot cannot last,
For violent fires soon burn out themselves;
Small showers last long, but sudden storms are
    short;
He tires betimes that spurs too fast betimes;
With eager feeding food doth choke the feeder:
Light vanity, insatiate cormorant,
Consuming means, soon preys upon itself.
This royal throne of kings, this scepter'd isle,
This earth of majesty, this seat of Mars,
This other Eden, demi-paradise,
This fortress built by Nature for herself
Against infection and the hand of war,
This happy breed of men, this little world,
This precious stone set in the silver sea,
Which serves it in the office of a wall,
Or as a moat defensive to a house,
Against the envy of less happier lands,
This blessed plot, this earth, this realm, this
    England,
This nurse, this teeming womb of royal kings,
Fear'd by their breed and famous by their birth,
Renowned for their deeds as far from home,—
For Christian service and true chivalry,—
As is the sepulchre in stubborn Jewry
Of the world's ransom, blessed Mary's Son:
This land of such dear souls, this dear, dear land,
Dear for her reputation through the world,

Is now leas'd out,—I die pronouncing it,—
Like to a tenement, or pelting farm :
England, bound in with the triumphant sea,
Whose rocky shore beats back the envious siege
Of watery Neptune, is now bound in with shame,
With inky blots, and rotten parchment bonds :
That England, that was wont to conquer others,
Hath made a shameful conquest of itself.
Ah ! would the scandal vanish with my life,
How happy then were my ensuing death.

Richard II, II. i.

ENGLAND AT WAR

(1) *Agincourt*

Chorus. O ! for a Muse of fire, that would ascend
The brightest heaven of invention ;
A kingdom for a stage, princes to act
And monarchs to behold the swelling scene.
Then should the war-like Harry, like himself,
Assume the port of Mars ; and at his heels,
Leash'd in like hounds, should famine, sword,
    and fire
Crouch for employment. But pardon, gentles all,
The flat unraised spirits that hath dar'd
On this unworthy scaffold to bring forth
So great an object : can this cockpit hold
The vasty fields of France ? or may we cram
Within this wooden O the very casques
That did affright the air at Agincourt ?
O, pardon ! since a crooked figure may
Attest in little place a million ;

pelting] paltry.
wooden O] perhaps pit.

And let us, ciphers to this great accompt,
On your imaginary forces work.
Suppose within the girdle of these walls
Are now confin'd two mighty monarchies,
Whose high upreared and abutting fronts
The perilous narrow ocean parts asunder:
Piece out our imperfections with your thoughts:
Into a thousand parts divide one man,
And make imaginary puissance;
Think when we talk of horses that you see them
Printing their proud hoofs i' the receiving earth;
For 'tis your thoughts that now must deck our
　　kings,
Carry them here and there, jumping o'er times,
Turning the accomplishment of many years
Into an hour-glass: for the which supply,
Admit me Chorus to this history;
Who prologue-like your humble patience pray,
Gently to hear, kindly to judge, our play.

(2) *Preparation and Conspiracy*

　Chorus. Now all the youth of England are on fire
And silken dalliance in the wardrobe lies;
Now thrive the armourers, and honour's thought
Reigns solely in the breast of every man:
They sell the pasture now to buy the horse,
Following the mirror of all Christian kings,
With winged heels, as English Mercuries.
For now sits Expectation in the air
And hides a sword from hilts unto the point
With crowns imperial, crowns and coronets,
Promis'd to Harry and his followers.
The French, advis'd by good intelligence

Of this most dreadful preparation,
Shake in their fear, and with pale policy
Seek to divert the English purposes.
O England! model to thy inward greatness,
Like little body with a mighty heart,
What mightst thou do, that honour would thee do,
Were all thy children kind and natural!
But see thy fault! France hath in thee found out
A nest of hollow bosoms, which he fills
With treacherous crowns; and three corrupted
    men,
One, Richard Earl of Cambridge, and the second,
Henry Lord Scroop of Masham, and the third,
Sir Thomas Grey, knight, of Northumberland,
Have, for the gilt of France,—O guilt, indeed!—
Confirm'd conspiracy with fearful France;
And by their hands this grace of kings must die,—
If hell and treason hold their promises,—
Ere he take ship for France, and in Southampton.
Linger your patience on; and well digest
The abuse of distance while we force a play.
The sum is paid; the traitors are agreed;
The king is set from London; and the scene
Is now transported, gentles, to Southampton:
There is the playhouse now, there must you sit:
And thence to France shall we convey you safe,
And bring you back, charming the narrow seas
To give you gentle pass; for, if we may,
We'll not offend one stomach with our play.
But, till the king come forth and not till then,
Unto Southampton do we shift our scene.

(3) *The Fleet's course to Harfleur*

Chorus. Thus with imagin'd wing our swift scene
    flies
In motion of no less celerity
Than that of thought. Suppose that you have seen
The well-appointed king at Hampton pier
Embark his royalty ; and his brave fleet
With silken streamers the young Phœbus fanning :
Play with your fancies, and in them behold
Upon the hempen tackle ship-boys climbing ;
Hear the shrill whistle which doth order give
To sounds confus'd ; behold the threaden sails,
Borne with the invisible and creeping wind,
Draw the huge bottoms through the furrow'd sea,
Breasting the lofty surge.   O ! do but think
You stand upon the rivage and behold
A city on the inconstant billows dancing ;
For so appears this fleet majestical,
Holding due course to Harfleur.   Follow, follow !
Grapple your minds to sternage of this navy,
And leave your England, as dead midnight still,
Guarded with grandsires, babies, and old women,
Either past or not arriv'd to pith and puissance :
For who is he, whose chin is but enrich'd
With one appearing hair, that will not follow
Those cull'd and choice-drawn cavaliers to France ?
Work, work your thoughts, and therein see a siege ;
Behold the ordenance on their carriages,
With fatal mouths gaping on girded Harfleur.
Suppose the ambassador from the French comes
    back ;
Tells Harry that the king doth offer him
Katharine his daughter ; and with her, to dowry,

Some petty and unprofitable dukedoms :
The offer likes not : and the nimble gunner
With linstock now the devilish cannon touches,

        [Alarum ; and chambers go off.
And down goes all before them. Still be kind,
And eke out our performance with your mind.

   (4) *Harfleur. England and St. George*

  King Henry. Once more unto the breach, dear
    friends, once more ;
Or close the wall up with our English dead !
In peace there 's nothing so becomes a man
As modest stillness and humility :
But when the blast of war blows in our ears,
Then imitate the action of the tiger ;
Stiffen the sinews, summon up the blood,
Disguise fair nature with hard-favour'd rage ;
Then lend the eye a terrible aspect ;
Let it pry through the portage of the head
Like the brass cannon ; let the brow o'erwhelm it
As fearfully as doth a galled rock
O'erhang and jutty his confounded base,
Swill'd with the wild and wasteful ocean.
Now set the teeth and stretch the nostril wide,
Hold hard the breath, and bend up every spirit
To his full height ! On, on, you noblest English !
Whose blood is fet from fathers of war-proof ;
Fathers that, like so many Alexanders,
Have in these parts from morn till even fought,
And sheath'd their swords for lack of argument.
Dishonour not your mothers, now attest
That those whom you call'd fathers did beget you.

linstock] the stick for holding a gunner's match.   galled
rock] rock worn by the action of the waves.   fet] fetched.

Be copy now to men of grosser blood,
And teach them how to war.　And you, good
　　yeomen,
Whose limbs were made in England, show us here
The mettle of your pasture; let us swear
That you are worth your breeding; which I doubt
　　not;
For there is none of you so mean and base
That hath not noble lustre in your eyes.
I see you stand like greyhounds in the slips,
Straining upon the start. The game's afoot:
Follow your spirit; and, upon this charge
Cry 'God for Harry! England and Saint George!'

(5) *The Eve of Agincourt*

Chorus. Now entertain conjecture of a time
When creeping murmur and the poring dark
Fills the wide vessel of the universe.
From camp to camp, through the foul womb of
　　night,
The hum of either army stilly sounds,
That the fix'd sentinels almost receive
The secret whispers of each other's watch:
Fire answers fire, and through their paly flames
Each battle sees the other's umber'd face:
Steed threatens steed, in high and boastful neighs
Piercing the night's dull ear; and from the tents
The armourers, accomplishing the knights,
With busy hammers closing rivets up,
Give dreadful note of preparation.
The country cocks do crow, the clocks do toll,
And the third hour of drowsy morning name.

poring dark] darkness which makes one strain one's eyes.

Proud of their numbers, and secure in soul,
The confident and over-lusty French
Do the low-rated English play at dice ;
And chide the cripple tardy-gaited night
Who, like a foul and ugly witch, doth limp
So tediously away. The poor condemned English,
Like sacrifices, by their watchful fires
Sit patiently, and inly ruminate
The morning's danger, and their gesture sad
Investing lank-lean cheeks and war-worn coats
Presenteth them unto the gazing moon
So many horrid ghosts. O ! now, who will behold
The royal captain of this ruin'd band
Walking from watch to watch, from tent to tent,
Let him cry ' Praise and glory on his head ! '
For forth he goes and visits all his host,
Bids them good morrow with a modest smile,
And calls them brothers, friends, and countrymen.
Upon his royal face there is no note
How dread an army hath enrounded him ;
Nor doth he dedicate one jot of colour
Unto the weary and all-watched night :
But freshly looks and overbears attaint
With cheerful semblance and sweet majesty ;
That every wretch, pining and pale before,
Beholding him, plucks comfort from his looks.
A largess universal, like the sun
His liberal eye doth give to every one,
Thawing cold fear. Then mean and gentle all,
Behold, as may unworthiness define,
A little touch of Harry in the night.
And so our scene must to the battle fly ;
Where,—O for pity,—we shall much disgrace,
With four or five most vile and ragged foils,

Right ill dispos'd in brawl ridiculous,
The name of Agincourt. Yet sit and see;
Minding true things by what their mockeries be.

(6) *St. Crispin's Day*

Westmoreland. O! that we now had here
But one ten thousand of those men in England
That do no work to-day.

    K. Henry. What's he that wishes so?
My cousin Westmoreland? No, my fair cousin:
If we are mark'd to die, we are enow
To do our country loss; and if to live,
The fewer men, the greater share of honour.
God's will! I pray thee, wish not one man more.
By Jove, I am not covetous for gold,
Nor care I who doth feed upon my cost;
It yearns me not if men my garments wear;
Such outward things dwell not in my desires:
But if it be a sin to covet honour,
I am the most offending soul alive.
No, faith, my coz, wish not a man from England:
God's peace! I would not lose so great an honour
As one man more, methinks, would share from me,
For the best hope I have. O! do not wish one more:
Rather proclaim it, Westmoreland, through my
    host,
That he which hath no stomach to this fight,
Let him depart: his passport shall be made,
And crowns for convoy put into his purse:
We would not die in that man's company
That fears his fellowship to die with us.
This day is call'd the feast of Crispian:
He that outlives this day, and comes safe home,

Will stand a tip-toe when this day is nam'd,
And rouse him at the name of Crispian.
He that shall live this day, and see old age,
Will yearly on the vigil feast his neighbours,
And say, 'To-morrow is Saint Crispian:'
Then will he strip his sleeve and show his scars,
And say, 'These wounds I had on Crispin's day.'
Old men forget: yet all shall be forgot,
But he'll remember with advantages
What feats he did that day. Then shall our names,
Familiar in his mouth as household words,
Harry the king, Bedford and Exeter,
Warwick and Talbot, Salisbury and Gloucester,
Be in their flowing cups freshly remember'd.
This story shall the good man teach his son;
And Crispin Crispian shall ne'er go by,
From this day to the ending of the world,
But we in it shall be remembered;
We few, we happy few, we band of brothers;
For he to-day that sheds his blood with me
Shall be my brother; be he ne'er so vile
This day shall gentle his condition:
And gentlemen in England, now a-bed,
Shall think themselves accurs'd they were not here,
And hold their manhoods cheap whiles any speaks
That fought with us upon Saint Crispin's day.

(7) *The return to England*

Chorus. Now we bear the king
Toward Calais: grant him there; there seen,
Heave him away upon your winged thoughts
Athwart the sea. Behold, the English beach

gentle] *v.t.* to ennoble.

Pales in the flood with men, with wives, and boys,
Whose shouts and claps out-voice the deep-
    mouth'd sea,
Which, like a mighty whiffler 'fore the king,
Seems to prepare his way : so let him land
And solemnly see him set on to London.
So swift a pace hath thought that even now
You may imagine him upon Blackheath ;
Where that his lords desire him to have borne
His bruised helmet and his bended sword
Before him through the city : he forbids it,
Being free from vainness and self-glorious pride ;
Giving full trophy, signal and ostent,
Quite from himself, to God. But now behold,
In the quick forge and working-house of thought,
How London doth pour out her citizens.
The mayor and all his brethren in best sort,
Like to the senators of the antique Rome,
With the plebeians swarming at their heels,
Go forth and fetch their conquering Cæsar in.

Henry V.

ENGLAND AT PEACE. A VISION

(1) *The Christening of the infant Elizabeth*

Cranmer. This royal infant,—heaven still move
    about her !—
Though in her cradle, yet now promises
Upon this land a thousand thousand blessings,
Which time shall bring to ripeness : she shall be—
But few now living can behold that goodness—
A pattern to all princes living with her,

    whiffler] one who cleared the way in a procession.

And all that shall succeed : Saba was never
More covetous of wisdom and fair virtue
Than this pure soul shall be : all princely graces,
That mould up such a mighty piece as this is,
With all the virtues that attend the good,
Shall still be doubled on her; truth shall nurse her;
Holy and heavenly thoughts still counsel her;
She shall be lov'd and fear'd ; her own shall bless
    her ;
Her foes shake like a field of beaten corn,
And hang their heads with sorrow ; good grows
    with her.
In her days every man shall eat in safety
Under his own vine what he plants ; and sing
The merry songs of peace to all his neighbours.
God shall be truly known ; and those about her
From her shall read the perfect ways of honour,
And by those claim their greatness, not by blood.
Nor shall this peace sleep with her ; but as when
The bird of wonder dies, the maiden phœnix,
Her ashes new-create another heir
As great in admiration as herself,
So shall she leave her blessedness to one,—
When heaven shall call her from this cloud of dark-
    ness,—
Who, from the sacred ashes of her honour,
Shall star-like rise, as great in fame as she was,
And so stand fix'd. Peace, plenty, love, truth,
    terror,
That were the servants to this chosen infant,
Shall then be his, and like a vine grow to him :
Wherever the bright sun of heaven shall shine,
His honour and the greatness of his name
Shall be, and make new nations ; he shall flourish,

And, like a mountain cedar, reach his branches
To all the plains about him ; our children's children
Shall see this, and bless heaven.

Henry VIII, v. v.

KINGSHIP

(1) *Sad Stories of the death of Kings*

King Richard II. Let's talk of graves, of worms,
    and epitaphs ;
Make dust our paper, and with rainy eyes
Write sorrow on the bosom of the earth ;
Let's choose executors and talk of wills :
And yet not so—for what can we bequeath
Save our deposed bodies to the ground ?
Our lands, our lives, and all are Bolingbroke's,
And nothing can we call our own but death,
And that small model of the barren earth
Which serves as paste and cover to our bones.
For God's sake, let us sit upon the ground
And tell sad stories of the death of kings :
How some have been depos'd, some slain in war,
Some haunted by the ghosts they have depos'd,
Some poison'd by their wives, some sleeping kill'd ;
All murder'd : for within the hollow crown
That rounds the mortal temples of a king
Keeps Death his court, and there the antick sits,
Scoffing his state and grinning at his pomp ;
Allowing him a breath, a little scene,
To monarchize, be fear'd, and kill with looks,
Infusing him with self and vain conceit
As if this flesh which walls about our life
Were brass impregnable ; and humour'd thus

antick] *sub.* the buffoon of the old plays.

Comes at the last, and with a little pin
Bores through his castle wall, and farewell king !
Cover your heads, and mock not flesh and blood.
With solemn reverence : throw away respect,
Tradition, form, and ceremonious duty,
For you have but mistook me all this while :
I live with bread like you, feel want,
Taste grief, need friends : subjected thus,
How can you say to me I am a king ?

Richard II, III. ii.

(2) *Kingship and the Shepherd's Life*

K. Henry VI. O God ! methinks it were a happy life,
To be no better than a homely swain ;
To sit upon a hill, as I do now,
To carve out dials quaintly, point by point,
Thereby to see the minutes how they run,
How many make the hour full complete ;
How many hours bring about the day ;
How many days will finish up the year ;
How many years a mortal man may live.
When this is known, then to divide the times :
So many hours must I tend my flock ;
So many hours must I take my rest ;
So many hours must I contemplate ;
So many hours must I sport myself ;
So many days my ewes have been with young ;
So many weeks ere the poor fools will ean ;
So many years ere I shall shear the fleece :
So minutes, hours, days, months, and years,
Pass'd over to the end they were created,

ean] *v.t.* to yean, to bring forth young.

Would bring white hairs unto a quiet grave.
Ah! what a life were this! how sweet! how lovely!
Gives not the hawthorn bush a sweeter shade
To shepherds, looking on their silly sheep,
Than doth a rich embroider'd canopy
To kings, that fear their subjects' treachery?
O, yes! it doth; a thousand-fold it doth.
And to conclude, the shepherd's homely curds,
His cold thin drink out of his leather bottle,
His wonted sleep under a fresh tree's shade,
All which secure and sweetly he enjoys,
Is far beyond a prince's delicates,
His viands sparkling in a golden cup,
His body couched in a curious bed,
When care, mistrust, and treason wait on him.

Henry VI, Part III, II. v,

SLEEP

(1) *Uneasy lies the head that wears a crown*

K. Henry IV. How many thousand of my
    poorest subjects
Are at this hour asleep! O sleep! O gentle sleep!
Nature's soft nurse, how have I frighted thee,
That thou no more wilt weigh my eyelids down
And steep my senses in forgetfulness?
Why rather, sleep, liest thou in smoky cribs,
Upon uneasy pallets stretching thee,
And hush'd with buzzing night-flies to thy slumber,
Than in the perfum'd chambers of the great,
Under the canopies of costly state,
And lull'd with sound of sweetest melody?

O thou dull god ! why liest thou with the vile
In loathsome beds, and leav'st the kingly couch
A watch-case or a common 'larum bell ?
Wilt thou upon the high and giddy mast
Seal up the ship-boy's eyes, and rock his brains
In cradle of the rude imperious surge,
And in the visitation of the winds,
Who take the ruffian billows by the top,
Curling their monstrous heads, and hanging them
With deaf'ning clamour in the slippery clouds,
That with the hurly death itself awakes ?
Canst thou, O partial sleep ! give thy repose
To the wet sea-boy in an hour so rude,
And in the calmest and most stillest night,
With all appliances and means to boot,
Deny it to a king ? Then, happy low, lie down !
Uneasy lies the head that wears a crown.

Henry IV, Part II, III. i.

(2) *Innocent Sleep*

Macbeth. Methought I heard a voice cry 'Sleep
    no more !
Macbeth does murder sleep', the innocent sleep,
Sleep that knits up the ravell'd sleave of care,
The death of each day's life, sore labour's bath,
Balm of hurt minds, great nature's second course,
Chief nourisher in life's feast.

Macbeth, II. ii.

FLOWERS

Perdita

Perdita. Give me those flowers there, Dorcas.
Reverend sirs,
For you there 's rosemary and rue ; these keep
Seeming and savour all the winter long :
Grace and remembrance be to you both,
And welcome to our shearing !

Polixenes. Shepherdess,—
A fair one are you,—well you fit our ages
With flowers of winter.

Perdita. Sir, the year growing ancient,
Not yet on summer's death, nor on the birth
Of trembling winter, the fairest flowers o' the season
Are our carnations, and streak'd gillyvors,
Which some call nature's bastards : of that kind
Our rustic garden 's barren, and I care not
To get slips of them.

Polixenes. Wherefore, gentle maiden,
Do you neglect them ?

Perdita. For I have heard it said
There is an art which in their piedness shares
With great creating nature.

Polixenes. Say there be ;
Yet nature is made better by no mean
But nature makes that mean : so, over that art,
Which you say adds to nature, is an art
That nature makes. You see, sweet maid, we
marry
A gentler scion to the wildest stock,
And make conceive a bark of baser kind
By bud of nobler race : this is an art

Which does mend nature, change it rather, but
The art itself is nature.

    Perdita.   So it is.

    Polixenes. Then make your garden rich in
    gillyvors,
And do not call them bastards.

    Perdita.   I'll not put
The dibble in earth to set one slip of them;
No more than, were I painted, I would wish
This youth should say, 'twere well, and only there-
    fore
Desire to breed by me. Here's flowers for you;
Hot lavender, mints, savory, marjoram;
The marigold, that goes to bed wi' the sun,
And with him rises weeping: these are flowers
Of middle summer, and I think they are given
To men of middle age. You're very welcome.

    Camillo. I should leave grazing, were I of your
    flock,
And only live by gazing.

    Perdita.   Out, alas!
You'd be so lean, that blasts of January
Would blow you through and through. Now, my
    fair'st friend,
I would I had some flowers o' the spring that might
Become your time of day; and yours, and yours,
That wear upon your virgin branches yet
Your maidenheads growing: O Proserpina!
For the flowers now that frighted thou let'st fall
From Dis's waggon! daffodils,
That come before the swallow dares, and take
The winds of March with beauty; violets dim,
But sweeter than the lids of Juno's eyes
Or Cytherea's breath; pale prime-roses,

That die unmarried, ere they can behold
Bright Phœbus in his strength, a malady
Most incident to maids; bold oxlips and
The crown imperial; lilies of all kinds,
The flower-de-luce being one. O! these I lack
To make you garlands of, and my sweet friend,
To strew him o'er and o'er!

Winter's Tale, IV. iii.

THE FOREST OF ARDEN

Enter DUKE *Senior,* AMIENS, *and other* Lords,
like Foresters.

Duke S. Now, my co-mates and brothers in exile,
Hath not old custom made this life more sweet
Than that of painted pomp? Are not these woods
More free from peril than the envious court?
Here feel we but the penalty of Adam,
The seasons' difference; as, the icy fang
And churlish chiding of the winter's wind,
Which, when it bites and blows upon my body,
Even till I shrink with cold, I smile and say
'This is no flattery: these are counsellors
That feelingly persuade me what I am.'
Sweet are the uses of adversity,
Which like the toad, ugly and venomous,
Wears yet a precious jewel in his head;
And this our life exempt from public haunt,
Finds tongues in trees, books in the running brooks,
Sermons in stones, and good in every thing.

As You Like It, II. i.

THE CONSTANT SERVICE OF THE
ANTIQUE WORLD

Adam.   I have five hundred crowns,
The thrifty hire I sav'd under your father,
Which I did store to be my foster-nurse
When service should in my old limbs lie lame,
And unregarded age in corners thrown.
Take that; and He that doth the ravens feed,
Yea, providently caters for the sparrow,
Be comfort to my age! Here is the gold;
All this I give you. Let me be your servant:
Though I look old, yet I am strong and lusty;
For in my youth I never did apply
Hot and rebellious liquors in my blood,
Nor did not with unbashful forehead woo
The means of weakness and debility;
Therefore my age is as a lusty winter,
Frosty, but kindly. Let me go with you;
I'll do the service of a younger man
In all your business and necessities.

    Orlando.   O good old man! how well in thee
       appears
The constant service of the antique world,
When service sweat for duty, not for meed!
Thou art not for the fashion of these times,
Where none will sweat but for promotion,
And having that, do choke their service up
Even with the having.

As You Like It, II. iii

THE SEVEN AGES OF MAN

Jaques.   All the world's a stage,
And all the men and women merely players :
They have their exits and their entrances ;
And one man in his time plays many parts,
His acts being seven ages. At first the infant,
Mewling and puking in the nurse's arms.
And then the whining school-boy, with his satchel,
And shining morning face, creeping like snail
Unwillingly to school. And then the lover,
Sighing like furnace, with a woful ballad
Made to his mistress' eyebrow. Then a soldier,
Full of strange oaths, and bearded like the pard,
Jealous in honour, sudden and quick in quarrel,
Seeking the bubble reputation
Even in the cannon's mouth. And then the justice,
In fair round belly with good capon lin'd,
With eyes severe, and beard of formal cut,
Full of wise saws and modern instances ;
And so he plays his part. The sixth age shifts
Into the lean and slipper'd pantaloon,
With spectacles on nose and pouch on side,
His youthful hose well sav'd, a world too wide
For his shrunk shank ; and his big manly voice,
Turning again toward childish treble, pipes
And whistles in his sound. Last scene of all,
That ends this strange eventful history,
Is second childishness and mere oblivion,
Sans teeth, sans eyes, sans taste, sans everything.

As You Like It, II. vii.

pard] leopard.

HER INFINITE VARIETY

Age cannot wither her, nor custom stale
Her infinite variety; other women cloy
The appetites they feed, but she makes hungry
Where most she satisfies.

Antony and Cleopatra, II. ii.

QUEEN MAB

Mercutio. O! then, I see, Queen Mab hath been
    with you.
Benvolio. Queen Mab! What's she?
Mercutio. She is the fairies' midwife, and she
    comes
In shape no bigger than an agate-stone
On the fore-finger of an alderman,
Drawn with a team of little atomies
Athwart men's noses as they lie asleep:
Her waggon-spokes made of long spinners' legs;
The cover, of the wings of grasshoppers;
The traces, of the smallest spider's web;
The collars, of the moonshine's watery beams;
Her whip, of cricket's bone; the lash, of film;
Her waggoner, a small grey-coated gnat,
Not half so big as a round little worm
Prick'd from the lazy finger of a maid;
Her chariot is an empty hazel-nut,
Made by the joiner squirrel or old grub,
Time out o' mind the fairies' coach-makers.
And in this state she gallops night by night
Through lovers' brains, and then they dream of
    love;

O'er courtiers' knees, that dream on curtsies
    straight ;
O'er lawyers' fingers, who straight dream on fees ;
O'er ladies' lips, who straight on kisses dream ;
Which oft the angry Mab with blisters plagues,
Because their breaths with sweetmeats tainted are.
Sometimes she gallops o'er a courtier's nose,
And then dreams he of smelling out a suit ;
And sometimes comes she with a tithe-pig's tail,
Tickling a parson's nose as a' lies asleep,
Then dreams he of another benefice ;
Sometime she driveth o'er a soldier's neck,
And then dreams he of cutting foreign throats,
Of breaches, ambuscadoes, Spanish blades,
Of healths five fathom deep ; and then anon
Drums in his ear, at which he starts and wakes ;
And, being thus frighted, swears a prayer or two,
And sleeps again.

Romeo and Juliet, i. iv.

PATIENCE AND SORROW

'TIS all men's office to speak patience
To those that wring under the load of sorrow,
But no man's virtue nor sufficiency
To be so moral when he shall endure
The like himself.

Much Ado About Nothing, v. i.

MERCY

    Angelo. Your brother is a forfeit of the law,
And you but waste your words.
    Isabella.   Alas ! alas !
Why, all the souls that were were forfeit once ;
And He that might the vantage best have took,

Found out the remedy. How would you be,
If He, which is the top of judgment, should
But judge you as you are? O! think on that,
And mercy then will breathe within your lips,
Like man new made.

Measure for Measure, II. ii.

THE QUALITY OF MERCY

Portia. The quality of mercy is not strain'd,
It droppeth as the gentle rain from heaven
Upon the place beneath: it is twice bless'd;
It blesseth him that gives and him that takes:
'Tis mightiest in the mightiest; it becomes
The throned monarch better than his crown;
His sceptre shows the force of temporal power,
The attribute to awe and majesty,
Wherein doth sit the dread and fear of kings;
But mercy is above this sceptred sway,
It is enthroned in the hearts of kings,
It is an attribute to God himself,
And earthly power doth then show likest God's
When mercy seasons justice.

Merchant of Venice, IV. i.

MUSIC

Lorenzo. How sweet the moonlight sleeps upon
    this bank!
Here will we sit, and let the sounds of music
Creep in our ears: soft stillness and the night
Become the touches of sweet harmony.
Sit, Jessica: look, how the floor of heaven
Is thick inlaid with patines of bright gold:
There's not the smallest orb which thou behold'st

But in his motion like an angel sings,
Still quiring to the young-eyed cherubins;
Such harmony is in immortal souls;
But, whilst this muddy vesture of decay
Doth grossly close it in, we cannot hear it.

Enter Musicians.

Come, ho! and wake Diana with a hymn:
With sweetest touches pierce your mistress' ear,
And draw her home with music.   [*Music.*

　Jessica. I am never merry when I hear sweet
music.

　Lorenzo. The reason is, your spirits are attentive:
For do but note a wild and wanton herd,
Or race of youthful and unhandled colts,
Fetching mad bounds, bellowing and neighing
　　loud,
Which is the hot condition of their blood;
If they but hear perchance a trumpet sound,
Or any air of music touch their ears,
You shall perceive them make a mutual stand,
Their savage eyes turn'd to a modest gaze
By the sweet power of music: therefore the
　　poet
Did feign that Orpheus drew trees, stones, and
　　floods;
Since naught so stockish, hard, and full of rage,
But music for the time doth change his nature.
The man that hath no music in himself,
Nor is not mov'd with concord of sweet sounds,
Is fit for treasons, stratagems, and spoils;
The motions of his spirit are dull as night,
And his affections dark as Erebus:
Let no such man be trusted. Mark the music.

Enter PORTIA *and* NERISSA, *at a distance.*

Portia. That light we see is burning in my hall.
How far that little candle throws his beams !
So shines a good deed in a naughty world.

    Nerissa. When the moon shone, we did not see
      the candle.

    Portia. So doth the greater glory dim the less :
A substitute shines brightly as a king
Until a king be by, and then his state
Empties itself, as doth an inland brook
Into the main of waters. Music ! hark !

    Nerissa. It is your music, madam, of the house.

    Portia. Nothing is good, I see, without respect :
Methinks it sounds much sweeter than by day.

    Nerissa. Silence bestows that virtue on it, madam.

    Portia. The crow doth sing as sweetly as the lark
When neither is attended, and I think
The nightingale, if she should sing by day,
When every goose is cackling, would be thought
No better a musician than the wren.
How many things by season season'd are
To their right praise and true perfection !
Peace, ho ! the moon sleeps with Endymion,
And would not be awak'd !

                Merchant of Venice, **v. i.**

IF MUSIC BE THE FOOD OF LOVE

    Duke of Illyria. If music be the food of love,
      play on ;
Give me excess of it, that, surfeiting,
The appetite may sicken, and so die.
That strain again ! it had a dying fall :
O ! it came o'er my ear like the sweet sound
That breathes upon a bank of violets,

Stealing and giving odour. Enough ! no more :
'Tis not so sweet now as it was before.
O spirit of love ! how quick and fresh art thou,
That, notwithstanding thy capacity
Receiveth as the sea, nought enters there,
Of what validity and pitch soe'er,
But falls into abatement and low price,
Even in a minute : so full of shapes is fancy,
That it alone is high fantastical.

Twelfth Night, I. i.

THE MUSIC OF HOUNDS

Theseus. Go, one of you, find out the forester ;
For now our observation is perform'd ;
And since we have the vaward of the day,
My love shall hear the music of my hounds.
Uncouple in the western valley ; let them go :
Dispatch, I say, and find the forester.
We will, fair queen, up to the mountain's top,
And mark the musical confusion
Of hounds and echo in conjunction.

Hippolyta. I was with Hercules and Cadmus
once,
When in a wood of Crete they bay'd the bear
With hounds of Sparta : never did I hear
Such gallant chiding ; for, besides the groves,
The skies, the fountains, every region near
Seem'd all one mutual cry. I never heard
So musical a discord, such sweet thunder.

Theseus. My hounds are bred out of the Spartan
kind,
So flew'd, so sanded ; and their heads are hung

vaward] vanguard, the first part.   flew'd] *adj.* ' flews '
are the large hanging chaps of a hound.   sanded] *adj.*
of a sandy colour.

With ears that sweep away the morning dew ;
Crook-knee'd, and dew-lapp'd like Thessalian
    bulls ;
Slow in pursuit, but match'd in mouth like bells,
Each under each. A cry more tuneable
Was never holla'd to, nor cheer'd with horn,
In Crete, in Sparta, nor in Thessaly :
Judge, when you hear.

A Midsummer-Night's Dream, IV. i.

IMAGINATION

THE lunatic, the lover, and the poet,
Are of imagination all compact :
One sees more devils than vast hell can hold,
That is, the madman ; the lover, all as frantic,
Sees Helen's beauty in a brow of Egypt :
The poet's eye, in a fine frenzy rolling,
Doth glance from heaven to earth, from earth to
    heaven ;
And, as imagination bodies forth
The forms of things unknown, the poet's pen
Turns them to shapes, and gives to airy nothing
A local habitation and a name.

A Midsummer-Night's Dream, v. i.

BANISHMENT

Gaunt. All places that the eye of heaven visits
Are to a wise man ports and happy havens.
Teach thy necessity to reason thus ;
There is no virtue like necessity.
Think not the king did banish thee,
But thou the king. Woe doth the heavier sit,
Where it perceives it is but faintly borne.

Go, say I sent thee forth to purchase honour,
And not the king exil'd thee ; or suppose
Devouring pestilence hangs in our air,
And thou art flying to a fresher clime.
Look, what thy soul holds dear, imagine it
To lie that way thou go'st, not whence thou com'st.
Suppose the singing birds musicians,
The grass whereon thou tread'st the presence
    strew'd,
The flowers fair ladies, and thy steps no more
Than a delightful measure or a dance ;
For gnarling sorrow hath less power to bite
The man that mocks at it and sets it light.
   Bolingbroke. O ! who can hold a fire in his hand
By thinking on the frosty Caucasus ?
Or cloy the hungry edge of appetite
By bare imagination of a feast ?
Or wallow naked in December snow
By thinking on fantastic summer's heat ?
O, no ! the apprehension of the good
Gives but the greater feeling to the worse :
Fell sorrow's tooth doth never rankle more
Than when it bites, but lanceth not the sore.

Richard II, I. iii.

WOLSEY'S FAREWELL TO CROMWELL

CROMWELL, I did not think to shed a tear
In all my miseries ; but thou hast forc'd me,
Out of thy honest truth, to play the woman.
Let's dry our eyes : and thus far hear me, Cromwell;
And, when I am forgotten, as I shall be,
And sleep in dull cold marble, where no mention

gnarling] *adj.* snarling.

Of me more must be heard of, say, I taught thee,
Say, Wolsey, that once trod the ways of glory,
And sounded all the depths and shoals of honour,
Found thee a way, out of his wrack, to rise in ;
A sure and safe one, though thy master miss'd it.
Mark but my fall, and that that ruin'd me.
Cromwell, I charge thee, fling away ambition :
By that sin fell the angels ; how can man then,
The image of his Maker, hope to win by 't ?
Love thyself last : cherish those hearts that hate
    thee ;
Corruption wins not more than honesty.
Still in thy right hand carry gentle peace,
To silence envious tongues : be just, and fear not.
Let all the ends thou aim'st at be thy country's,
Thy God's, and truth's ; then if thou fall'st, O
    Cromwell !
Thou fall'st a blessed martyr. Serve the king ;
And,—prithee, lead me in :
There take an inventory of all I have,
To the last penny ; 'tis the king's : my robe,
And my integrity to heaven is all
I dare now call mine own. O Cromwell, Cromwell !
Had I but serv'd my God with half the zeal
I serv'd my king, he would not in mine age
Have left me naked to mine enemies.

Henry VIII, III. ii.

GOODNESS IN THINGS EVIL

Henry V. There is some soul of goodness in
    things evil,
Would men observingly distil it out;
For our bad neighbour makes us early stirrers,
Which is both healthful, and good husbandry:
Besides, they are our outward consciences,
And preachers to us all; admonishing
That we should dress us fairly for our end.
Thus may we gather honey from the weed,
And make a moral of the devil himself.

Henry V, IV. i.

CHRISTMAS

Marcellus. Some say that ever 'gainst that
    season comes
Wherein our Saviour's birth is celebrated,
The bird of dawning singeth all night long;
And then, they say, no spirit can walk abroad;
The nights are wholesome; then no planets strike,
No fairy takes, nor witch hath power to charm,
So hallow'd and so gracious is the time.

Hamlet. I. i.

THESE FEW PRECEPTS

Polonius. There, my blessing with thee !
And these few precepts in thy memory
Look thou character. Give thy thoughts no tongue,
Nor any unproportion'd thought his act.
Be thou familiar, but by no means vulgar;
The friends thou hast, and their adoption tried,
Grapple them to thy soul with hoops of steel;
But do not dull thy palm with entertainment

      bird of dawning] the cock.
      character] *v.t.* to inscribe, engrave.

Of each new-hatch'd, unfledg'd comrade. Beware
Of entrance to a quarrel, but, being in,
Bear 't that th' opposed may beware of thee.
Give every man thine ear, but few thy voice;
Take each man's censure, but reserve thy judgment.
Costly thy habit as thy purse can buy,
But not express'd in fancy; rich, not gaudy;
For the apparel oft proclaims the man,
And they in France of the best rank and station
Are most select and generous, chief in that.
Neither a borrower, nor a lender be;
For loan oft loses both itself and friend,
And borrowing dulls the edge of husbandry.
This above all: to thine own self be true,
And it must follow, as the night the day,
Thou canst not then be false to any man.

Hamlet, I. iii.

TO BE OR NOT TO BE

Hamlet. To be, or not to be: that is the question:
Whether 'tis nobler in the mind to suffer
The slings and arrows of outrageous fortune,
Or to take arms against a sea of troubles,
And by opposing end them? To die: to sleep;
No more; and, by a sleep to say we end
The heart-ache and the thousand natural shocks
That flesh is heir to, 'tis a consummation
Devoutly to be wish'd. To die, to sleep;
To sleep: perchance to dream: ay, there's the
     rub;
For in that sleep of death what dreams may come
When we have shuffled off this mortal coil,

Must give us pause. There's the respect
That makes calamity of so long life ;
For who would bear the whips and scorns of time,
The oppressor's wrong, the proud man's contumely,
The pangs of dispriz'd love, the law's delay,
The insolence of office, and the spurns
That patient merit of the unworthy takes,
When he himself might his quietus make
With a bare bodkin ? who would fardels bear,
To grunt and sweat under a weary life,
But that the dread of something after death,
The undiscover'd country from whose bourn
No traveller returns, puzzles the will,
And makes us rather bear those ills we have
Than fly to others that we know not of ?
Thus conscience does make cowards of us all ;
And thus the native hue of resolution
Is sicklied o'er with the pale cast of thought,
And enterprises of great pith and moment
With this regard their currents turn awry,
And lose the name of action.

Hamlet, III. i.

A NOBLE FRIENDSHIP. HAMLET AND HORATIO

Hamlet. Horatio, thou art e'en as just a man
As e'er my conversation cop'd withal.
    Horatio. O ! my dear lord,—
    Hamlet.   Nay, do not think I flatter ;
For what advancement may I hope from thee,
That no revenue hast but thy good spirits

---

    fardels] *sub.* burdens, packs.   pith] (pitch) importance,
gravity, weight.
    just] honest.   conversation] experience, intercourse.

To feed and clothe thee ? Why should the poor be
    flatter'd ?
No ; let the candied tongue lick absurd pomp,
And crook the pregnant hinges of the knee
Where thrift may follow fawning. Dost thou hear ?
Since my dear soul was mistress of her choice
And could of men distinguish, her election
Hath seal'd thee for herself ; for thou hast been
As one, in suffering all, that suffers nothing,
A man that fortune's buffets and rewards
Hast ta'en with equal thanks ; and bless'd are those
Whose blood and judgment are so well co-mingled
That they are not a pipe for fortune's finger
To sound what stop she please. Give me that man
That is not passion's slave, and I will wear him
In my heart's core, ay, in my heart of heart,
As I do thee.

Hamlet, III. ii.

HAMLET (dying) to HORATIO.

If thou didst ever hold me in thy heart,
Absent thee from felicity awhile,
And in this harsh world draw thy breath in pain,
To tell my story.

Hamlet, v. ii.

candied] flattering.   pregnant] ready, prompt.   thrift]
gain.   blood] passion.

DUNCAN'S MURDER

i. *Vaulting Ambition.*

Macbeth. If it were done when 'tis done, then
   'twere well
It were done quickly ; if the assassination
Could trammel up the consequence, and catch
With his surcease success ; that but this blow
Might be the be-all and the end-all here,
But here, upon this bank and shoal of time,
We'd jump the life to come. But in these cases
We still have judgment here ; that we but teach
Bloody instructions, which, being taught, return
To plague the inventor ; this even-handed justice
Commends the ingredients of our poison'd chalice
To our own lips. He's here in double trust :
First, as I am his kinsman and his subject,
Strong both against the deed ; then, as his host,
Who should against his murderer shut the door,
Not bear the knife myself. Besides, this Duncan
Hath borne his faculties so meek, hath been
So clear in his great office, that his virtues
Will plead like angels trumpet-tongu'd against
The deep damnation of his taking-off ;
And pity, like a naked new-born babe,
Striding the blast, or heaven's cherubin, hors'd
Upon the sightless couriers of the air,
Shall blow the horrid deed in every eye,
That tears shall drown the wind. I have no spur
To prick the sides of my intent, but only
Vaulting ambition, which o'er-leaps itself
And falls on the other.—

trammel up] to net up, to enmesh.   surcease] cessation,
conclusion.   jump] hazard.   commends] offers.

Enter LADY MACBETH.

How now ! what news ?

Lady Macbeth. He has almost supp'd : why have
you left the chamber ?

Macbeth. Hath he ask'd for me ?

Lady Macbeth. Know you not he has ?

Macbeth. We will proceed no further in this
business :
He hath honour'd me of late ; and I have bought
Golden opinions from all sorts of people,
Which would be worn now in their newest gloss,
Not cast aside so soon.

Lady Macbeth. Was the hope drunk,
Wherein you dress'd yourself ? hath it slept since,
And wakes it now, to look so green and pale
At what it did so freely ? From this time
Such I account thy love. Art thou afeard
To be the same in thine own act and valour
As thou art in desire ? Wouldst thou have that
Which thou esteem'st the ornament of life,
And live a coward in thine own esteem,
Letting ' I dare not ' wait upon ' I would ',
Like the poor cat i' the adage ?

Macbeth. Prithee, peace.
I dare do all that may become a man ;
Who dares do more is none.

Lady Macbeth. What beast was 't, then,
That made you break this enterprise to me ?
When you durst do it then you were a man ;
And, to be more than what you were, you would
Be so much more the man. Nor time nor place

bought] won, acquired.   break] impart, disclose.

Did then adhere, and yet you would make both :
They have made themselves, and that their fitness now
Does unmake you. I have given suck, and know
How tender 'tis to love the babe that milks me :
I would, while it was smiling in my face,
Have pluck'd my nipple from his boneless gums,
And dash'd the brains out, had I so sworn as you
Have done to this.

  Macbeth.   If we should fail,—

  Lady Macbeth.   We fail !
But screw your courage to the sticking-place,
And we 'll not fail. When Duncan is asleep,
Whereto the rather shall his day's hard journey
Soundly invite him, his two chamberlains
Will I with wine and wassail so convince
That memory, the warder of the brain,
Shall be a fume, and the receipt of reason
A limbeck only ; when in swinish sleep
Their drenched natures lie, as in a death,
What cannot you and I perform upon
The unguarded Duncan ? what not put upon
His spongy officers, who shall bear the guilt
Of our great quell ?

  Macbeth.   Bring forth men-children only ;
For thy undaunted mettle should compose
Nothing but males. Will it not be receiv'd,
When we have mark'd with blood those sleepy two
Of his own chamber and us'd their very daggers,
That they have done 't ?

  Lady Macbeth.   Who dares receive it other,
As we shall make our griefs and clamour roar
Upon his death ?

      adhere] favour.   quell] murder.

Macbeth.   I am settled, and bend up
Each corporal agent to this terrible feat.
Away, and mock the time with fairest show :
False face must hide what the false heart doth
    know.

Macbeth, I. vii.

ii. *Is this a dagger ?*

Macbeth. Is this a dagger which I see before me,
The handle toward my hand ? Come, let me clutch
    thee :
I have thee not, and yet I see thee still.
Art thou not, fatal vision, sensible
To feeling as to sight ? or art thou but
A dagger of the mind, a false creation,
Proceeding from the heat-oppressed brain ?
I see thee yet, in form as palpable
As this which now I draw.
Thou marshall'st me the way that I was going ;
And such an instrument I was to use.
Mine eyes are made the fools o' the other senses,
Or else worth all the rest : I see thee still ;
And on thy blade and dudgeon gouts of blood,
Which was not so before. There 's no such thing :
It is the bloody business which informs
Thus to mine eyes. Now o'er the one half-world
Nature seems dead, and wicked dreams abuse
The curtain'd sleep ; witchcraft celebrates
Pale Hecate's offerings ; and wither'd murder,
Alarum'd by his sentinel, the wolf,
Whose howl 's his watch, thus with his stealthy
    pace,

dudgeon] haft.   wither'd] ghastly, spectre-like.

With Tarquin's ravishing strides, toward his design
Moves like a ghost. Thou sure and firm-set earth,
Hear not my steps, which way they walk, for fear
Thy very stones prate of my whereabout,
And take the present horror from the time,
Which now suits with it. Whiles I threat he lives :
Words to the heat of deeds too cold breath gives.

　　　　　　　　　　　　　　　　[*A bell rings.*

I go, and it is done ; the bell invites me.
Hear it not, Duncan ; for it is a knell
That summons thee to heaven or to hell.

　　　　　　　　　　　　　　　　　Macbeth, II. i.

iii. *The deed.*

　　Lady Macbeth. That which hath made them
　　　　drunk hath made me bold,
What hath quench'd them hath given me fire.
　　　　Hark !
Peace !
It was that owl that shriek'd, the fatal bellman,
Which gives the stern'st good-night. He is about it :
The doors are open, and the surfeited grooms
Do mock their charge with snores : I have drugg'd
　　　　their possets,
That death and nature do contend about them,
Whether they live or die.
　　Macbeth [*Within.*] Who's there ? what, ho !
　　Lady Macbeth. Alack ! I am afraid they have
　　　　awak'd,
And 'tis not done ; the attempt and not the deed
Confounds us. Hark ! I laid their daggers ready ;
He could not miss them. Had he not resembled
My father as he slept I had done 't. My husband !

　　　　　　　Confounds] ruins.

Enter MACBETH.

Macbeth. I have done the deed.   Didst thou not
  hear a noise ?

Lady Macbeth. I heard the owl scream and the
  crickets cry.

Did not you speak ?

Macbeth.   When ?

Lady Macbeth.   Now.

Macbeth.   As I descended ?

Lady Macbeth. Ay.

Macbeth. Hark !

Who lies i' the second chamber ?

Lady Macbeth.   Donalbain.

Macbeth [*Looking on his hands.*] This is a sorry
  sight.

Lady Macbeth. A foolish thought to say a sorry
  sight.

Macbeth. There's one did laugh in 's sleep, and
  one cried 'Murder !'

That they did wake each other : I stood and heard
  them ;

But they did say their prayers, and address'd them
Again to sleep.

  Lady Macbeth.   There are two lodg'd together.

  Macbeth. One cried 'God bless us !' and 'Amen'
    the other :

As they had seen me with these hangman's hands.
Listening their fear, I could not say 'Amen',
When they did say 'God bless us !'

  Lady Macbeth.   Consider it not so deeply.

  Macbeth. But wherefore could not I pronounce
    ' Amen ? '

I had most need of blessing, and 'Amen'

Stuck in my throat.

Lady Macbeth. These deeds must not be thought
After these ways ; so, it will make us mad.

Macbeth. Methought I heard a voice cry 'Sleep
no more !

Macbeth does murder sleep,' the innocent sleep,
Sleep that knits up the ravell'd sleave of care,
The death of each day's life, sore labour's bath,
Balm of hurt minds, great nature's second course,
Chief nourisher in life's feast,—

Lady Macbeth.   What do you mean ?

Macbeth. Still it cried, 'Sleep no more !' to all
the house :

'Glamis hath murder'd sleep, and therefore
Cawdor

Shall sleep no more, Macbeth shall sleep no more !'

Lady Macbeth. Who was it that thus cried ?
Why, worthy thane,

You do unbend your noble strength to think
So brainsickly of things. Go get some water,
And wash this filthy witness from your hand.
Why did you bring these daggers from the place ?
They must lie there : go carry them, and smear
The sleepy grooms with blood.

Macbeth.   I'll go no more :
I am afraid to think what I have done ;
Look on 't again I dare not.

Lady Macbeth.   Infirm of purpose !
Give me the daggers. The sleeping and the dead
Are but as pictures ; 'tis the eye of childhood
That fears a painted devil. If he do bleed,
I'll gild the faces of the grooms withal ;
For it must seem their guilt.

[*Exit. Knocking within.*

Macbeth.   Whence is that knocking?
How is 't with me, when every noise appals me?
What hands are here! Ha! they pluck out mine
    eyes.
Will all great Neptune's ocean wash this blood
Clean from my hand? No, this my hand will
    rather
The multitudinous seas incarnadine,
Making the green one red.

Re-enter LADY MACBETH.

Lady Macbeth. My hands are of your colour, but
    I shame
To wear a heart so white.—[*Knocking within.*] I
    hear a knocking
At the south entry; retire we to our chamber;
A little water clears us of this deed;
How easy is it, then! Your constancy
Hath left you unattended.   [*Knocking within.*]
        Hark! more knocking.
Get on your night-gown, lest occasion call us,
And show us to be watchers. Be not lost
So poorly in your thoughts.

Macbeth. To know my deed 'twere best not
    know myself.   [*Knocking within.*
Wake Duncan with thy knocking! I would thou
    couldst!

                            Macbeth, II. ii.

THE WAY TO DUSTY DEATH

Macbeth. To morrow, and to-morrow, and to
    morrow,
Creeps in this petty pace from day to day,
To the last syllable of recorded time;
And all our yesterdays have lighted fools

The way to dusty death. Out out, brief candle!
Life's but a walking shadow, a poor player
That struts and frets his hour upon the stage,
And then is heard no more; it is a tale
Told by an idiot, full of sound and fury,
Signifying nothing.

Macbeth, v. v.

MURDER OF JULIUS CAESAR

*Between the acting of a dreadful thing and the first
motion.*

Brutus. It must be by his death: and, for my
part,
I know no personal cause to spurn at him,
But for the general. He would be crown'd:
How that might change his nature, there's the
question:
It is the bright day that brings forth the adder
And that craves wary walking. Crown him?—
that!
And then, I grant, we put a sting in him,
That at his will he may do danger with.
The abuse of greatness is when it disjoins
Remorse from power; and, to speak truth of
Caesar,
I have not known when his affections sway'd
More than his reason. But 'tis a common proof,
That lowliness is young ambition's ladder,
Whereto the climber-upward turns his face;
But when he once attains the upmost round,
He then unto the ladder turns his back,
Looks in the clouds, scorning the base degrees

general] general public.

By which he did ascend. So Caesar may:
Then, lest he may, prevent. And, since the quarrel
Will bear no colour for the thing he is,
Fashion it thus; that what he is, augmented,
Would run to these and these extremities;
And therefore think him as a serpent's egg
Which, hatch'd, would, as his kind, grow mis-
chievous,
And kill him in the shell. . . .
Since Cassius first did whet me against Caesar,
I have not slept.
Between the acting of a dreadful thing
And the first motion, all the interim is
Like a phantasma, or a hideous dream:
The genius and the mortal instruments
Are then in council; and the state of man,
Like to a little kingdom, suffers then
The nature of an insurrection.

Julius Caesar, II. i.

SOME SPEECHES

I. ANTONY'S ORATION OVER THE BODY OF CAESAR

Antony. Friends, Romans, countrymen, lend me
your ears;
I come to bury Caesar, not to praise him.
The evil that men do lives after them,
The good is often interred with their bones;
So let it be with Caesar. The noble Brutus
Hath told you Caesar was ambitious;
If it were so, it was a grievous fault,
And grievously hath Caesar answer'd it.
Here, under leave of Brutus and the rest,—
For Brutus is an honourable man;
So are they all, all honourable men,—

Come I to speak in Caesar's funeral.
He was my friend, faithful and just to me:
But Brutus says he was ambitious;
And Brutus is an honourable man.
He hath brought many captives home to Rome,
Whose ransoms did the general coffers fill:
Did this in Caesar seem ambitious?
When that the poor have cried, Caesar hath wept;
Ambition should be made of sterner stuff:
Yet Brutus says he was ambitious;
And Brutus is an honourable man.
You all did see that on the Lupercal
I thrice presented him a kingly crown,
Which he did thrice refuse: was this ambition?
Yet Brutus says he was ambitious:
And, sure, he is an honourable man.
I speak not to disprove what Brutus spoke,
But here I am to speak what I do know.
You all did love him once, not without cause:
What cause withholds you then to mourn for him?
O judgment! thou art fled to brutish beasts,
And men have lost their reason. Bear with me;
My heart is in the coffin there with Caesar,
And I must pause till it come back to me.

> *First Citizen.* Methinks there is much reason in
> his sayings.
> *Second Citizen.* If thou consider rightly of the
> matter,
Caesar has had great wrong.
> *Third Citizen.*   Has he, masters?
I fear there will a worse come in his place.
> *Fourth Citizen.* Mark'd ye his words? He would
> not take the crown;
Therefore 'tis certain he was not ambitious.

First Citizen. If it be found so, some will dear
abide it.

Second Citizen. Poor soul! his eyes are red as
fire with weeping.

Third Citizen. There's not a nobler man in
Rome than Antony.

Fourth Citizen. Now mark him; he begins again
to speak.

Antony. But yesterday the word of Caesar might
Have stood against the world; now lies he there,
And none so poor to do him reverence.
O masters! if I were dispos'd to stir
Your hearts and minds to mutiny and rage,
I should do Brutus wrong, and Cassius wrong,
Who, you all know, are honourable men.
I will not do them wrong; I rather choose
To wrong the dead, to wrong myself, and you,
Than I will wrong such honourable men.
But here's a parchment with the seal of Caesar;
I found it in his closet, 'tis his will.
Let but the commons hear this testament—
Which, pardon me, I do not mean to read—
And they would go and kiss dead Caesar's wounds,
And dip their napkins in his sacred blood,
Yea, beg a hair of him for memory,
And, dying, mention it within their wills,
Bequeathing it as a rich legacy
Unto their issue.

Fourth Citizen. We'll hear the will: read it,
Mark Antony.

Citizens. The will, the will! we will hear
Caesar's will.

Antony. Have patience, gentle friends; I must
not read it:

It is not meet you know how Caesar lov'd you.
You are not wood, you are not stones, but men ;
And, being men, hearing the will of Caesar,
It will inflame you, it will make you mad.
'Tis good you know not that you are his heirs ;
For if you should, O ! what would come of it.

 Fourth Citizen. Read the will ! we'll hear it,
  Antony ;
You shall read us the will, Caesar's will.

 Antony. Will you be patient ? Will you stay
  awhile ?
I have o'ershot myself to tell you of it.
I fear I wrong the honourable men
Whose daggers have stabb'd Caesar ; I do fear it.

 Fourth Citizen. They were traitors : honourable
  men !

 Citizens. The will ! the testament !

 Second Citizen. They were villains, murderers.
  The will ! read the will.

 Antony. You will compel me then to read the
  will ?
Then make a ring about the corpse of Caesar,
And let me show you him that made the will.
Shall I descend ? and will you give me leave ?

 Citizens. Come down.

 Second Citizen. Descend. [ANTONY *comes down.*

 Third Citizen. You shall have leave.

 Fourth Citizen. A ring ; stand round.

 First Citizen. Stand from the hearse ; stand
  from the body.

 Second Citizen. Room for Antony ; most noble
  Antony.

 Antony. Nay, press not so upon me ; stand far
  off.

Citizens. Stand back! room! bear back!

Antony. If you have tears, prepare to shed them
now.

You all do know this mantle: I remember
The first time ever Caesar put it on;
'Twas on a summer's evening, in his tent,
That day he overcame the Nervii.
Look! in this place ran Cassius' dagger through:
See what a rent the envious Casca made:
Through this the well-beloved Brutus stabb'd:
And, as he pluck'd his cursed steel away,
Mark how the blood of Caesar follow'd it,
As rushing out of doors, to be resolv'd
If Brutus so unkindly knock'd or no;
For Brutus, as you know, was Caesar's angel:
Judge, O you gods! how dearly Caesar lov'd him.
This was the most unkindest cut of all;
For when the noble Caesar saw him stab,
Ingratitude, more strong than traitors' arms,
Quite vanquish'd him: then burst his mighty
heart;
And, in his mantle muffling up his face,
Even at the base of Pompey's statua,
Which all the while ran blood, great Caesar fell.
O! what a fall was there, my countrymen;
Then I, and you, and all of us fell down,
Whilst bloody treason flourish'd over us,
O! now you weep, and I perceive you feel
The dint of pity; these are gracious drops.
Kind souls, what! weep you when you but behold
Our Caesar's vesture wounded? Look you here,
Here is himself, marr'd, as you see, with traitors.

First Citizen. O piteous spectacle!

Second Citizen. O noble Caesar!

Third Citizen. O woeful day!

Fourth Citizen. O traitors! villains!

First Citizen. O most bloody sight!

Second Citizen. We will be revenged.

Citizens. Revenge!—About!—Seek!—Burn!
Fire!—Kill!—Slay! Let not a traitor live.

Antony. Stay, countrymen!

First Citizen. Peace there! Hear the noble
Antony.

Second Citizen. We'll hear him, we'll follow
him, we'll die with him.

Antony. Good friends, sweet friends, let me not
stir you up
To such a sudden flood of mutiny.
They that have done this deed are honourable:
What private griefs they have, alas! I know not,
That made them do it; they are wise and honour-
able,
And will, no doubt, with reasons answer you.
I come not, friends, to steal away your hearts:
I am no orator, as Brutus is;
But, as you know me all, a plain blunt man,
That love my friend; and that they know full well
That gave me public leave to speak of him.
For I have neither wit, nor words, nor worth,
Action, nor utterance, nor the power of speech,
To stir men's blood: I only speak right on;
I tell you that which you yourselves do know,
Show you sweet Caesar's wounds, poor poor dumb
mouths,
And bid them speak for me: but were I Brutus,
And Brutus Antony, there were an Antony
Would ruffle up your spirits, and put a tongue
In every wound of Caesar, that should move

The stones of Rome to rise and mutiny.

Citizens. We'll mutiny.

First Citizen. We'll burn the house of Brutus.

Third Citizen. Away, then! come, seek the
conspirators.

Antony. Yet hear me, countrymen; yet hear
me speak.

Citizens. Peace, ho!—Hear Antony,—most
noble Antony.

Antony. Why, friends, you go to do you know
not what.

Wherein hath Caesar thus deserv'd your loves?

Alas! you know not: I must tell you then.

You have forgot the will I told you of.

Citizens. Most true. The will! let's stay and
hear the will.

Antony. Here is the will, and under Caesar's seal,

To every Roman citizen he gives,

To every several man, seventy-five drachmas.

Second Citizen. Most noble Caesar! we'll revenge
his death.

Third Citizen. O royal Caesar!

Antony. Hear me with patience.

Citizens. 'Peace, ho!

Antony. Moreover, he hath left you all his walks,

His private arbours, and new-planted orchards,

On this side Tiber; he hath left them you,

And to your heirs for ever; common pleasures,

To walk abroad, and recreate yourselves.

Here was a Caesar! when comes such another?

First Citizen. Never, never! Come, away, away!

We'll burn his body in the holy place,

And with the brands fire the traitors' houses.

Take up the body.

Second Citizen. Go fetch fire.

Third Citizen. Pluck down benches.

Fourth Citizen. Pluck down forms, windows, any thing.   [*Exeunt* Citizens, *with the body.*

Antony. Now let it work: mischief, thou art afoot,

Take thou what course thou wilt!

Julius Cæsar, III. ii.

II. OTHELLO. HOW HE WON THE LOVE OF DESDEMONA

Most potent, grave, and reverend signiors,
My very noble and approv'd good masters,
That I have ta'en away this old man's daughter,
It is most true; true, I have married her:
The very head and front of my offending
Hath this extent, no more. Rude am I in my
   speech,
And little bless'd with the soft phrase of peace;
For since these arms of mine had seven years' pith,
Till now some nine moons wasted, they have us'd
Their dearest action in the tented field;
And little of this great world can I speak,
More than pertains to feats of broil and battle;
And therefore little shall I grace my cause
In speaking for myself. Yet, by your gracious
   patience,
I will a round unvarnish'd tale deliver
Of my whole course of love; what drugs, what
   charms,
What conjuration, and what mighty magic,
For such proceeding I am charg'd withal,
I won his daughter. . . .

          pith] strength, vigour.

Her father lov'd me ; oft invited me ;
Still question'd me the story of my life
From year to year, the battles, sieges, fortunes
That I have pass'd.
I ran it through, even from my boyish days
To the very moment that he bade me tell it ;
Wherein I spake of most disastrous chances,
Of moving accidents by flood and field,
Of hair-breadth 'scapes i' the imminent deadly
    breach,
Of being taken by the insolent foe
And sold to slavery, of my redemption thence
And portance in my travel's history ;
Wherein of antres vast and desarts idle,
Rough quarries, rocks and hills whose heads touch
    heaven,
It was my hint to speak, such was the process ;
And of the Cannibals that each other eat,
The Anthropophagi, and men whose heads
Do grow beneath their shoulders. This to hear
Would Desdemona seriously incline ;
But still the house-affairs would draw her thence ;
Which ever as she could with haste dispatch,
She'd come again, and with a greedy ear
Devour up my discourse. Which I observing,
Took once a pliant hour, and found good means
To draw from her a prayer of earnest heart
That I would all my pilgrimage dilate,
Whereof by parcels she had something heard,
But not intentively ; I did consent ;
And often did beguile her of her tears,
When I did speak of some distressful stroke

portance] conduct.   antres] caverns.   idle] barren.
intentively] with unbroken attention.

That my youth suffer'd. My story being done,
She gave me for my pains a world of sighs:
She swore, in faith, 'twas strange, 'twas passing
    strange;
'Twas pitiful, 'twas wondrous pitiful:
She wish'd she had not heard it, yet she wish'd
That heaven had made her such a man; she
    thank'd me,
And bade me, if I had a friend that lov'd her,
I should but teach him how to tell my story,
And that would woo her. Upon this hint I spake:
She lov'd me for the dangers I had pass'd,
And I lov'd her that she did pity them.
This only is the witchcraft I have us'd:
Here comes the lady; let her witness it.

Othello, I. iii.

III. AGAMEMNON AND NESTOR

Agamemnon. Princes,
What grief hath set the jaundice on your cheeks?
The ample proposition that hope makes
In all designs begun on earth below
Fails in the promis'd largeness: checks and
    disasters
Grow in the veins of actions highest rear'd;
As knots, by the conflux of meeting sap,
Infect the sound pine and divert his grain
Tortive and errant from his course of growth.
Nor, princes, is it matter new to us
That we come short of our suppose so far

Tortive] distorted.   suppose] supposition.

That after seven years' siege yet Troy walls stand ;
Sith every action that hath gone before,
Whereof we have record, trial did draw
Bias and thwart, not answering the aim,
And that unbodied figure of the thought
That gave 't surmised shape. Why then, you princes,
Do you with cheeks abash'd behold our works,
And call them shames ? which are indeed nought
    else
But the protractive trials of great Jove,
To find persistive constancy in men :
The fineness of which metal is not found
In Fortune's love ; for then, the bold and coward,
The wise and fool, the artist and unread,
The hard and soft, seem all affin'd and kin :
But, in the wind and tempest of her frown,
Distinction, with a broad and powerful fan,
Puffing at all, winnows the light away ;
And what hath mass or matter, by itself
Lies rich in virtue and unmingled.
    Nestor. With due observance of thy god-like seat,
Great Agamemnon, Nestor shall apply
Thy latest words. In the reproof of chance
Lies the true proof of men : the sea being smooth
How many shallow bauble boats dare sail
Upon her patient breast, making their way
With those of nobler bulk !
But let the ruffian Boreas once enrage
The gentle Thetis, and anon behold
The strong-ribb'd bark through liquid mountains
    cut,
Bounding between the two moist elements,
Like Perseus' horse : where 's then the saucy boat

reproof] confutation, refutation.

Whose weak untimber'd sides but even now
Co-rivall'd greatness ? either to harbour fled,
Or made a toast for Neptune. Even so
Doth valour's show and valour's worth divide
In storms of fortune ; for in her ray and brightness
The herd hath more annoyance by the breese
Than by the tiger ; but when the splitting wind
Makes flexible the knees of knotted oaks,
And flies fled under shade, why then the thing of
　　courage,
As rous'd with rage, with rage doth sympathize,
And with an accent tun'd in self-same key,
Retorts to chiding fortune.

Troilus and Cressida, I. iii.

IV. ULYSSES. ON DEGREE

THE heavens themselves, the planets, and this
　　centre
Observe degree, priority, and place,
Insisture, course, proportion, season, form,
Office, and custom, in all line of order :
And therefore is the glorious planet Sol
In noble eminence enthron'd and spher'd
Amidst the other ; whose med'cinable eye
Corrects the ill aspects of planets evil,
And posts, like the commandment of a king,
Sans check, to good and bad : but when the planets
In evil mixture to disorder wander,
What plagues, and what portents, what mutiny,
What raging of the sea, shaking of earth,
Commotion in the winds, frights, changes, horrors,
Divert and crack, rend and deracinate

Insisture] persistency, constancy.　　deracinate] uproot.

The unity and married calm of states
Quite from their fixure! O! when degree is shak'd,
Which is the ladder to all high designs,
The enterprise is sick. How could communities,
Degrees in schools, and brotherhoods in cities,
Peaceful commerce from dividable shores,
The primogenitive and due of birth,
Prerogative of age, crowns, sceptres, laurels,
But by degree, stand in authentic place?
Take but degree away, untune that string,
And, hark! what discord follows; each thing meets
In mere oppugnancy; the bounded waters
Should lift their bosoms higher than the shores,
And make a sop of all this solid globe:
Strength should be lord of imbecility,
And the rude son should strike his father dead:
Force should be right; or rather, right and wrong
Between whose endless jar justice resides—
Should lose their names, and so should justice too.
Then every thing includes itself in power,
Power into will, will into appetite;
And appetite, a universal wolf,
So doubly seconded with will and power,
Must make perforce a universal prey,
And last eat up himself. Great Agamemnon,
This chaos, when degree is suffocate,
Follows the choking.
And this neglection of degree it is
That by a pace goes backward, with a purpose
It hath to climb. The general's disdain'd
By him one step below, he by the next,
That next by him beneath; so every step,
Exampled by the first pace that is sick

oppugnancy] opposition.

Of his superior, grows to an envious fever
Of pale and bloodless emulation :
And 'tis this fever that keeps Troy on foot,
Not her own sinews. To end a tale of length,
Troy in our weakness lives, not in her strength.

Troilus and Cressida, I. iii.

ULYSSES (TO ACHILLES). THE INSTANT WAY

TIME hath, my lord, a wallet at his back,
Wherein he puts alms for oblivion,
A great-siz'd monster of ingratitudes :
Those scraps are good deeds past ; which are
    devour'd
As fast as they are made, forgot as soon
As done : perseverance, dear my lord,
Keeps honour bright : to have done, is to hang
Quite out of fashion, like a rusty mail
In monumental mockery. Take the instant way ;
For honour travels in a strait so narrow
Where one but goes abreast : keep, then, the path ;
For emulation hath a thousand sons
That one by one pursue : if you give way,
Or hedge aside from the direct forthright,
Like to an enter'd tide they all rush by
And leave you hindmost ;
Or, like a gallant horse fall'n in first rank,
Lie there for pavement to the abject rear,
O'errun and trampled on : then what they do in
    present,
Though less than yours in past, must o'ertop yours ;
For time is like a fashionable host,
That slightly shakes his parting guest by the hand,

And with his arms outstretch'd, as he would fly,
Grasps in the comer : welcome ever smiles,
And farewell goes out sighing. O ! let not virtue
  seek
Remuneration for the thing it was ;
For beauty, wit,
High birth, vigour of bone, desert in service,
Love, friendship, charity, are subjects all
To envious and calumniating time.
One touch of nature makes the whole world kin,
That all with one consent praise new-born gawds,
Though they are made and moulded of things past,
And give to dust that is a little gilt
More laud than gilt o'er-dusted.
The present eye praises the present object :
Then marvel not, thou great and complete man,
That all the Greeks begin to worship Ajax ;
Since things in motion sooner catch the eye
Than what not stirs. The cry went once on thee,
And still it might, and yet it may again,
If thou wouldst not entomb thyself alive,
And case thy reputation in thy tent ;
Whose glorious deeds, but in these fields of late,
Made emulous missions 'mongst the gods them-
  selves,
And drave great Mars to faction.

Troilus and Cressida, III. iii.

SUCH STUFF AS DREAMS ARE MADE ON

Prospero. You do look, my son, in a mov'd sort,
As if you were dismay'd : be cheerful, sir :
Our revels now are ended. These our actors,
As I foretold you, were all spirits and

Are melted into air, into thin air :
And, like the baseless fabric of this vision,
The cloud-capp'd towers, the gorgeous palaces,
The solemn temples, the great globe itself,
Yea, all which it inherit, shall dissolve
And, like this insubstantial pageant faded,
Leave not a rack behind. We are such stuff
As dreams are made on, and our little life
Is rounded with a sleep.

The Tempest, IV. i.

SONGS

ORPHEUS

ORPHEUS with his lute made trees,
And the mountain tops that freeze,
  Bow themselves, when he did sing :
To his music plants and flowers
Ever sprung ; as sun and showers
  There had made a lasting spring.

Every thing that heard him play,
Even the billows of the sea,
  Hung their heads, and then lay by.
In sweet music is such art,
Killing care and grief of heart
  Fall asleep, or hearing, die.

King Henry VIII, III. i.

TELL ME WHERE IS FANCY BRED

TELL me where is fancy bred,
Or in the heart or in the head?
How begot, how nourished?
    Reply, reply.

It is engender'd in the eyes,
With gazing fed; and fancy dies
In the cradle where it lies.
    Let us all ring fancy's knell:
    I'll begin it,—Ding, dong, bell.
All. Ding, dong, bell.

                 Merchant of Venice, III. ii.

SIGH NO MORE

SIGH no more, ladies, sigh no more,
  Men were deceivers ever;
One foot in sea, and one on shore,
  To one thing constant never.
    Then sigh not so,
    But let them go,
And be you blithe and bonny,
Converting all your sounds of woe
  Into Hey nonny, nonny.

Sing no more ditties, sing no mo
  Of dumps so dull and heavy;
The fraud of men was ever so,
  Since summer first was leavy.
    Then sigh not so,
    But let them go,
And be you blithe and bonny,
Converting all your sounds of woe
  Into Hey nonny, nonny.

            Much Ado About Nothing, II. iii.

SPRING

I

WHEN daisies pied and violets blue
  And lady-smocks all silver-white
And cuckoo-buds of yellow hue
  Do paint the meadows with delight,
The cuckoo then, on every tree,
Mocks married men ; for thus sings he,
                          Cuckoo ;
Cuckoo, cuckoo : O, word of fear,
Unpleasing to a married ear !

II

When shepherds pipe on oaten straws,
  And merry larks are ploughmen's clocks,
When turtles tread, and rooks, and daws,
  And maidens bleach their summer smocks,
The cuckoo then, on every tree,
Mocks married men ; for thus sings he,
                          Cuckoo ;
Cuckoo, cuckoo : O, word of fear,
Unpleasing to a married ear !

Love's Labour's Lost. v. ii.

WINTER

III

WHEN icicles hang by the wall,
  And Dick the shepherd blows his nail,
And Tom bears logs into the hall,
  And milk comes frozen home in pail,
When blood is nipp'd, and ways be foul,
Then nightly sings the staring owl,
                          Tu-who ;
To-whit, tu-who—a merry note,
While greasy Joan doth keel the pot.

IV

When all aloud the wind doth blow,
   And coughing drowns the parson's saw,
And birds sit brooding in the snow,
   And Marian's nose looks red and raw,
When roasted crabs hiss in the bowl,
Then nightly sings the staring owl,
                Tu-who;
Tu-whit, tu-who—a merry note,
While greasy Joan doth keel the pot.

Love's Labour's Lost, **v. ii.**

SILVIA

Who is Silvia? what is she?
   That all our swains commend her?
Holy, fair, and wise is she;
   The heaven such grace did lend her,
That she might admired be.

Is she kind as she is fair?
   For beauty lives with kindness:
Love doth to her eyes repair,
   To help him of his blindness;
And, being help'd, inhabits there.

Then to Silvia let us sing,
   That Silvia is excelling;
She excels each mortal thing
   Upon the dull earth dwelling;
To her let us garlands bring.

Two Gentlemen of Verona, **iv. ii.**

A LOVER'S LAMENT

Come away, come away, death,
    And in sad cypress let me be laid;
Fly away, fly away, breath;
    I am slain by a fair cruel maid.
My shroud of white, stuck all with yew,
        O! prepare it.
My part of death, no one so true
        Did share it.

Not a flower, not a flower sweet,
    On my black coffin let there be strown;
Not a friend, not a friend greet
    My poor corse, where my bones shall be thrown.
A thousand thousand sighs to save,
        Lay me, O! where
Sad true lover never find my grave,
        To weep there.

                                        Twelfth Night, II. iv.

TAKE, O TAKE

Take, O take those lips away,
    That so sweetly were forsworn;
And those eyes, the break of day,
    Lights that do mislead the morn:
But my kisses bring again,
                        bring again,
Seals of love, but seal'd in vain,
                        seal'd in vain.

                                        Measure for Measure, IV. i.

OVER HILL, OVER DALE

OVER hill, over dale,
　　Thorough bush, thorough brier,
Over park, over pale,
　　Thorough flood, thorough fire,
I do wander every where,
Swifter than the moone's sphere;
And I serve the fairy queen,
To dew her orbs upon the green:
The cowslips tall her pensioners be;
In their gold coats spots you see;
Those be rubies, fairy favours,
In their freckles live their savours:
I must go seek some dew-drops here
And hang a pearl in every cowslip's ear.

　　　　　　　　A Midsummer Night's Dream, II. i.

A MORNING SONG

HARK! hark! the lark at heaven's gate sings,
　　And Phœbus 'gins arise,
His steeds to water at those springs
　　On chalic'd flowers that lies;
And winking Mary-buds begin
　　To ope their golden eyes:
With every thing that pretty is,
　　My lady sweet, arise:
　　　　Arise, arise!

　　　　　　　　Cymbeline, II. iii.

A FAIRIES' SONG

I

You spotted snakes with double tongue,
    Thorny hedge-hogs, be not seen;
Newts, and blind-worms, do no wrong;
    Come not near our fairy queen.

Philomel, with melody,
    Sing in our sweet lullaby:
Lulla, lulla, lullaby; lulla, lulla, lullaby:
    Never harm,
    Nor spell, nor charm,
Come our lovely lady nigh;
So, good night, with lullaby.

II

Weaving spiders come not here;
    Hence, you long-legg'd spinners, hence!
Beetles black, approach not near;
    Worm nor snail, do no offence.

Philomel, with melody, &c.

A Midsummer Night's Dream, **II. ii.**

BLOW, BLOW, THOU WINTER WIND

Blow, blow, thou winter wind,
Thou art not so unkind
    As man's ingratitude;
Thy tooth is not so keen,
Because thou art not seen,
    Although thy breath be rude.

Heigh-ho ! sing, heigh-ho ! unto the green holly :
Most friendship is feigning, most loving mere folly.
    Then heigh-ho ! the holly !
      This life is most jolly.

    Freeze, freeze, thou bitter sky,
    That dost not bite so nigh
     As benefits forgot :
    Though thou the waters warp,
    Thy sting is not so sharp
     As friend remember'd not.
Heigh-ho ! sing, heigh-ho ! unto the green holly :
Most friendship is feigning, most loving mere folly.
    Then heigh-ho ! the holly !
      This life is most jolly.

As You Like It, II. vii.

ARIEL'S SONGS

I

Come unto these yellow sands,
    And then take hands :
Curtsied when you have, and kiss'd,—
    The wild waves whist,—
Foot it featly here and there ;
And, sweet sprites, the burden bear.
    Hark, hark !
      [*Burden* : Bow, wow, *dispersedly.*
    The watch-dogs bark :
      [*Burden* : Bow, wow, *dispersedly.*
    Hark, hark ! I hear
The strain of strutting Chanticleer
      [*Cry*, Cock-a-diddle-dow.

The Tempest, I. ii.

II

Full fathom five thy father lies ;
　Of his bones are coral made :
Those are pearls that were his eyes :
　Nothing of him that doth fade,
But doth suffer a sea-change
Into something rich and strange.
Sea-nymphs hourly ring his knell :
　　　　　　[*Burden :* ding-dong.
Hark ! now I hear them,—ding-dong, bell.

The Tempest, I. ii.

III

Where the bee sucks, there suck I
In a cowslip's bell I lie ;
There I couch when owls do cry.
On the bat's back I do fly
After summer merrily :
Merrily, merrily shall I live now
Under the blossom that hangs on the bough.

The Tempest, V. i.

AUTOLYCUS

WHEN daffodils begin to peer,
　With heigh ! the doxy, over the dale,
Why, then comes in the sweet o' the year ;
　For the red blood reigns in the winter's pale.

The white sheet bleaching on the hedge,
　With heigh ! the sweet birds, O, how they sing !
Doth set my pugging tooth on edge ;
　For a quart of ale is a dish for a king.

The lark, that tirra-lirra chants,
　With, heigh ! with, heigh ! the thrush and the jay,

Are summer songs for me and my aunts,
  While we lie tumbling in the hay.

[I have served Prince Florizel, and in my time wore
three-pile ; but now I am out of service :]

But shall I go mourn for that, my dear ?
  The pale moon shines by night ;
And when I wander here and there,
  I then do most go right.

If tinkers may have leave to live,
  And bear the sow-skin bowget,
Then my account I well may give,
  And in the stocks avouch it.

Jog on, jog on, the footpath way,
  And merrily hent the stile-a :
A merry heart goes all the day,
  Your sad tires in a mile-a.

Winter's Tale, IV. ii.

THE GREENWOOD

UNDER the greenwood tree
Who loves to lie with me,
And turn his merry note
Unto the sweet bird's throat,
Come hither, come hither, come hither :
  Here shall he see
  No enemy
But winter and rough weather.

Who doth ambition shun,
And loves to live i' the sun,
Seeking the food he eats,
And pleas'd with what he gets,

  bowget] a leathern pouch.

Come hither, come hither, come hither :
   Here shall he see
     No enemy
But winter and rough weather.

As You Like It, II. v.

IT WAS A LOVER

It was a lover and his lass,
 With a hey, and a ho, and a hey nonino,
That o'er the green corn-field did pass,
 In the spring time, the only pretty ring time,
When birds do sing, hey ding a ding, ding ;
Sweet lovers love the spring.

Between the acres of the rye,
 With a hey, and a ho, and a hey nonino,
These pretty country folks would lie,
 In the spring time, &c.

This carol they began that hour,
 With a hey, and a ho, and a hey nonino,
How that a life was but a flower
 In the spring time, &c.

And therefore take the present time,
 With a hey, and a ho, and a hey nonino ;
For love is crowned with the prime
 In the spring time, &c.

As You Like It, v. iii.

HOW SHOULD I YOUR TRUE LOVE KNOW

  How should I your true love know
   From another one ?
  By his cockle hat and staff,
   And his sandal shoon.

He is dead and gone, lady,
    He is dead and gone ;
At his head a grass-green turf ;
    At his heels a stone.

White his shroud as the mountain snow
    Larded with sweet flowers ;
Which bewept to the grave did go
    With true-love showers.

Hamlet, IV. V.

O MISTRESS MINE

O MISTRESS mine ! where are you roaming ?
O ! stay and hear ; your true love 's coming,
    That can sing both high and low.
Trip no further, pretty sweeting ;
Journeys end in lovers meeting,
    Every wise man's son doth know.

What is love ? 'tis not hereafter ;
Present mirth hath present laughter ;
    What 's to come is still unsure :
In delay there lies no plenty ;
Then come kiss me, sweet-and-twenty,
    Youth 's a stuff will not endure.

Twelfth Night, II. iii.

LAWN AS WHITE AS DRIVEN SNOW

    LAWN as white as driven snow ;
    Cyprus black as e'er was crow ;
    Gloves as sweet as damask roses :
    Masks for faces and for noses :
    Bugle-bracelet, necklace-amber,
    Perfume for a lady's chamber ;

Golden quoifs and stomachers,
For my lads to give their dears ;
Pins and poking-sticks of steel ;
What maids lack from head to heel :
Come buy of me, come ; come buy, come buy ;
Buy, lads, or else your lasses cry :
Come buy.

Winter's Tale, IV. iii.

ON A DAY

On a day, alack the day !
Love, whose month is ever May,
Spied a blossom passing fair
Playing in the wanton air ;
Through the velvet leaves the wind,
All unseen, 'gan passage find ;
That the lover, sick to death,
Wish'd himself the heaven's breath.
Air, quoth he, thy cheeks may blow
Air, would I might triumph so !
But alack ! my hand is sworn
Ne'er to pluck thee from thy thorn
Vow, alack ! for youth unmeet,
Youth so apt to pluck a sweet.
Do not call it sin in me,
That I am forsworn for thee ;
Thou for whom e'en Jove would swear
Juno but an Ethiop were ;
And deny himself for Jove,
Turning mortal for thy love.

Love's Labour 's Lost, IV. iii.

ROSES, THEIR SHARP SPINES BEING GONE

Roses, their sharp spines being gone,
Not royal in their smells alone,
But in their hue.
Maiden pinks, of odour faint,
Daisies smelless, yet most quaint,
And sweet thyme true.

Primrose, firstborn child of Ver,
Merry springtime's harbinger,
With her bells dim.
Oxlips, in their cradles growing,
Marigolds, on deathbeds blowing,
Lark's heels trim.

All dear Nature's children sweet,
Lie 'fore bride and bridegroom's feet,
Blessing their sense.
Not an angel of the air,
Bird melodious or bird fair,
Is absent hence.

The crow, the slanderous cuckoo, nor
The boding raven, nor chough hoar
Nor chattering pie,
May on our bridehouse perch or sing,
Or with them any discord bring,
But from it fly.

The Two Noble Kinsmen, I. i
(Shakespeare and Fletcher).

CRABBED AGE AND YOUTH

CRABBED age and youth cannot live together :
Youth is full of pleasure, age is full of care ;
Youth like summer morn, age like winter weather ;
Youth like summer brave, age like winter bare.
Youth is full of sport, age's breath is short ;
    Youth is nimble, age is lame ;
Youth is hot and bold, age is weak and cold ;
Youth is wild, and age is tame.
Age, I do abhor thee, youth, I do adore thee ;
    O ! my love, my love is young :
Age, I do defy thee : O ! sweet shepherd, hie thee,
    For methinks thou stay'st too long.

The Passionate Pilgrim.

DIRGE

FEAR no more the heat o' the sun,
    Nor the furious winter's rages ;
Thou thy worldly task hast done,
    Home art gone, and ta'en thy wages ;
Golden lads and girls all must,
As chimney-sweepers, come to dust.

Fear no more the frown o' the great,
    Thou art past the tyrant's stroke :
Care no more to clothe and eat ;
    To thee the reed is as the oak :
The sceptre, learning, physic, must
All follow this, and come to dust.

Fear no more the lightning-flash,
    Nor the all-dreaded thunder-stone;
Fear not slander, censure rash;
    Thou hast finish'd joy and moan:
All lovers young, all lovers must
Consign to thee, and come to dust.

No exorciser harm thee!
    Nor no witchcraft charm thee!
Ghost unlaid forbear thee!
    Nothing ill come near thee!
Quiet consummation have;
And renowned be thy grave!

Cymbeline, IV. ii.

SONNETS

XII

WHEN I do count the clock that tells the time,
And see the brave day sunk in hideous night;
When I behold the violet past prime,
And sable curls, all silver'd o'er with white;
When lofty trees I see barren of leaves,
Which erst from heat did canopy the herd,
And summer's green all girded up in sheaves,
Borne on the bier with white and bristly beard,
Then of thy beauty do I question make,
That thou among the wastes of time must go,
Since sweets and beauties do themselves forsake
And die as fast as they see others grow;
    And nothing 'gainst Time's scythe can make
        defence
    Save breed, to brave him when he takes thee
        hence.

breed] offspring.

XVIII

Shall I compare thee to a summer's day ?
Thou art more lovely and more temperate :
Rough winds do shake the darling buds of May,
And summer's lease hath all too short a date :
Sometime too hot the eye of heaven shines,
And often is his gold complexion dimm'd ;
And every fair from fair sometime declines,
By chance, or nature's changing course untrimm'd
But thy eternal summer shall not fade,
Nor lose possession of that fair thou ow'st,
Nor shall death brag thou wander'st in his shade,
When in eternal lines to time thou grow'st ;
   So long as men can breathe, or eyes can see,
   So long lives this, and this gives life to thee.

XXIX

When in disgrace with fortune and men's eyes
I all alone beweep my outcast state,
And trouble deaf heaven with my bootless cries,
And look upon myself, and curse my fate,
Wishing me like to one more rich in hope,
Featur'd like him, like him with friends possess'd,
Desiring this man's art, and that man's scope,
With what I most enjoy contented least ;
Yet in these thoughts myself almost despising,
Haply I think on thee,—and then my state,
Like to the lark at break of day arising
From sullen earth, sings hymns at heaven's gate ;
   For thy **sweet love** remember'd such wealth
    brings
   That then I scorn to change my state with kings.

XXX

When to the sessions of sweet silent thought
I summon up remembrance of things past,
I sigh the lack of many a thing I sought,
And with old woes new wail my dear times' waste :
Then can I drown an eye, unus'd to flow,
For precious friends hid in death's dateless night,
And weep afresh love's long since cancell'd woe,
And moan the expense of many a vanish'd sight :
Then can I grieve at grievances foregone,
And heavily from woe to woe tell o'er
The sad account of fore-bemoaned moan,
Which I new pay as if not paid before.
    But if the while I think on thee, dear friend,
      All losses are restor'd and sorrows end.

XXXII

If thou survive my well-contented day,
When that churl Death my bones with dust shall
    cover,
And shalt by fortune once more re-survey
These poor rude lines of thy deceased lover,
Compare them with the bettering of the time,
And though they be outstripp'd by every pen,
Reserve them for my love, not for their rime,
Exceeded by the height of happier men.
O ! then vouchsafe me but this loving thought :
'Had my friend's Muse grown with this growing
    age,
A dearer birth than this his love had brought,
To march in ranks of better equipage :
    But since he died, and poets better prove,
      Theirs for their style I'll read, his for his love.'

XXXIII

Full many a glorious morning have I seen
Flatter the mountain-tops with sovereign eye,
Kissing with golden face the meadows green,
Gilding pale streams with heavenly alchymy;
Anon permit the basest clouds to ride
With ugly rack on his celestial face,
And from the forlorn world his visage hide,
Stealing unseen to west with this disgrace:
Even so my sun one early morn did shine,
With all-triumphant splendour on my brow;
But, out! alack! he was but one hour mine,
The region cloud hath mask'd him from me now.

    Yet him for this my love no whit disdaineth;
    Suns of the world may stain when heaven's sun
      staineth.

LIII

What is your substance, whereof are you made,
That millions of strange shadows on you tend?
Since every one hath, every one, one shade,
And you, but one, can every shadow lend.
Describe Adonis, and the counterfeit
Is poorly imitated after you;
On Helen's cheek all art of beauty set,
And you in Grecian tires are painted new:
Speak of the spring and foison of the year,
The one doth shadow of your beauty show,
The other as your bounty doth appear;
And you in every blessed shape we know.

    In all external grace you have some part,
    But you like none, none you, for constant heart.

    tires] head-dresses.   foison] plenty.

LIV

O ! how much more doth beauty beauteous seem
By that sweet ornament which truth doth give !
The rose looks fair, but fairer we it deem
For that sweet odour which doth in it live.
The canker-blooms have full as deep a dye
As the perfumed tincture of the roses,
Hang on such thorns, and play as wantonly
When summer's breath their masked buds dis-
    closes :
But, for their virtue only is their show,
They live unwoo'd, and unrespected fade ;
Die to themselves. Sweet roses do not so ;
Of their sweet deaths are sweetest odours made :
  And so of you, beauteous and lovely youth,
    When that shall vade, my verse distils your
    truth.

LVII

Being your slave, what should I do but tend
Upon the hours and times of your desire ?
I have no precious time at all to spend,
Nor services to do, till you require.
Nor dare I chide the world-without-end hour
Whilst I, my sovereign, watch the clock for you,
Nor think the bitterness of absence sour
When you have bid your servant once adieu ;
Nor dare I question with my jealous thought
Where you may be, or your affairs suppose,
But, like a sad slave, stay and think of nought
Save, where you are how happy you make those.
  So true a fool is love that in your will,
    Though you do anything, he thinks no ill.

vade] fade.

LX

Like as the waves make towards the pebbled shore,
So do our minutes hasten to their end ;
Each changing place with that which goes before,
In sequent toil all forwards do contend.
Nativity, once in the main of light,
Crawls to maturity, wherewith being crown'd,
Crooked eclipses 'gainst his glory fight,
And Time that gave doth now his gift confound.
Time doth transfix the flourish set on youth
And delves the parallels in beauty's brow,
Feeds on the rarities of nature's truth,
And nothing stands but for his scythe to mow :
   And yet to times in hope my verse shall stand,
   Praising thy worth, despite his cruel hand.

LXIV

When I have seen by Time's fell hand defac'd
The rich-proud cost of outworn buried age ;
When sometime lofty towers I see down-raz'd,
And brass eternal slave to mortal rage ;
When I have seen the hungry ocean gain
Advantage on the kingdom of the shore,
And the firm soil win of the watery main,
Increasing store with loss, and loss with store ;
When I have seen such interchange of state,
Or state itself confounded to decay ;
Ruin hath taught me thus to ruminate—
That Time will come and take my love away.
   This thought is as a death, which cannot choose
   But weep to have that which it fears to lose.

delves the parallels] makes furrows.

LXV

Since brass, nor stone, nor earth, nor boundless sea,
But sad mortality o'ersways their power,
How with this rage shall beauty hold a plea,
Whose action is no stronger than a flower ?
O ! how shall summer's honey breath hold out
Against the wrackful siege of battering days,
When rocks impregnable are not so stout,
Nor gates of steel so strong, but Time decays ?
O fearful meditation ! where, alack,
Shall Time's best jewel from Time's chest lie hid ?
Or what strong hand can hold his swift foot back ?
Or who his spoil of beauty can forbid ?
   O ! none, unless this miracle have might,
   That in black ink my love may still shine bright.

LXVI

Tir'd with all these, for restful death I cry
As to behold desert a beggar born,
And needy nothing trimm'd in jollity,
And purest faith unhappily forsworn,
And gilded honour shamefully misplac'd,
And maiden virtue rudely strumpeted,
And right perfection wrongfully disgraced,
And strength by limping sway disabled,
And art made tongue-tied by authority,
And folly—doctor-like—controlling skill,
And simple truth miscall'd simplicity,
And captive good attending captain ill :
   Tir'd with all these, from these would I be gone,
   Save that, to die, I leave my love alone.

LXXI

No longer mourn for me when I am dead
Than you shall hear the surly sullen bell
Give warning to the world that I am fled
From this vile world, with vilest worms to dwell:
Nay, if you read this line, remember not
The hand that writ it; for I love you so,
That I in your sweet thoughts would be forgot,
If thinking on me then should make you woe.
O! if,—I say, you look upon this verse,
When I perhaps compounded am with clay,
Do not so much as my poor name rehearse,
But let your love even with my life decay;
　　Lest the wise world should look into your moan,
　　And mock you with me after I am gone.

LXXIII

That time of year thou mayst in me behold
When yellow leaves, or none, or few, do hang
Upon those boughs which shake against the cold,
Bare ruin'd choirs, where late the sweet birds sang.
In me thou see'st the twilight of such day
As after sunset fadeth in the west;
Which by and by black night doth take away,
Death's second self, that seals up all in rest.
In me thou see'st the glowing of such fire,
That on the ashes of his youth doth lie,
As the death-bed whereon it must expire
Consum'd with that which it was nourish'd by.
　　This thou perceiv'st, which makes thy love more
　　　strong,
　　To love that well which thou must leave ere long.

LXXXVII

Farewell! thou art too dear for my possessing,
And like enough thou know'st thy estimate:
The charter of thy worth gives thee releasing;
My bonds in thee are all determinate.
For how do I hold thee but by thy granting?
And for that riches where is my deserving?
The cause of this fair gift in me is wanting,
And so my patent back again is swerving.
Thyself thou gav'st, thy own worth then not
    knowing,
Or me, to whom thou gav'st it, else mistaking;
So thy great gift, upon misprision growing,
Comes home again, on better judgement making.
    Thus have I had thee, as a dream doth flatter,
    In sleep a king, but, waking, no such matter.

XC

Then hate me when thou wilt; if ever, now;
Now, while the world is bent my deeds to cross,
Join with the spite of fortune, make me bow,
And do not drop in for an after-loss:
Ah! do not, when my heart hath 'scap'd this
    sorrow,
Come in the rearward of a conquer'd woe;
Give not a windy night a rainy morrow,
To linger out a purpos'd overthrow.
If thou wilt leave me, do not leave me last,
When other petty griefs have done their spite,
But in the onset come: so shall I taste
At first the very worst of fortune's might;
    And other strains of woe, which now seem woe,
    Compar'd with loss of thee will not seem so.

        misprision] error, mistake.

XCIV

They that have power to hurt and will do none,
That do not do the thing they most do show,
Who, moving others, are themselves as stone,
Unmoved, cold, and to temptation slow;
They rightly do inherit heaven's graces,
And husband nature's riches from expense;
They are the lords and owners of their faces,
Others but stewards of their excellence.
The summer's flower is to the summer sweet,
Though to itself it only live and die,
But if that flower with base infection meet,
The basest weed outbraves his dignity:
    For sweetest things turn sourest by their deeds;
    Lilies that fester smell far worse than weeds.

XCVII

How like a winter hath my absence been
From thee, the pleasure of the fleeting year!
What freezings have I felt, what dark days seen!
What old December's bareness every where!
And yet this time remov'd was summer's time;
The teeming autumn, big with rich increase,
Bearing the wanton burden of the prime,
Like widow'd wombs after their lords' decease:
Yet this abundant issue seem'd to me
But hope of orphans and unfather'd fruit;
For summer and his pleasures wait on thee,
And, thou away, the very birds are mute:
    Or, if they sing, 'tis with so dull a cheer,
    That leaves look pale, dreading the winter's near.

CIV

To me, fair friend, you never can be old,
For as you were when first your eye I ey'd,
Such seems your beauty still. Three winters cold
Have from the forests shook three summers' pride,
Three beauteous springs to yellow autumn turn'd
In process of the seasons have I seen,
Three April perfumes in three hot Junes burn'd,
Since first I saw you fresh, which yet are green.
Ah! yet doth beauty, like a dial-hand,
Steal from his figure, and no pace perceiv'd;
So your sweet hue, which methinks still doth stand,
Hath motion, and mine eye may be deceiv'd:
   For fear of which, hear this, thou age unbred:
   Ere you were born was beauty's summer dead.

CVI

When in the chronicle of wasted time
I see descriptions of the fairest wights,
And beauty making beautiful old rime,
In praise of ladies dead and lovely knights,
Then, in the blazon of sweet beauty's best,
Of hand, of foot, of lip, of eye, of brow,
I see their antique pen would have express'd
Even such a beauty as you master now.
So all their praises are but prophecies
Of this our time, all you prefiguring;
And, for they look'd but with divining eyes,
They had not skill enough your worth to sing:
   For we, which now behold these present days,
   Have eyes to wonder, but lack tongues to praise.

CVII

Not mine own fears, nor the prophetic soul
Of the wide world dreaming on things to come,
Can yet the lease of my true love control,
Suppos'd as forfeit to a confin'd doom.
The mortal moon hath her eclipse endur'd,
And the sad augurs mock their own presage;
Incertainties now crown themselves assur'd,
And peace proclaims olives of endless age.
Now with the drops of this most balmy time
My love looks fresh, and Death to me subscribes,
Since, spite of him, I'll live in this poor rime,
While he insults o'er dull and speechless tribes:
    And thou in this shalt find thy monument,
    When tyrants' crests and tombs of brass are
        spent.

CIX

O! never say that I was false of heart,
Though absence seem'd my flame to qualify.
As easy might I from myself depart
As from my soul, which in thy breast doth lie:
That is my home of love: if I have rang'd,
Like him that travels, I return again;
Just to the time, not with the time exchang'd,
So that myself bring water for my stain.
Never believe, though in my nature reign'd
All frailties that besiege all kinds of blood,
That it could so preposterously be stain'd,
To leave for nothing all thy sum of good;
    For nothing this wide universe I call,
    Save thou. my rose; in it thou art my all.

CX

Alas ! 'tis true I have gone here and there,
And made myself a motley to the view,
Gor'd mine own thoughts, sold cheap what is most
  dear,
Made old offences of affections new ;
Most true it is that I have look'd on truth
Askance and strangely ; but, by all above,
These blenches gave my heart another youth,
And worse essays prov'd thee my best of love.
Now all is done, save what shall have no end :
Mine appetite I never more will grind
On newer proof, to try an older friend,
A god in love, to whom I am confin'd.
  Then give me welcome, next my heaven the best,
  Even to thy pure and most most loving breast.

CXI

O ! for my sake do you with Fortune chide
The guilty goddess of my harmful deeds,
That did not better for my life provide
Than public means which public manners breeds.
Thence comes it that my name receives a brand,
And almost thence my nature is subdu'd
To what it works in, like the dyer's hand :
Pity me, then, and wish I were renew'd ;
Whilst, like a willing patient, I will drink
Potions of eisel 'gainst my strong infection ;
No bitterness that I will bitter think,
Nor double penance, to correct correction.
  Pity me, then, dear friend, and I assure ye
  Even that your pity is enough to cure me.

Gor'd mine own thoughts] gored or wounded my self-
esteem. eisel] vinegar.

CXVI

Let me not to the marriage of true minds
Admit impediments. Love is not love
Which alters when it alteration finds,
Or bends with the remover to remove:
O, no ! it is an ever-fixed mark,
That looks on tempests and is never shaken ;
It is the star to every wandering bark,
Whose worth's unknown, although his height be
    taken.
Love 's not Time's fool, though rosy lips and cheeks
Within his bending sickle's compass come ;
Love alters not with his brief hours and weeks,
But bears it out even to the edge of doom.
    If this be error, and upon me prov'd,
    I never writ, nor no man ever lov'd.

CXIX

What potions have I drunk of Siren tears,
Distill'd from limbecks foul as hell within,
Applying fears to hopes, and hopes to fears,
Still losing when I saw myself to win !
What wretched errors hath my heart committed,
Whilst it hath thought itself so blessed never !
How have mine eyes out of their spheres been
    fitted,
In the distraction of this madding fever !
O benefit of ill ! now I find true
That better is by evil still made better ;
And ruin'd love, when it is built anew,
Grows fairer than at first, more strong, far greater.
    So I return rebuk'd to my content,
    And gain by ill thrice more than I have spent.

CXLVI

Poor soul, the centre of my sinful earth,
Fool'd by these rebel powers that thee array,
Why dost thou pine within and suffer dearth,
Painting thy outward walls so costly gay?
Why so large cost, having so short a lease,
Dost thou upon thy fading mansion spend?
Shall worms, inheritors of this excess,
Eat up thy charge? Is this thy body's end?
Then, soul, live thou upon thy servant's loss,
And let that pine to aggravate thy store;
Buy terms divine in selling hours of dross;
Within be fed, without be rich no more:
  So shalt thou feed on Death, that feeds on men,
  And Death once dead, there's no more dying
    then.

CXLVIII

O me! what eyes hath Love put in my head,
Which have no correspondence with true sight;
Or, if they have, where is my judgement fled,
That censures falsely what they see aright?
If that be fair whereon my false eyes dote,
What means the world to say it is not so?
If it be not, then love doth well denote
Love's eye is not so true as all men's: no.
How can it? O! how can Love's eye be true,
That is so vex'd with watching and with tears?
No marvel then, though I mistake my view;
The sun itself sees not till heaven clears.
  O cunning Love! with tears thou keep'st me blind,
  Lest eyes well-seeing thy foul faults should find.

INDEX OF FIRST LINES

*Set at the University Press, Oxford
and reprinted from plates by
Neill and Co. Ltd., Edinburgh*